O CANADA
CROSSWORDS
BOOK 15

T0151441

O CANADA CROSSWORDS

BOOK 15

85 ALL NEW Crosswords

GWEN SJOGREN

NIGHTWOOD EDITIONS

Nightwood Editions
P.O. Box 1779
Gibsons, BC
V0N 1V0
www.nightwoodeditions.com

Edited by Margaret Tessman
Proofread by Patricia Wolfe
Printed in China

ISBN 978-0-88971-304-8

Contents

Name That City

Decode these Canadian nicknames

ACROSS

1. Remove one's whiskers
6. Short-term committee type
11. Facets
18. Jeopardy
19. Rottweiler's rumble
20. Caesar's horse-drawn transport
21. Smart fellow?
22. Indian subcontinent currency
23. **Cowtown**
24. Tiff
25. **The Queen City**
26. Something that's painful to look at?
27. Curved architectural mouldings
29. Place to put a heat pack
31. Fawcett's final documentary: _____ *Story*
34. Turn away trouble
36. 1970 Vanity Fare hit: "Hitchin' _____"
41. Banff National Park place: Lake _____
42. Separately
43. More absurd
44. Figure skater Kim who won 2010 Olympic gold
45. Office tasks, for short
47. Narrow the circumstances?
49. One _____ time
50. Pained expression
52. Horse's headgear
53. Canadian _____ Association
55. **The Big Smoke**
57. Equipment for a Canadian men's eight member
58. Use it or _____
60. It burns at Christmas
62. Feel terrible
65. Roof
67. Foxy lady?
68. Women's magazine since 1945

69. Purpose
70. That is, to Mark Antony
72. Former NHLer Shack, et al.
74. Aphids and ants
75. On guard
76. Natural fuel source
77. Hamilton newspaper, for short
78. Canadian Juno winners: Blue _____
79. Law of the land, say
84. **Bytown**
87. Adam's apple area
91. **City of Trees**
92. Red, in Rémigny
93. Like a hives sufferer
94. _____ Company of Canada
95. Pre-Confederation name: _____ Canada
96. Organisms that thrive on a reef
97. Gives a sworn statement
98. Unkempt
99. Get accustomed to

DOWN

1. Places to get pampered
2. Assistance
3. Bailiwick
4. **The Garden City**
5. Common Canadian mammal
6. Sees eye to eye
7. National pharmacy chain: London _____
8. Arizona Indian
9. _____ Sound ON
10. Maid or janitor
11. Willingly receive
12. Canadian "Happy Baby" band
13. White as a sheet
14. Work units
15. Goodbye, in Genoa
16. Vacuum pressure measurement
17. Peeper problem

25. Consider again, in court
28. Esso product
30. Royal Canadian Academy of _____
31. "Go _____ kite!"
32. Summer month, in Abitibi
33. Small boats that get around?
34. Bees' building
35. **Hollywood North**
36. Like non-digital clocks
37. East Indian side dish
38. Among other things, to Tiberius
39. They play with the antelope
40. Beach bird (var.)
42. Armoury inventory
43. Lyricist Gershwin
46. "Same for me"
48. Gunwale adjunct
50. Colourful salad ingredients?
51. Sign up for service
54. RRSP, say
56. It's only words?
58. Solitary
59. *Addams Family* cousin
61. Ontario Native group
63. Sept-_____ QC
64. Subtracted by
65. Cool
66. Stack
68. **City of Champions**
71. Propriety
73. Bambi's mom, say
75. Summits
76. Seedy NYC neighbourhood, in olden days
77. Begin to get skittish?
78. Carries on angrily?
79. *Transformers* star LaBeouf
80. Floozie's sweet treat?
81. "Thanks _____"
82. Pitchfork point
83. Strange sights in the sky

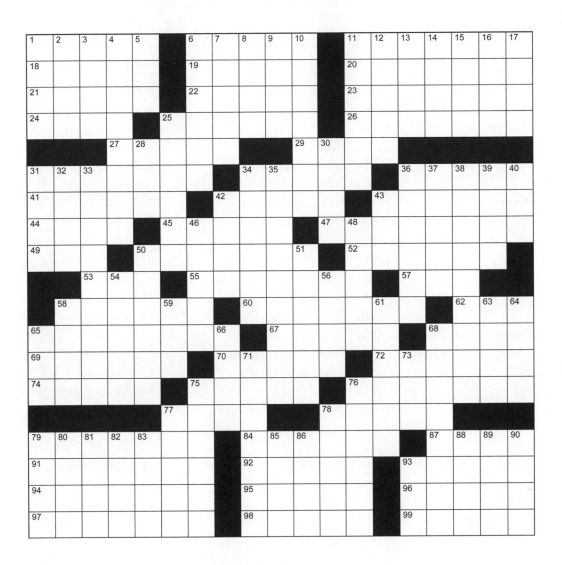

85. Drink too many daiquiris
86. Male sheep
88. Light brown shade

89. Burn a bit
90. Olympic golden Canadian gymnast Shewfelt

93. Here, in Hull

2 Hip to Be Square

Think inside the box with this one

ACROSS

1. Hoofbeat sound
5. *American Beauty* actress Suvari
9. Buy/sell agreement
13. Caesar and Waldorf
19. Ready
20. Skating jump type
21. Osprey kin
22. Edmonton's main drag: Jasper _____
23. Not locked
24. Cast one's ballot
25. Swine
26. 1960s Canadian Olympic swimmer Elaine
27. Where pilots sit
29. New Orleans Saints quarterback Drew
30. Third-person pronoun
31. *Decree* _____
32. Publishing submission encl.
33. "Queen of Mean" Helmsley
35. Emotionally disengaged
38. **Square for a solver?**
41. Bar mitzvah participant
46. Chinwag
48. Cruel
49. Greek letter
51. Communion, say
52. *La Bohème*, for example
54. Snow abode
57. House topper
58. Pie _____ mode
59. Surrealist painter Salvador
60. Patron
61. Ice cream holder
62. Pizza sausage
65. City in Italy
66. Australian cattle dog, for example
68. Canadian band: Our _____ Peace

69. **Postie's square?**
71. Fairway holler
72. Fit in
75. Driver's honk
76. Sallow complected
81. Condo complex dwelling
82. Make an accusation
84. Some pops?
85. _____-Gothic
86. Carry on complaining
87. Finish for a photo
88. Skiers' trail
90. _____ Jemima
91. Go up in price?
93. Bridget Fonda, to Jane
95. Frenchman who wrote *Phèdre*
97. _____ firma
98. **Bridge players' square?**
102. Based on eight
103. Brunch blini
105. Pitcher's asset
106. Bill Clinton's attorney general Janet
108. Caress
112. Certain shapes
114. Berton or Kennedy on *Front Page Challenge* (var.)
118. Gentleman's jewellery item
119. Dolly who said hello?
120. 1990 Colin James hit: "_____ Came Back"
121. Soprano's choir neighbour
122. Cite evidence
123. Worldly, not spiritual
124. Copier
125. Good piece of paper?
126. Affirmatives (var.)
127. Ransom's ride?
128. Suspicious
129. 1967 Montréal event

DOWN

1. Capt. Hook's nemesis
2. Cosmetic surgery procedure, for short
3. International oil grp.
4. Pocket gadget
5. Canadian writer Gallant
6. Unusual
7. Basketball hoops
8. Sleeman Cream _____
9. Cause spirits to sink
10. Port Dover's body of water
11. Mosca who won five Grey Cups with the Ti-Cats
12. _____ Slave Lake
13. Shimmery fabric
14. Hindu manifestations
15. Microscope part
16. Former federal justice minister McLellan
17. Fight for two
18. Old slave
28. Type type
29. Iraqi city
32. Rise above it?
34. "_____ a Grecian Urn"
35. Remnant
36. Scenic linen
37. Like pub draft
39. Bonn's name for its river
40. Erstwhile synonym
42. WestJet staff, in flight
43. Red Cross fluid
44. 1950s singing star Pat
45. Reach a reasonable conclusion
47. **Colonel Mustard's square?**
50. **Square for a chef?**
53. Ruse
55. Lame, colloquially
56. BC-born Olympic gold downhill champ: Kerrin _____-Gartner

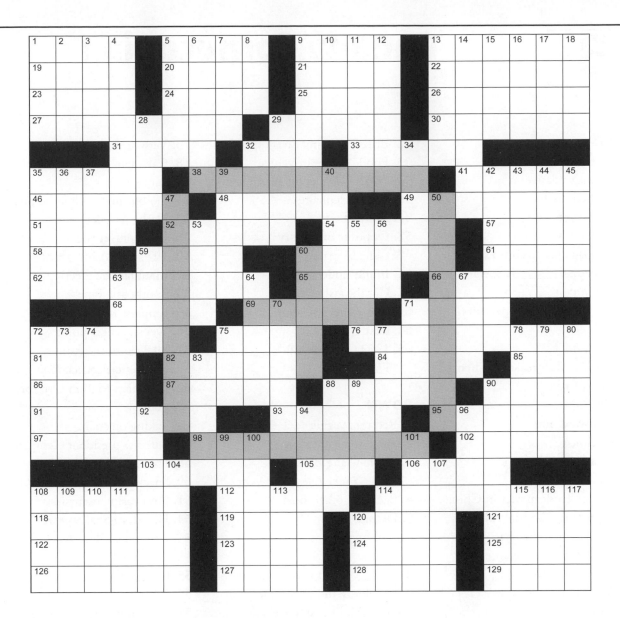

59. University official
60. **Square for stuff?**
63. Conspirator
64. Atoll
67. Greek god of love
70. See 35-D
71. Not sharp
72. Explode
73. Maternally related
74. *Britannic* or *Baltic*
75. Short order for a short-order cook?
77. 1950s Ford
78. Northern Canadian group

79. Medicinal plant
80. Toronto's Royal York, for example
83. Jouster's stick
88. Two pieces of fruit?
89. Nuclear weapon, for short
90. Éclat
92. Arctic Ocean covering
94. Slanted letters style
96. Best of the best
99. Name of many NASA missions
100. Show one's true colours?
101. Pencil end

104. Quebecers Lévesque and Robert
107. Foyer
108. Corset stiffener
109. Bay of Fundy motion
110. Crimson and candy apple
111. Creator's output
113. Gung-ho
114. Insect developmental stage
115. Berry-bearing shrub
116. Stride
117. Fuss
120. Moose _____ SK

3 Canada Cornucopia 1

ACROSS

1. Some scale notes
4. Herring's relative
8. Fortified ditch
14. Map abbr.
15. Narrator's story
16. Fish that fastens onto sharks
17. Canadian _____ Association
19. Not hip
20. Go with The Co-operators?
21. Guise
23. Derision
24. Former Montréal Canadiens coach Blake
25. Hardens
26. Farmyard birds
27. Precipice
29. First claim, in slang
31. From the get-go
34. Leader Trudeau met in China
35. It precedes "lies the rub"
38. Dandelion destroyers
40. Geological time span
41. Without reason?
43. Asian nurse, old style
45. Judge's mallet
46. East Indian flatbread
50. Middle East dignitary
52. British policing division (abbr.)
53. Public square in Venice
54. *HMS Pinafore*, for example
56. Stupid elephants?
57. Mottled cat
58. Opposite of cursory
60. Canada Space _____
61. Inning enders
62. Get the gist
63. Bog plants
64. Take a break
65. 1963 Chiffons hit: "_____ So Fine"

DOWN

1. Red root veggie
2. Show some emotion
3. Marie-Claire Blais book: *A _____ in the Life of Emmanuel*
4. Back end of the boat
5. Despise
6. Molson offering
7. Loot
8. "_____ North strong and free"
9. Landlords' monthly collections
10. Hosted, like Alex Trebek?
11. Lunch hour
12. Goalpost part
13. Very healthy
18. Canadian university official
22. Famous
24. Do business with a thespian?
27. Flashy jewellery
28. Use a prayer rug
30. 1975 ABBA hit
32. Maui tarmac greeting
33. Toothpaste type
35. Empress Hotel tradition
36. Website entry point
37. Like cloisonné (var.)
39. Energetic electrician?
42. Canadian Marion Orr, for example
44. Taking on staff
47. Surprise president George?
48. Highest orbital point
49. Snacks on
51. Joint casing excursion
53. Hexed, to Shakespeare
54. Ontario College Application Service (abbr.)
55. Child's playthings
56. Periods
59. _____ and cry

4. Picturesque Places

Get your camera ready!

ACROSS

1. Wood-shaping machine
6. *Nota* _____
10. Game you might want to check, mate
15. NHL's Staals, for short
19. Poet's heavens
20. Nursery rhyme line: "Pretty maids all in _____"
21. Slowly, on a music score
22. Sheltie's cry
23. Breakfast dish: Eggs _____
25. Passion, in Palm Springs
26. Road Runner's foe: _____ E. Coyote
27. Letter that follows sigma
28. Baby's minder
29. **Yukon peak**
31. Research facility (abbr.)
33. 1970s talk-show host Griffin
34. Fury
35. Surrealist artist Max
36. Begin
38. Bulrush type
42. Young man
43. Lunatic
45. Negative particles
46. Official Albanian currency
47. Women's _____
50. Prescription amounts
52. Matador's opponent
53. Periodic table element #85
55. BC winter resort
58. Poured
60. Halloween spectre
61. "For _____ a jolly good fellow"
62. Upper New York Bay island
64. _____ instant
65. Planters icon: Mr. _____
66. Adverse conditions?
68. **Québec city centre**
71. L'_____-Verte QC
72. Checkered fabrics
74. DNA bit
75. French Albert who wrote *The Stranger*
77. Needlefish
78. Tubular noodles
79. Pearls and peridots
81. Metal tea urns
83. Won over by wooing?
85. Group of London galleries
87. Bus station
88. Yours, in Pierreville
89. Carey Price's domain
90. Taking a shine to
92. Johannesburg township
95. XX or XY indicator
96. Governor _____ Awards
98. Old-style fiddle
99. Part of a flight?
102. Chicken _____ king
103. Nocturnal flyer
105. "Darn!"
106. **Nova Scotia shore spot**
109. Shania Twain's C&W all-time bestseller: _____ *Over*
111. *Rosemary's Baby* scribe Levin
112. Lust for life, say
113. Heart chambers (var.)
114. Mother of all battles
116. Top spot?
117. Harness adjunct
118. Supply vittles
119. Racist
120. Old CBC series: _____ *to Avonlea*
121. "Share and share alike," e.g.
122. Whirlpool
123. Appears to be

DOWN

1. Some political leanings?
2. Georgia's largest city
3. **Ontario archipelago**
4. Feminine pronoun
5. 1974 hit: "_____ Tú"
6. Pancake mix
7. Sudan's eastern neighbour
8. Much to-do about nothing
9. Jug with a big mouth
10. _____ chowder
11. Derring-do, say
12. Withstand
13. 2001 Giller nominee: *The _____ Carvers*
14. Classify
15. Writer's pithy saying?
16. Monarch's prime time
17. Pueblo pots
18. Exhausted all funds?
24. Game played with matchsticks
30. Fluid discharge
32. Canada's Rush, et al.
37. Good culinary sense?
39. Fashion house: Christian _____
40. **Banff National Park place**
41. Consecrate
42. Lease
44. String section instruments
46. Psychedelic drug
47. **Vancouver landmark**
48. Xenophobic, say
49. Improves upon
51. Broker's order
53. Virgil protagonist
54. Local cuisine, in Bangkok
55. Greyhound dog's descendant
56. Greek
57. Like Ruffles
59. Drug cop
63. Small merganser
65. Feather clusters
67. Trig function
69. 1969 hit from Calgary's Original Caste: "_____ Soldier"
70. In _____ rush
73. British manse
76. Deep sleep

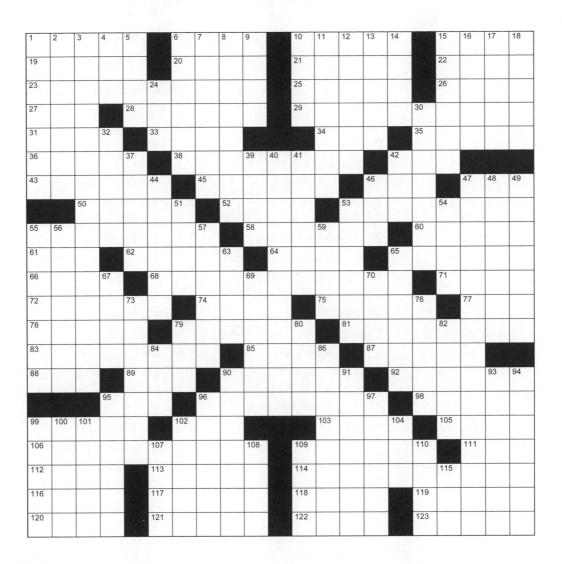

79. Winnipeg NHLer
80. Baker's brouhaha?
82. Promised
84. CBC stalwart Murphy
86. Attracted by (var.)
90. Going out the door
91. Latched onto
93. Place to drink Darjeeling?

94. Eighths
95. Inked on the dotted line
96. *Titanic* Oscar nominee Stuart
97. Supportive boyfriend?
99. Impale a piece of asparagus?
100. Phone service provider, for example
101. Lizard type

102. Played the fool?
104. Pig out?
107. Nobody doesn't like this Lee
108. Lighten up?
109. CBC radio show: *The Vinyl* _____
110. Birds' bills
115. Monopoly cube

5 Ships Ahoy!

They sailed the seven seas

ACROSS

1. Gorillas
5. Kimono closer
8. G8 member
11. Fishing stick
14. Metal fastening device
18. Michael Bublé song: "_____ the Last Dance for Me"
19. Doomed ocean liner
21. Before, archaically
22. Display apathy
23. Like excluded evidence
25. Bag for Beaujolais?
27. 20th-C. art movement
28. _____ fink
29. Electrician's basic training?
30. Revise text
31. Profess
33. Former Netherlands currency
34. Jordan who judged on *Canadian Idol*
35. Very, in Ville-Marie
36. Short military jacket
37. New newts
41. Deal with the devil?
42. They might wear sheeps' clothing?
43. Lively old-style dance
44. Toronto's Air Canada Centre has one
48. Chinese mammals
49. Until now
50. Shrivelled
51. Canadian Armed _____
52. Like some houses on Halloween?
53. 1960s skirt style
54. Top beef cut
56. Copy, for short
57. Go on a shopping spree
59. It landed at Plymouth Rock
61. Rotterdam language
65. Not smooth
67. Pet smell neutralizing product
69. Apple type
70. Fitting
73. Red-_____ woodpecker
74. Rubbish bin
76. Catcalled?
77. Alberta motto: _____ *et Liber*
78. French ethnic group
79. Figurehead locales
80. Vassal's free labour
81. Huffed and puffed
82. _____ precedent
83. Pressed shirts, say
84. 1960s CBC show: *This _____ Has Seven Days*
85. Female parent
89. Hand-held PVR devices
91. Postal _____
92. Beatles song: "Here _____ the Sun"
93. Mechanic's extra piece
96. Emeril Lagasse interjection!
97. Some carpentry guns
99. Marine invertebrate
100. Impossible to reconcile
102. Tuscany region river
103. Fleur-de-_____ (var.)
104. Cousteau's research vessel
105. This can spoil an outdoor wedding
106. Kokanee cold one
107. 1995 k.d. lang album: *All You Can _____*
108. YWG posting
109. See 49-A
110. Transmitted

DOWN

1. 45 hits
2. Central American country
3. Avoids
4. Comfy cars
5. Singer Redding
6. WWII German battleship
7. Third-person pronoun
8. Open up, say
9. Lake sediment
10. One of 52
11. Pens again
12. Yellow birds
13. Bare all?
14. Royal Navy battleship
15. World Golf Hall of Fame inductee Isao
16. Rotate
17. Iron ring wearer, for short
20. Buenos _____
24. _____-term
26. Compass point (abbr.)
29. Tropical fruits
32. Dog's doc
33. Retro tune
35. Military vehicles
36. Gained goodwill
38. Like Fanta without fizz
39. Shopping carryall
40. Went apace
41. Affix a brooch?
42. Psychologist's battle?
43. Calabash, for example
44. Doctrines, for short
45. Pringle
46. Marine bird
47. Greenpeace schooner
48. Lie detection test, for short
49. Dance form
51. Skirmish
52. Beloved public figure
55. Folklore rascals
56. Comedian Foxx
58. Deceived ones
60. Troubles
62. Tortilla kin
63. Tartan indicator
64. Austrian pediatrician Asperger
66. Chic

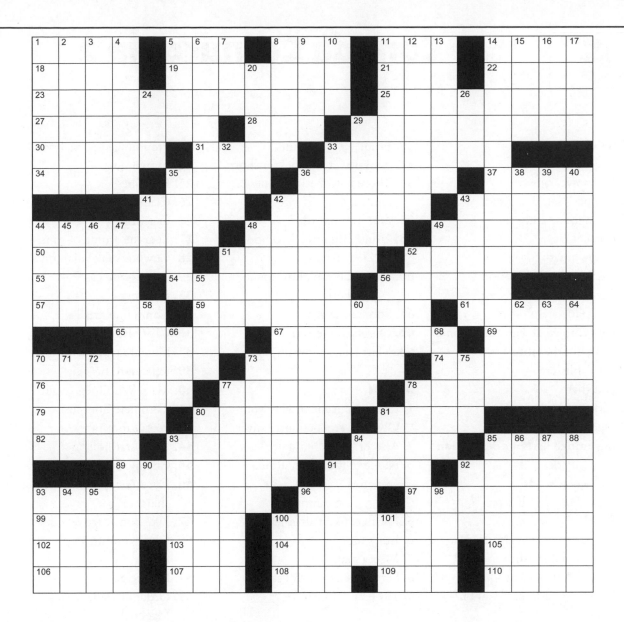

68. Less usual

70. National charitable org: The War _____

71. Dad, in Dorval

72. Cheer for

73. Royal Canadian Air Force CF-18

75. Stitch

77. Place to put one's tootsies up

78. Classic Canadian schooner

80. Adriatic Sea country

81. Physique, in slang

83. Pierce

84. Snug

85. Some teeth

86. Water organisms (var.)

87. Arthurian wand waver

88. Agree

90. Post WWII org., in Europe

91. Rhea played her on *Cheers*

92. 104, to Tiberius

93. See 83-D

94. Like the driven snow?

95. Murray who sings "Snowbird"

96. Rotten little kid

98. Oodles

100. History channel offering: _____ *Pilots NWT*

101. Intelligence agent

Canada Cornucopia 2

ACROSS

1. Ice cream serving
6. Post-shower powder
10. Trapper's saleable good
14. Change the church?
15. Russian city
16. Raspy breath
17. Backwards, in astronomy
19. Genie-winning director Reitman
20. L'Assemblée de la francophonie de l'Ontario (abbr.)
21. Petite blister
22. Not there
24. Tart to the tongue
25. Opera passages
26. Big Smoke harbour destination: _____ Park
30. Some mackerels
31. Tampa Bay MLB team
32. WWII flying force
35. Similar to your relatives?
36. Big-topped mushroom
37. Desert that borders China
38. Jewish worship place (abbr.)
39. Magnum _____
41. Prime minister Stephen
43. Blackmailers
46. Ant, old style
48. Popular German card game
49. Canadian insurance company
50. From _____ to nuts
51. National "taxman," for short
54. Those born between July 22 and August 23
55. Not in proportion
58. "Rule, Britannia!" composer
59. Hockey match
60. Saskatchewan ghost town: _____ Fork
61. Some rural rds.
62. Observer, old style
63. Matt Lauer morning show

DOWN

1. Canadian Renner who won Olympic cross-country silver
2. Alto or bass, on a staff
3. Name of four Holy Roman emperors
4. "_____ the ramparts . . ."
5. For free, to an attorney
6. Bull's foe
7. Mecca man
8. Served as a maestro, say
9. 1972 hit: "I Can See _____ Now"
10. Kingston Pen, formerly
11. Listens in secret
12. Gaucho's grassland
13. Portable shelters
18. Surpluses
23. Pronounced partiality
24. In two ticks
25. ER abbr.
26. Clement Clark Moore poem first word
27. Like the aroma of some wine
28. Cowboy's fake diamond?
29. "_____ my case"
33. Help out
34. Coniferous trees
36. CIBC Run for the _____
37. Liberal's true fortitude?
39. Related to hearing
40. Main Winnipeg street?
41. Complete nonsense
42. Poetry foot type
44. Short stat holidays?
45. Chemical compound
46. *For Whom the Bells Tolls* female character
47. Like non-reactive gases
50. Juno-winning graphic artist Hugh
51. Engine gunk
52. Order of Canada singer MacNeil
53. Sore
56. Declare
57. As well

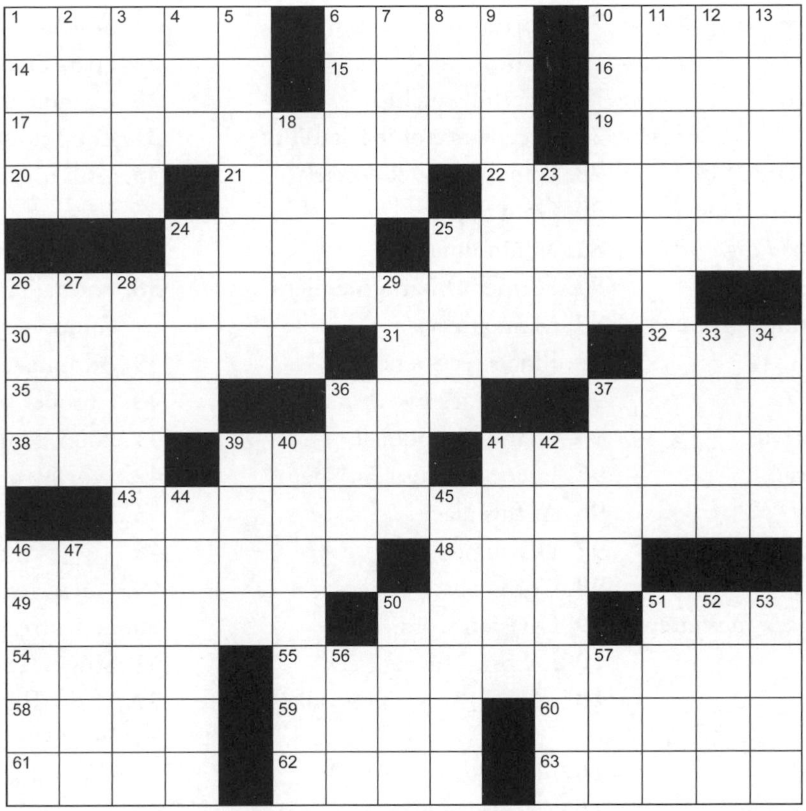

Solution on page 178

7 They Hail from Hamilton

Born in Steeltown

ACROSS

1. 1960s CFL star Jackson
5. Trudge
9. 1990s sitcom: *Dharma &* _____
13. Dutch cheese
17. 2.54 centimetres
18. Helper
19. Nestlé bar manufactured in Canada
20. *The Postman Always Rings Twice* star Turner
21. A Shetland pony might graze here
22. Leaves
23. Breakfast dish: Huevos _____
25. California tech area: _____ Valley
27. Military unit
29. Pizzeria appliances
30. Like much of Canada in winter
31. Boyfriend
32. Large book
34. With firm resolve
37. Writing buddy?
41. Psychic's talent, for short
44. It secretes formic acid
45. Exterior
47. Santa _____
48. Roping a dogie
52. Sacred Islamic book
53. Boast
54. Like a pilot's unkempt hair?
55. Well-endowed?
56. *Mea culpa*, say
57. **Political trailblazer Fairclough**
58. Dupes
59. **Ballerina Kain**
60. Big bashes
61. Short song
62. Strands in the Sahara?
64. Bibliographical note abbr.
65. Molars, et al.
66. Eastern white, in Ontario
67. H1N1, for one
68. Petro-Canada competitor
69. Spelling contest
70. North American time zone (abbr.)
71. Place of worship
73. Acceptance of inevitability
78. Bring up the children
80. Gold filigree
81. Minimum
84. Former Ontario premier Eves
87. Main artery
89. Illness recurrence
91. New Year's Eve drink
93. Grand, colloquially
95. Jazz/salsa musician Puente
96. At this place
97. Distribute
98. Corn cobs
99. Division word
100. Acorn-bearing trees
101. " . . . _____ 'til he takes a wife . . ."
102. Dick Van _____
103. **Rush drummer Peart**

DOWN

1. The Keg serves these
2. Dismantle an oil well?
3. E-F-G-A-B-C-D-E
4. **Former deputy prime minister Copps**
5. Asian building
6. Maned beast
7. Poem
8. Journey down a mountain
9. Very verbosely
10. Harvest
11. Accounting firm _____ & Young
12. Federal government abbr.
13. Mark Messier's NHL number
14. Canadian "good food" company
15. Soon, old style
16. Muster at church?
24. Head of the household on *The Simpsons*
26. Spanish icon: El _____
28. Granola morsel
31. Loud noise
33. Golf tournament title word
35. Lots
36. Mongolian abodes
38. Formal flower garden component
39. Administered a sacrament
40. Croquet pitch
41. 2003 holiday film
42. Worthy of retail shelf space
43. Dietary fibre source
46. _____-Sachs disease
49. Chef's repast?
50. Is in arrears
51. **Singer Thomas**
52. What The Raven did?
53. Insertion mark, in text
55. Like some coloured glass?
56. Use a surgical beam
58. Yoho National Park place
59. **1970s Montréal Canadien Dryden**
60. Present
61. *Gidget* actress Sandra
62. Weight watcher's regime
63. Director's domain
65. *Top Chef Canada* season one host Andrews
66. Fuel source
68. Shut-eye
69. Like a tardy birthday card
72. Gets the pump ready?
74. Athletic
75. Treat poorly
76. Large body of water
77. *SCTV* star Short
79. Fits of fury

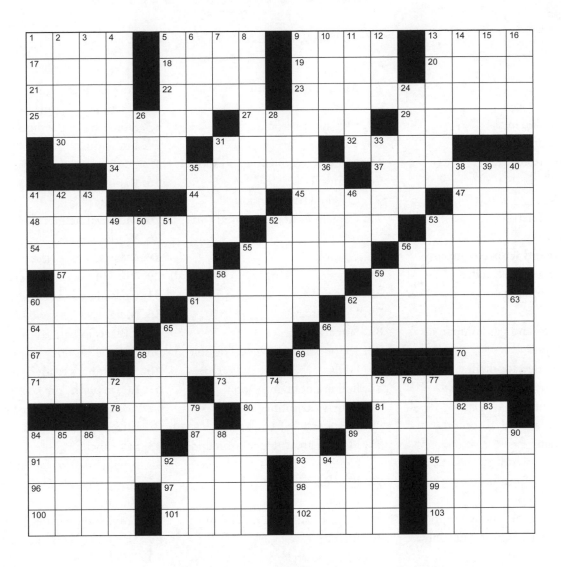

82. Fishnet

83. Little Richard hit: "_____ Frutti"

84. Bounce off the walls?

85. Canadian comedienne Caroline

86. British police informant

88. Not fooled by

89. Place setting implement

90. Dirty game?

92. AB motorists' assn.

94. Northwest Territories town: _____ River

8 Autobiographical

Men who made it big with cars

ACROSS

1. Biological bag
4. Lively folk dance
7. Third month
12. Support pole
17. "Yuck!"
18. Santa _____ winds
19. Daisy variety
20. Eclipse type
21. **Ferdinand whose company produced the Spyder**
23. _____ of soda
25. Rubes
27. Some oil and gas company employees
28. Insect's developmental stage
30. Norman _____ NWT
32. Garments for 47-D
33. 62nd mayor of Toronto Lastman
34. Word for word
36. On _____ and needles
37. Work without _____
39. 1940s PEI premier Campbell
40. Canadian TV host Mulroney, et al.
41. Snow White's medic?
44. Muslim religious teachers
46. Top quality
47. Lasso
48. Raised riverbanks
49. Laid low with grief
51. Doobie Brothers hit: "What _____ Believes"
54. **Ettore of early Grand Prix race cars**
56. Anoint, old style
57. Boring chants?
59. Canadian-born *Bonanza* star Greene
61. Official Québec flower: Blue flag _____
62. Play minigolf

63. American Revolutionary War warrior
67. Outlawed pesticide
68. Pans
69. Unexpected difficulty, in Dorset
70. Identical
71. Overlook the obvious
72. Captain & Tennille loved this rodent?
74. Glimpse
75. Butcher's offerings
78. Presew
79. Urban story?
81. Sumatran apes
83. 1970s *Saturday Night Live* star Gilda
85. Full of doom and gloom
87. **Sports car pioneer Enzo**
90. Despises
91. Hockey greats Henderson and Coffey
92. BC-born singer: Carly _____ Jepsen
93. Largest Canadian city (abbr.)
94. Big hit?
95. Kills, old style
96. Ocean Networks Canada (abbr.)
97. History channel show: _____ *Road Truckers*

DOWN

1. Eat dinner
2. Then
3. **Walter who founded one of the Big Three**
4. Coyote's African kin
5. Beneficiary
6. French tennis star Monfils
7. Social media event: Flash _____
8. Armpits
9. Remember
10. Some primary colours

11. Group on the range
12. "Here For Canada," et al.
13. Stereo system components
14. Ludicrous
15. Starbucks serving
16. Rapunzel's lock
22. Drunkard
24. Medieval helmet
26. Workout wear
28. Mosque prayer leader
29. "99 Luftballons" singer
31. Coastal avians (var.)
35. Metal fasteners with wings
36. CPP recipient, say
38. Societal no-nos
40. Shoeshiner's toady?
41. Adore (with "on")
42. **Adam of German automotive history**
43. Say "uncle"
45. Boxing or karate award
46. _____ Gallery of Greater Victoria
47. Royal Indian ladies (var.)
49. The _____ MB
50. Tirade
51. In the centre of
52. **Model T man Henry**
53. "Step _____!"
55. Receive
58. American marsupial
60. Pastoral parish head
63. Sailboat part
64. **Italian luxury car family name**
65. Prayer ending
66. Require
68. Like a greedy hog farmer?
69. With exacting meticulousness
71. Ministers' homes
72. 18th-C. gown
73. Madagascar mammal
75. Second-year students, for short
76. Best of the crop?

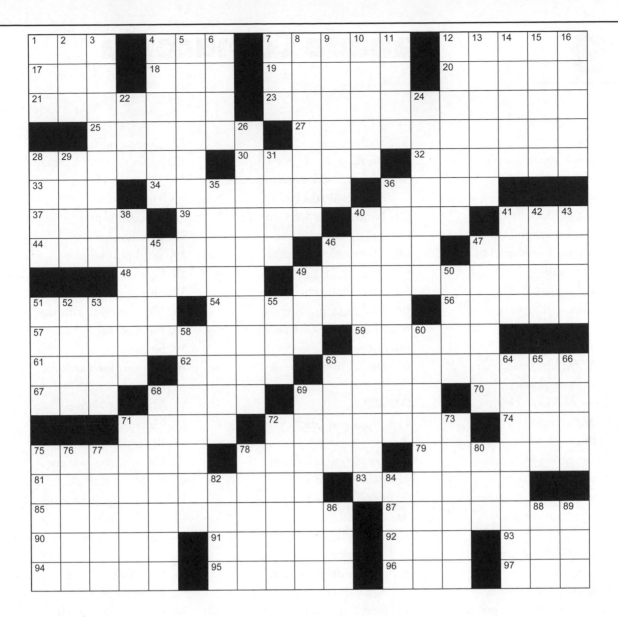

77. Bob Marley was one
78. Elementary
80. Bonn country (abbr.)

82. Inside info, say
84. Curly do
86. Canadian Sleep Society (abbr.)

88. *One Thousand and One Nights* bird
89. Rage

9 Canada Cornucopia 3

ACROSS

1. Canadian media family name
6. Farming machine
10. Nicholas II title
14. Fabric for some uniforms
15. Where an earring sits
16. Currency introduced in 2002
17. Wraps again
19. Body of poetry
20. Slalom turn type
21. Toys that fly
22. Loses fur
23. 1947 find in Leduc AB
24. *Peter Peter Pumpkin _____*
26. Western Russia city
31. Roman emperor
34. Extols
35. Congregation
37. Three, to an Italian
38. Insect world hill builders
39. Tender tootsies cause
40. _____ gras
41. Life story, for short
42. Ribs locale
43. Did electrical work
44. African wilderness trek
46. Lacking lodgings
48. Blueprint details
50. Belief system suffix
51. Slight incline
53. Breakfast food
56. AB agency: Environmental Appeals Board (abbr.)
59. Ninth Governor General: _____ Grey
60. Meaningless chatter
62. Penny _____
63. Australian gem export
64. Mulroney minister MacKay
65. Eliot of *The Untouchables*
66. Subside
67. Shades of blue-green

DOWN

1. 4,047 square metres
2. "_____ Always a Woman"
3. Gladys Knight's singers
4. *Bambi* character
5. Western Canada range
6. _____ du jour
7. Opera house box
8. Too plump
9. *Scream* director Craven
10. Small snicker
11. Real Canadian _____
12. Handle for NY Yankee Alex
13. Art _____ Trophy
18. Pottery firing appliance
22. Command to a collie
23. Town north of Calgary
25. It follows Gospels
26. Thick pieces
27. Mood disorder
28. Irritable
29. Wild plum type
30. Canadian photographer Yousuf
32. First Zodiac sign
33. Woodwind instrument sticks
36. Fond of, say
39. Swanky
40. Toronto International _____ Festival
42. Manitoba Natives
43. Canadian air carrier
45. BC produce export
47. Japanese soup choice
49. Buddhist shrine
51. Two-time Oscar winner Penn
52. Road segment
54. Muscat nation
55. Competent
56. Jane Austen novel
57. Biblical sibling
58. Round Table knight
60. Cut the grass
61. Suffix for nod or mod

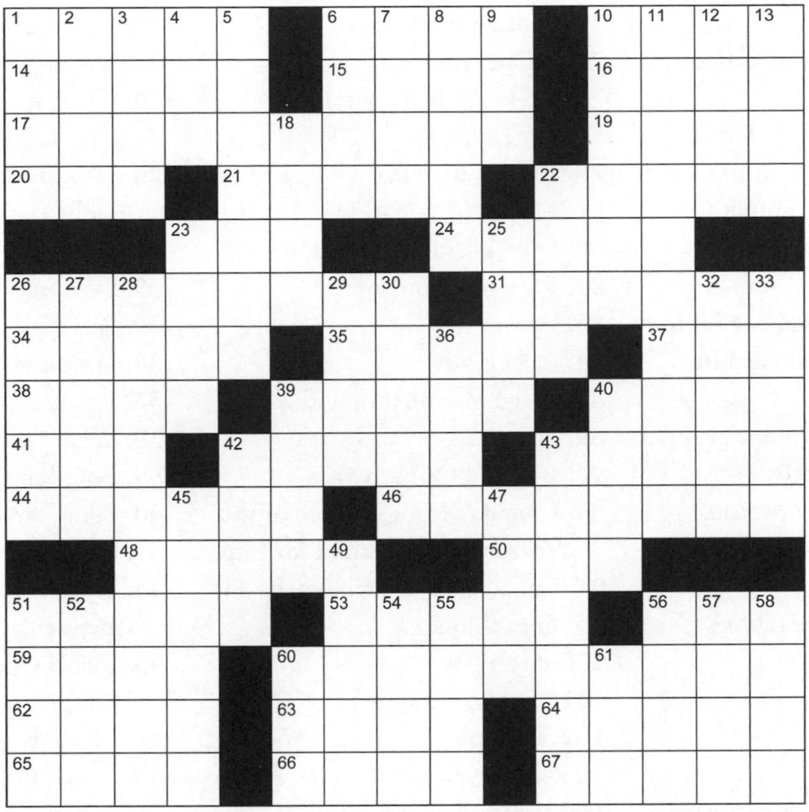

Solution on page 179

Better to Receive?

Some prized possessions

ACROSS

1. _____ Breton Highlands National Park
5. Japanese city
10. Some post-grad U of C degrees
13. Peel
17. With 100-A, *M*A*S*H* star
18. Himalayan snow creatures
19. Matterhorn, for example
20. Warts and all, in retail
21. Pigsty, say
22. **Canada's Memorial Medal for Humour is named for him**
25. Bits of hair
27. Small sewage treatment facilities
28. It played eight-tracks
31. Most tender, like a tootsie?
32. _____ wing and a prayer
33. Wall hanging
35. Our currency code (abbr.)
36. Prisoner without parole
41. Former New Brunswick premier Bernard
43. Angels
45. **Former TV excellence award**
46. Buffy Sainte-Marie hit: "_____ It's Time for You to Go"
48. Walks through a river
49. Becomes more heartfelt
50. Picked the perp from a lineup
52. When doubled, a ballroom dance
53. Gangster's "rod"
54. Turn (var.)
55. "The Beeb"
57. **Crime Writers of Canada present this annual award**
61. Cacophony
62. April shower, say
64. Stallone franchise film: *Rocky* _____
65. Become a plaintiff
66. Little kids
68. Sets goals
70. Rooftop panel type
72. Chastise
75. **Scotiabank literary prize**
76. Edible tree seed
78. Reese Witherspoon film: _____ *Off Place*
79. 1975 Paul Anka song: "I Don't Like to _____ Alone"
80. Spitz kin, at the dog show
81. Race for a foursome
83. By way of
84. Ear malady
87. Weighing the pros and cons
89. Some cats
94. Erie and Ontario
95. **Canada's Male Athlete of the Year award is named for him**
97. Canadian Little who made an impression?
100. See 17-A
101. Cardinal number
102. Pay up?
103. _____ *Dick*
104. Stelco detritus
105. 1982 Eddie Murphy movie: *48* _____
106. Cast out
107. Finger clicking sound

DOWN

1. Comox-born ex-Bruin Neely
2. Pub drink
3. Verb form
4. Follow
5. Rockefeller's seafood serving?
6. Gear-to-shaft fastener
7. Dined
8. Dosses, in Derby
9. Sackcloth and _____
10. Chants
11. Associated with, in NATO?
12. Glasses, for short
13. South American critter
14. "Well I'll be _____ of a gun!"
15. Canadian comedian Mercer
16. Edmonton CFLers, for short
23. Geological eras
24. Clement who came before and after Churchill
26. US consumer protection agency (abbr.)
28. Fragrant balsam
29. Ever and _____
30. Pakistani port city
34. Hindu religious figure
37. Rascals
38. What farmers see?
39. Boredom
40. Like Christ, on the third day
42. Completed a task
44. **Former cup for the Jays vs. the Expos**
45. Marvin Gaye hit: "Let's _____ On"
47. Meadow
49. East Indian lentil dish
51. Less moist
53. Gathered info, say
55. Boasts
56. Spice rack bottle label
58. Xmas carol contraction
59. 18th-C. Swiss math guru
60. *Titanic*'s Marconi msg.
63. Cleopatra's river
67. Early Air Canada name (abbr.)
69. Quiet period
70. Apelike
71. Unfettered, say
73. Stretched out
74. Gravitational force
76. Witches' brews
77. Silk upholstery fabric
80. Crustacean's claw
82. Chatty beast?
85. State of the soil

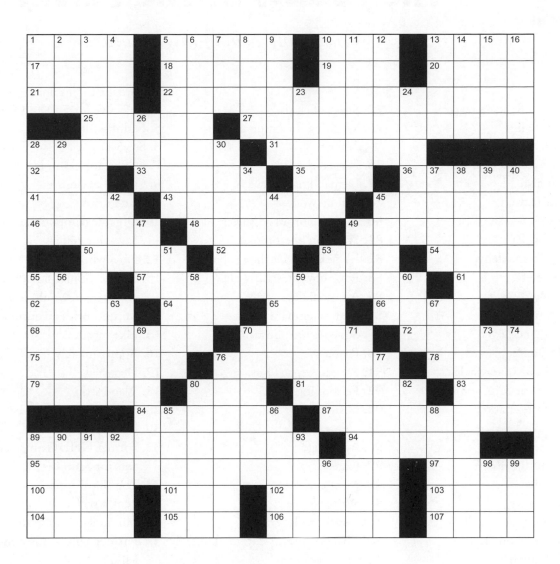

86. Drum type
88. Periods of endearment?
89. "With regret"
90. Ex BC premier Vander Zalm

91. *Star Wars* Jedi master
92. Setback
93. Heroin a.k.a. (var.)
96. Make tracks

98. National attorneys' org.
99. Triangle side (abbr.)

11   The Fabrics of Their Lives

What some people might wear?

ACROSS

1. Fourteenth Saskatchewan premier Wall
5. *Buenos* _____
9. Impoverished person
15. Cereal dish
19. Part of Hawaii
20. *Monty Python* star Eric
21. Book format
22. _____ formaldehyde
23. News brief?
24. Mrs. Mulroney
25. Ocean bird
26. "_____ She Lovely"
27. **Little Bo Peep?**
29. **Canadian singer Jacks?**
31. St. John's or Saint John
32. Post-injury mark
34. Deep hole
35. Short-sleeved tops
39. Kidlit author Roald
40. Like coins
45. Makes merry?
46. Pepsi, for one
47. Obsolete phone feature
48. Post-it square
49. Handbag
50. Convicted criminal
51. RONA used to be this in Canada
52. *Cats* cat: Rum _____ Tugger
53. Make a mistake
54. Not a soul
56. Watery-eyed
58. Perform better than
60. Sweeping story
62. 1980s Grammy winner Benatar
63. Basins
64. Not visible
65. Canadian winter boots brand
67. Heart part
68. Canadian Pointer, for example
69. Lemon-like fruit
71. Virile
72. Scrap of cloth
73. Wedding invitation answer (abbr.)
76. Not coupled?
77. Demanding
78. Choral work
80. Make amorous advances
81. Street, in Sherbrooke
82. It's next to a narthex
83. Loverboy hit: "Turn Me _____"
85. Ammonia derivative
87. Teapot remnant
89. Squeezes the most from
90. Primates
91. Pats down, at a bust
92. Persevering
94. Glance over
95. Contradict
96. Atlas page
97. Careen
98. Meat cut
99. **Writer Joyce?**
104. **Author Heyer?**
109. Beauty queen's cummerbund
110. Battery ends
112. Bookies' computations
113. Winnipeg-born magician Henning
114. Chauffeur's vehicle
115. Like a tough teacher
116. Metalware
117. Cow patty contents
118. NL historic site: L'_____ aux Meadows
119. Old CBC show: *Rick Mercer's _____ Report*
120. Quartz variety
121. Mars' opposite number

DOWN

1. Seethe
2. Pro _____
3. Throat clearer's noise
4. Adjective for 5-D and 6-D
5. Numbskulls
6. See 5-D
7. Pewter, for example
8. Official enclosure?
9. Dad's drink?
10. Organic compound
11. Say something
12. Final wife of Henry VIII
13. Robert Goulet signature song: "If _____ I Would Leave You"
14. Rotund Brit's favourite dessert?
15. Like most dishwashers
16. Approximately
17. Departed
18. Wood strip
28. Window netting
30. USSR follower
32. Former NHL Canuck and Senator Sami
33. **The Big Bopper?**
35. Tent type (var.)
36. Impolite diner's sound
37. **Former Ontario premier Mike?**
38. Bublé album: _____ *Time*
39. Charity, in Chichester
40. Stadium levels
41. Undulating
42. **Roger Federer?**
43. Pianist's practice piece
44. Fiend
46. Penny
47. Canadian rapper
50. Farm newborn
55. Ajar
57. Green-eyed spite
58. Single digit
59. Drug addict
61. Apple's centre
63. Without, in Hull
64. Instinctive desire

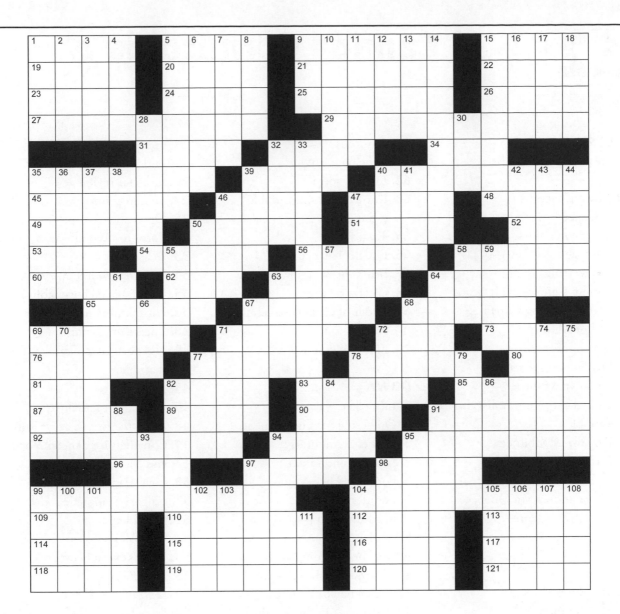

66. Gemini-nominated sports announcer Black
67. Flower holders
68. Diminish
69. They go with whey
70. Habituate
71. Shakes and shimmies
72. Supremes singer Diana
74. Clear alcohol
75. Old-style verse
77. Capital of Azerbaijan
78. Faucet brand
79. Exhausting

82. Tumour, say
84. October birthstone
86. Part of an hr.
88. Detective's galosh?
91. Equitable females?
93. _____-di-dah
94. Toronto college name
95. Considerable in size
97. Made over
98. Seduced
99. 1987 Madonna hit: "La _____ Bonita"
100. Precipitation

101. Schools of thought
102. Sondheim musical: _____ *the Woods*
103. Old Scandinavian language
104. Jazz standard: "You _____ My Head"
105. Icelandic literary ana
106. _____ de force
107. Harmonize an orchestra
108. Omelette components
111. Home for a hog

ACROSS

1. Like a chic Spice Girl?
5. Cry
8. Some crustaceans
13. Take heed
14. BC Lieutenant-Governor Campagnolo (2001–07)
15. Yellow fruit
16. Former Québec NHL team
18. Nobel-winning Canadian author Munro
19. Watch mechanism
20. Preplanned sports play
22. These, in Montréal
24. United Empire Loyalist, for example
25. Dog for a Dubliner?
30. Fertilizing soil
31. La Brea pit goo
32. Lady's address, in Québec
37. Use advantageously
39. Modern music style
41. Dangerous situation
42. Kind of block
44. Trig ratio
46. Not as much
47. CBC consumer advocacy show since 1972
50. Vow
54. Chai or camomile
55. Amorous
57. Acne blemish
62. *Carmen* form
63. Known for unfavourable exploits
65. Totally legal
66. Equally balanced
67. Brink
68. Clear a cassette
69. Order of Canada ballet dancer Harrington
70. Like a dilettante

DOWN

1. Little lake
2. Orchestral reed instrument
3. Dali contemporary
4. Famed London park
5. Former French coin
6. Loonies
7. Most disgusting
8. Audience's nonsense?
9. Got the fire going again
10. *Maclean's* writer Barbara
11. Lawn bowling game
12. Curl one's lip in disdain
14. Smarts evaluation tool
17. Small imperial measurement
21. Come down copiously
23. Burn the outside of a steak
25. He might have a Sunni outlook?
26. Five-star review
27. Tehran country
28. Open an envelope
29. Toronto's Woodbine, for one
33. PC brand
34. Length x width
35. Catch-all category (abbr.)
36. Ultimatum ending
38. Encase in plastic
40. NB-born Bliss Carman, for example
43. Endure
45. Crush, colloquially
48. *All in the Family* actor Rob
49. Canadian ice dancers Virtue and Moir, for example
50. Lowly labourer
51. Calgary Stampede rodeo pro
52. Greek letter
53. Baseball great Roger
56. Peggy's Nova Scotia place?
58. Mineral type
59. See 21-D
60. Sexual desire
61. See Mata Hari?
64. 1940s singer/actor Ritter

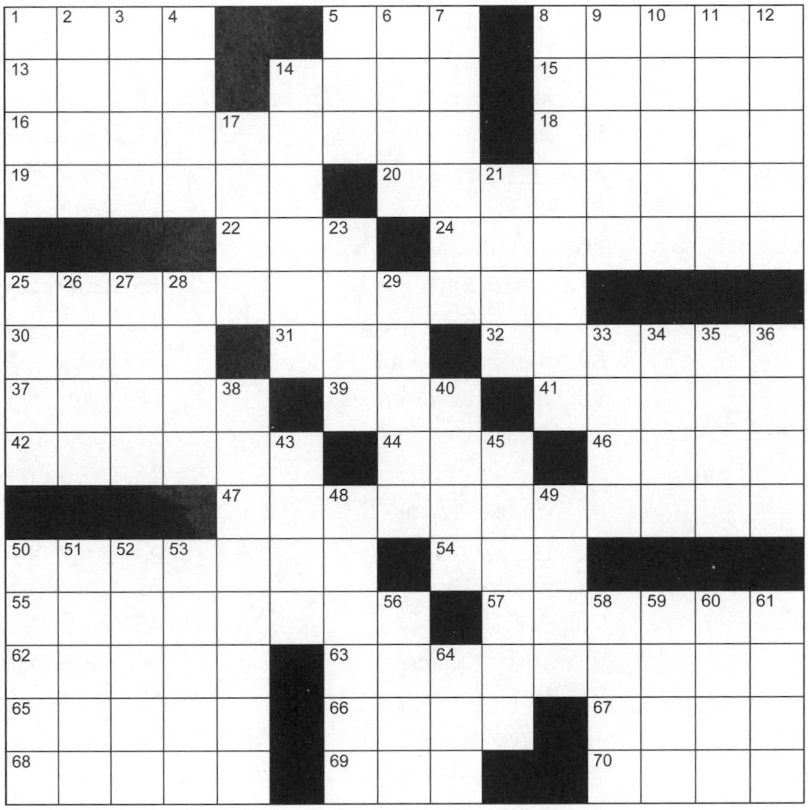

Solution on page 179

13   Stampede Parade Marshals

They led the annual festivities in Calgary

ACROSS

1. Fix Fifi, say
5. _____ Man's Flats AB
9. Ladies' crowns
15. Cello implements
19. Peruvian capital
20. Wight or Man
21. Like modern electronics
22. Flash of creativity
23. Not proven with evidence
25. **Nova Scotia singer (1991)**
27. **American comedian (1963)**
28. Kind of cross
30. Cold mist
31. Legislative passage
33. Canadian Thanksgiving mo.
34. _____-toe
38. Tractor-trailer
39. Woodworking tools
41. Northern BC city
42. More obscene
46. Sault Ste. _____
48. Bobby Hull, to Brett
49. Surprised sounds
50. Sense of community spirit
51. Hebrew letter
52. Asian carp
53. Jennies, et al.
54. Opposite of 58-D
55. Some horses
56. *Superman's* Lois
58. Spherical shape
59. Travellers' pit stop
61. Skin spuds
62. Heeding instructions
66. BIC fluid
67. **Comedic Canadian actor (1992)**
70. Long-time CBC hockey host MacLean
71. Euros replaced these in Spain
73. Carbonated quaff
74. Canadian restaurant chain: _____ Mario's
76. Actor DeLuise
77. Rosy colour
78. Anger
79. Small case, in Saint-Tropez
80. Deep pit
83. _____ de deux
84. Love
86. Uses a hammer
87. Gator's kin
88. Beanie Babies, e.g.
89. Oktoberfest mug
90. Merengue and mambo, in Montréal
91. Add weight restrictions?
93. Michael Smith's PEI-set series: _____ *at Home*
94. Modify text
96. Flew
97. Corral fodder
98. Ethiopian capital
104. Washed away, like a riverbank
106. Air conditioning energy unit (abbr.)
107. **Crazy Canuck (1979)**
108. **Ex-Calgary Flame (2004)**
112. Foot bone groups
114. Give a darn
115. Boulevard
116. Word of regret
117. Jackson 5 member
118. Not close
119. Like some butter
120. Construction project zone
121. Grasps

DOWN

1. Chunks of marble
2. _____ noir
3. Minute organism (var.)
4. Luxurious boat
5. Lens power measurement (var.)
6. Regard highly
7. _____ mode
8. Major US airline
9. By way of, briefly
10. Number on a sundial
11. Top stories?
12. Strike back
13. Zenith
14. Conned Isaac Hayes?
15. **American entertainer (1959)**
16. "_____ to Joy"
17. Former *W5* journalist Chen
18. "My Gal _____"
24. Puts out a fire
26. Coconut fibre
29. Sentient
32. Insignificant
33. Cheer for Real Madrid?
35. Southwest US artists' mecca
36. Head malady
37. Bad luck of the Irish?
40. Duo who toured Canada in 2011
41. Mai _____
42. Unleash a blue streak?
43. Flammable gas
44. Stirs eggs
45. "Stop it"
47. Morning hrs.
48. Anonymous John
51. Band out of Winnipeg: The _____ Who
52. Leg segment
53. Looks _____ everything
55. Pierre Berton book: *The National _____*
57. Solo at La Scala
58. Overweight
60. Some saxes
61. Low-level worker
62. US Plains Native

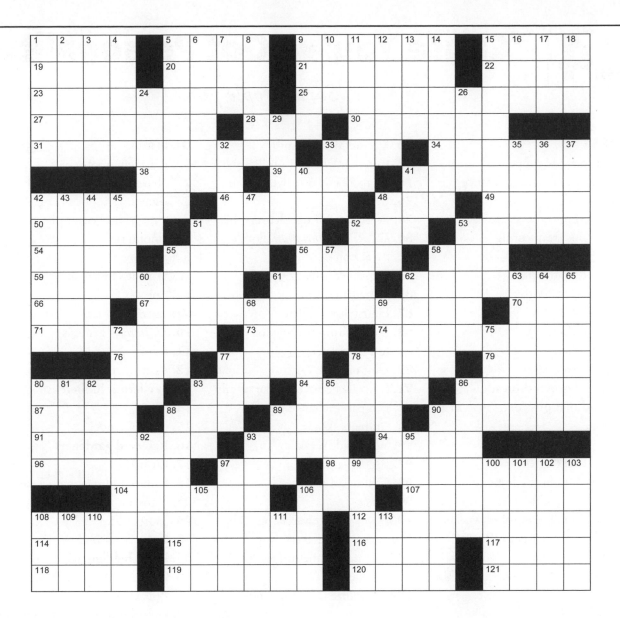

63. Eye ailment
64. Small bump
65. Metamorphic rock
68. She appears in hieroglyphs
69. Erudite
72. **Governor General (1981)**
75. James Bond portrayer Connery
77. Steno's need
78. King of Québec?
80. Play parts
81. Vivacity, in Veneto
82. Enlightening exercise?

83. Goat-legged Greek god
85. Remove lard
86. Floating
88. Brimmed hats
89. Reticent
90. Parkinson's or polio
92. Gull's relative
93. Rhythmical
95. Dogmatic decree
97. German philosopher Georg
99. *The Count of Monte Cristo* scribe
100. Young rascals

101. Hawk's perch
102. Moisten the chicken
103. Tijuana ta-ta
105. Hindu deity
106. Raised a baker?
108. _____ Victor
109. Big galoot
110. Car grille covering
111. Light shade
113. 1967 Governor General's
     literary award winner Mandel

14 'Cause You've Got Personality

Some people puns

ACROSS

1. MLB players' toppers
5. Elevator manufacturer since 1853
9. Sharpen one's razor
14. Abstains from eating
19. _____-bodied
20. Issued an order
21. Seaport in Dorset
22. Reddish yellow
23. **Fun fellow?**
26. Not urban
27. Bestow a quality
28. Hors d'oeuvres spread
29. Word that preceded "fizz" in a jingle
30. Stumbles
31. He always agrees
33. One-thousand kilograms
35. Des Moines citizen
37. Old ship's boiler room worker
39. *77 Sunset Strip* actor Byrnes
41. Modern prefix?
42. Canadian restaurant chain: The _____
45. _____ Mahal
48. Sun's beams
49. Star student
51. Ours has the Bluenose on one side
52. Great Plains tribe
54. Chevy Blazer, for example
55. Small insect
56. Shot of whisky, say
57. Belittle
58. Walk like Tiny Tim?
61. George Brown and Humber, in Toronto
63. H.H. Munro pen name
64. Over with
65. Wild
67. Neckline type
68. Architectural moulding
70. US president Grant
72. Ceremonial French military hat
74. England's WWII flyers
76. Crush
78. Peter Mansbridge delivers this
80. *WKRP in Cincinnati* blonde Anderson
83. Capable of change
85. Canadian opera star Stratas
87. Hairstylist's milieu
88. Former Toronto Maple Leaf John-Michael _____
89. Unit of work
91. His wife became a pillar of salt
92. Pen pals exchange these
94. Animal's skin
95. With wide scope
97. Bit of plankton
98. Confucian ideal
99. Shack
100. US aviation watchdog (abbr.)
101. Canada's smallest prov.
102. Gather on the surface, in chemistry
104. Organize the Irish dancers again?
106. Bell, e.g.
108. Russian plain
112. Canadian specialty channel
114. Woody Allen comedy: *Anything _____*
117. Farmer's field
119. War of 1812 heroine Secord
120. Equestrian, say
121. **First responder?**
124. Flip
125. Preside at the podium
126. Nevada casino city
127. Fragrance since 1932
128. Examinations
129. Barely beat out
130. June 6, 1944
131. Ooze

DOWN

1. Like a wily zookeeper?
2. "I have _____ to pick with you"
3. Trudges
4. Some ground cover plants
5. Kimono tie
6. Press down
7. Uses one's imagination
8. Zone
9. Jacuzzi
10. *Lusitania*'s nemesis
11. Bun
12. Assortment
13. **Lecherous looker?**
14. "Tea _____"
15. Honda model
16. **Reserved gardener?**
17. Ensnare
18. Some condiments, in Québec
24. Cups and saucers salver
25. Mother bird
32. Genesis ark builder
34. **Flustered female?**
36. Canada's Office of Energy Efficiency (abbr.)
38. Greenhouse gas treaty signed by Canada
40. Dental Therapy Assistant (abbr.)
43. Run the show?
44. Canadian honkers
45. Small amounts
46. Nevada's _____ 51
47. **Handy man?**
49. Place
50. Boxes up
51. Paul Gross TV show: _____ *South*
53. Prudish person
54. Type of wheat
56. _____ Worlde
59. Still to be born
60. Navy rank (abbr.)

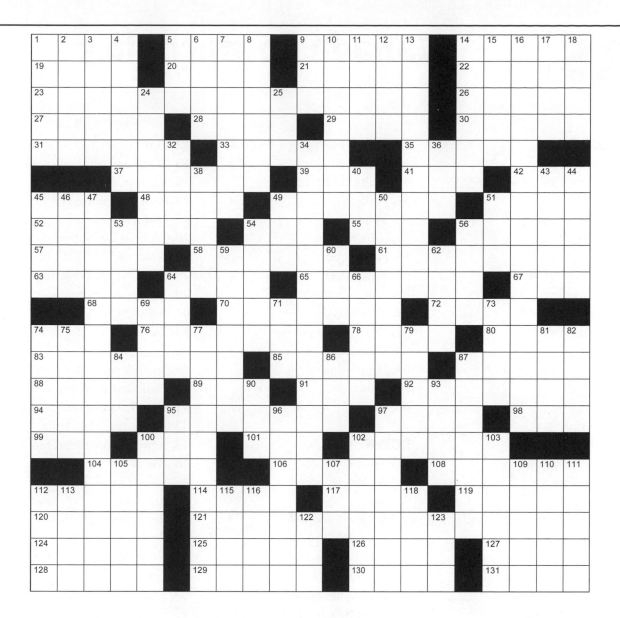

62. Albanian monetary units
64. Restaurant type
66. Religious principle
69. Minute amphibians
71. Up to now
73. Surveyor's document
74. Kramden played by Gleason
75. Frontenac farewell
77. **Regular guy?**
79. Room dividers
81. *Sleepless in Seattle* scribe Ephron
82. "Not _____ many words"
84. Most preferred pooch?

86. 1990s Saskatchewan premier Romanow
87. Scare
90. Space
93. Ids' neighbours
95. *Red Corner* co-star Ling
96. Diplomatic thaw
97. Festooned
100. Norway land features
102. See 15-D
103. Animals
105. Current happening?
107. Be situated, say

109. Cocoon dwellers
110. Intensive investigation
111. Consume?
112. Like some champagne
113. Ready for picking
115. The Cup's named after him: _____ Stanley
116. 1970s carpet style
118. Lab burner
122. 1998 film: *Waking _____ Devine*
123. Claire who wrote *Canadians in the Civil War*

15 Canada Cornucopia 5

ACROSS

1. Electrical flash
6. Southern Québec locale: _____-Sud
10. Loading zone
14. Poet W.H. _____
15. Zeus' spouse
16. Fairy tale baddy
17. Some Queen's instructors
19. Bearing in mind?
20. Group of six
21. *Mens* _____
22. Turgenev who wrote *Fathers and Sons*
23. Pulls
25. Adversary
26. Not whole
30. Transparent overlay
32. Intimidate
34. Plotter
38. Saskatchewan is the world's leading exporter of this
39. Red shade
40. Rather than
42. 2013 Avril Lavigne hit: "_____ Never Growing Up"
43. Consumed by, colloquially
45. Failing grades
46. Martin who judged on *Canada's Got Talent*
49. Calibri and Cambria
51. NHL award: _____ Smythe Trophy
52. It covers a pan
53. Forcible removal
58. Botany sacs
59. Line under text
61. Defrost
62. "It's _____ a pleasure"
63. Great Lake
64. Hunter's quarry
65. Tallies
66. Buddy Holly hit: "_____ Easy"

DOWN

1. Depletes
2. Like filtered water
3. Fusses
4. Plundered, old style
5. Poked with a patella
6. Canadian interjections
7. *Hockey Night in Canada* anchor Stroumboulopoulos
8. Takes into custody
9. Apollo mission org.
10. Tyrannized
11. Pointed arch type
12. Lotion
13. "Footloose" singer Loggins
18. Panama, for example
24. Easily succeed at
25. Old sedation gas
26. Western US Native
27. Stratford ON river
28. Tennis court do-agains
29. College social group
31. Bill of exchange signer
33. Take _____
35. _____ *en scène*
36. Spanish compass point
37. Antique automobiles
41. Gave meaning to
42. Endearment for Attila?
44. Agreed, with a head motion
46. Rascal
47. Bob or Doug McKenzie persona
48. Repentigny relative
50. Raw fish serving
52. *Royal Canadian Air Farce* actress Goy
54. Peter Rabbit's tail
55. Craggy peaks
56. Psyche loved him
57. Loverboy lead singer Mike
60. Dash types

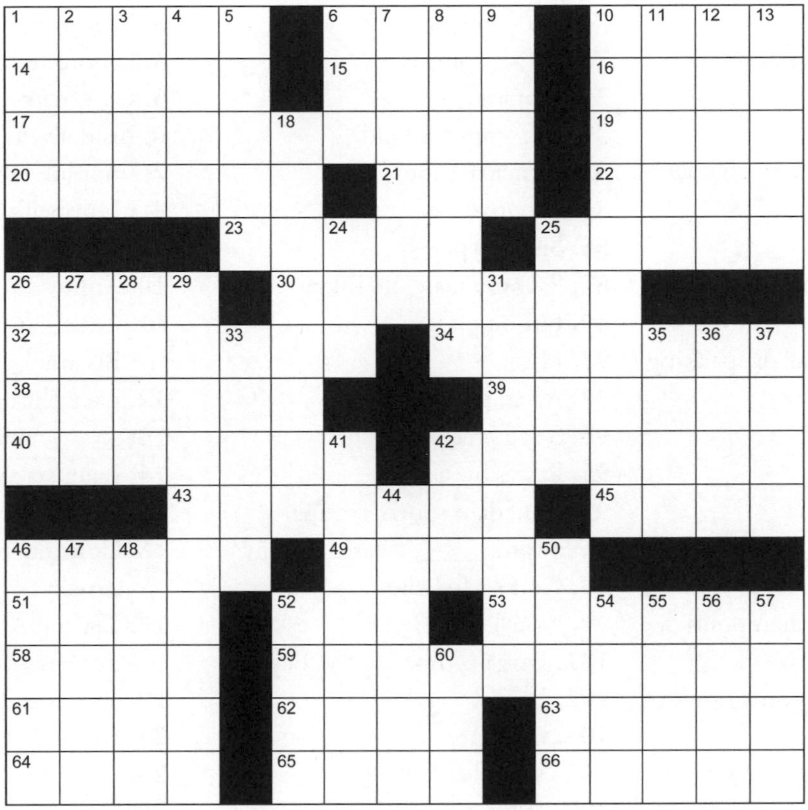

Solution on page 180

16 Canadian "Clan" Bands

They enjoyed relative success

ACROSS

1. Recipe spoonful (abbr.)
5. Hotel room sign: Do not _____
12. Short swim
15. Monroe movie: *The Seven Year _____*
19. Math measurement
20. *The Merchant of Venice* character
21. Yoko of note
22. "Get lost!"
23. **"Rise Again" Cape Breton group**
25. Person's unique way of speaking
27. Roundish
28. Make a speech
29. Kleenex thickness
30. Nigerian city
31. More brusque
33. Greek letter
34. Stockwell of Canadian politics
35. Get out of the army
36. You might pin this on a donkey
38. Sedum variety (var.)
40. Old CTV comedy: *Corner _____*
41. Reaction sound to a punch in the gut
43. Crop for cattle
46. Sang, in 51-D (var.)
48. 451, in Rome of old
49. East Indian bread
50. Snare in a sting
53. Bear type
54. Michigan place: Ann _____
55. Take _____ down memory lane
57. Sailboat's kin
59. Awesome woman?
61. Chinese dumplings
63. Irving Berlin composition: "_____ Simple Melody"
65. Nauseating
68. Weathervane pt.

69. **1990s Vancouver alt rock band**
73. Red Rose, for example
74. Old-style narcotic
76. _____ John NB
77. Hurries
79. Inn from the cold?
82. Principal pipes
84. Play part
85. Snake type
87. Savoury taste, in Tokyo
89. Put on plaster
91. Husk
92. Avian pouch
93. Salad green
95. Passes by, as time
97. Canadian sports excellence award: _____ Marsh Trophy
98. Golf's Michelle
99. Non-Jews, to Jews
101. Bargain time, at The Bay
102. Leered
104. Coop mama
105. Whistler trail
107. 1960s sitcom: _____ *Heroes*
111. Genus of plant pests
112. Outfield surface
113. More fitting
115. Irrigation water wheel
116. Bravery award
118. **Their signature song is "One More Astronaut"**
120. _____-do-well
121. Foot digit
122. Earn via merit
123. *Craft Wars* hostess Spelling
124. Goofs
125. Hogs' domain
126. Held by fiduciaries
127. Clean the deck (var.)

DOWN

1. Cosmic card?
2. Bold
3. La Mancha man
4. Lahore residents
5. CTV news name Matheson
6. Insider's dope?
7. Impolite look
8. Campbell's soup type
9. Like many African governments
10. Annoy
11. Canadian blues musician: King Biscuit _____
12. Lacy cloth
13. _____ 500
14. Luau staple
15. Muslims' religion
16. **Country band with a 40-year career**
17. Central American hardwood tree
18. Spicy candies: Red _____
24. Utopian
26. Bullring cheers
29. Juries
32. Disagreement
34. "Thank You" singer
35. Papa
37. Unseen spouse on *The Mary Tyler Moore Show*
39. **Their "Which Way You Goin' Billy?" hit in '69**
40. Noun formed from a verb
42. Douglas' favourite tree?
43. Head wreath
44. See 3-D
45. **They scored a #1 Canadian country hit in '96**
47. Riga country (abbr.)
48. Residential street abbr.
51. They cross Switzerland
52. Marco _____

54. Ill will
56. Aggressive drug seller?
58. Louts
60. Former Jordanian queen
62. Churn
64. Puccini's "Vissi d'arte," for example
66. Bieber duet with Kingston: "Eenie _____"
67. Artists' stands
70. CBC show: The _____ of Things
71. Camelot lady
72. Italian peak
75. "What a relief!" word
78. Whipping boys

80. Aussie ostrich
81. Shabby
83. Files a lawsuit
85. Knee ligament (abbr.)
86. More weary
88. Atomic particle
90. Uninspired
93. Help
94. Overseas mailing option
96. Not accompanied
98. One of Canada's coasts
100. Mumble
103. Untruthful people
104. Georgian Bay community: _____ Harbour

106. India's initial prime minister
108. 1950s Canadian plane: Avro _____
109. TNT component
110. Colonial India title
111. Teens' bane
112. Chimney dirt
113. Word of praise
114. Guns the engine
117. 1961 Shirelles hit: "Baby _____ You"
118. Former dictator Amin
119. Soak hemp

Exit Strategy

Find your way out with this one

ACROSS

1. "I _____ Was in Dixie"
6. Hunts for
11. Iditarod transport
15. Martial arts school
19. Pined for
20. Canadian Tire Centre, in Kanata
21. Yellow cab
22. All tied up
23. LDL or HDL
25. They say "safe" at Rogers Centre
26. Adorable
27. Without much motivation
28. Ask for, old style
30. Priests' vestments
31. Oil cartel grp.
34. Diva's shining moment
37. Southernmost South American point: Cape _____
38. Yonder
39. **From a building**
43. Maple syrup source
45. _____ Hortons
47. Butcher's balderdash?
48. Santa's rider?
49. Murderous act by Ivan the Terrible
51. Lay to rest
53. "It Don't Mean a Thing (If It _____ Got That Swing)"
54. Trudges
55. Causing stomach inflammation
57. Rockies lake
58. Underwear manufacturer since 1901
59. Cassandra, for example
60. Atlantic fish
61. With sincere conviction
64. Radio station revenue source
65. _____ annum
66. Lymphatic bumps
67. 1930s actress Myrna

68. Professor's degree (abbr.)
71. Iconic Athens temple
73. Received
74. _____ *Russia with Love*
75. Ready to swing a Louisville Slugger
78. _____ is not to wonder why
79. High-fashion designers
82. Counteracted
84. As a result
85. _____-potty
86. Authenticity
87. Boil over?
89. 2010 *The Talk* co-host: Holly Robinson _____
91. Oshawa-to-Kingston direction (abbr.)
92. Leave dumbfounded
93. **From the theatre**
95. Some Canadian military ranks (abbr.)
97. Pudding starch
99. Wild party
100. Old Greek portico
101. To be, in Terrebonne
102. Drank quickly
105. Secular
107. Famed primatologist Fossey
108. Roll call response
109. Ready for an annulment?
115. "What _____ is new?"
116. Banned orchard spray
117. Elephant training tool
118. Florida theme park
119. Birds' home
120. Colds and flus?
121. Kind of infection
122. Track and field competitions

DOWN

1. First three initials of former BC premier Bennett
2. "_____ bin ein Berliner"

3. Japanese reed instrument
4. **From a flood zone**
5. Fingered, say
6. Like a farcical faun?
7. Byron line: "Maid of Athens, _____ we part"
8. Eternally, poetically
9. Door handle
10. Pair skater Jamie
11. Dazed and confused state
12. Former Chief Justice of Canada Antonio
13. PC's circuit board port
14. Circular plate
15. Coffee option at 45-A
16. Conception time
17. **From the air terminal**
18. Snake eyes
24. Zagreb citizen, say
29. Christie classic: *One, Two, Buckle My _____*
31. Bit of food
32. Posed a threat (var.)
33. Clearly demonstrates
35. Put filigree on furniture
36. Colin James "best of" album: *Then _____*
38. How to emulate a gorilla?
40. Lascivious look
41. Castle cells
42. Dresden direction
44. Keyboard key (abbr.)
46. Officers' eyesore?
49. Come to the _____
50. Sculptor's medium
52. Canada's Paul Tracy, for example
54. Sports nuts
55. It's south of Canada (abbr.)
56. Cat type
57. Self-propelled digging machine
62. Tumult
63. Add, in Aylesbury

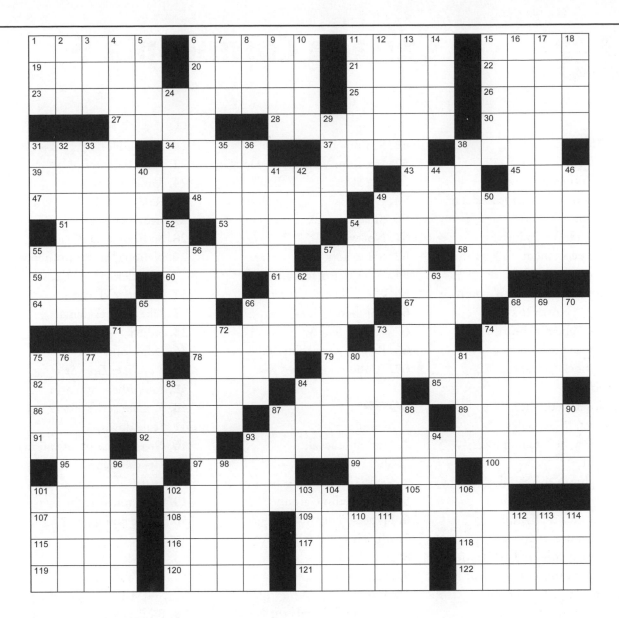

65. Metals' oxide coatings
66. Geek
68. Cover story, say
69. Famed admiral Nelson
70. Document Management System (abbr.)
71. White with fear
72. Shades
73. Copious oil well
74. **From a burning building**
75. Contribution to the kitty
76. **From the subway**

77. US country music genre
80. Expenditure
81. Of poor quality, in Portsmouth
83. Not a lot
84. Golf bag item
87. Industrial pollution
88. An official language in Canada
90. YVR posting
93. Dave who wrote *A Heartbreaking Work of Staggering Genius*
94. Greenish blue

96. Religious belief
98. Acoustic-related
101. 1960s TV star Barbara
102. Tea type
103. Important epochs
104. Fender damage
106. The same, to Tiberius
110. Jamaican music style
111. Grey _____
112. Bell's TSX handle
113. Place to park
114. UFO crew

Canada Cornucopia 6

ACROSS

1. "Wow!"
5. Take a turn in the tub
10. BC-born *This Is the End* star Rogen
14. New Haven university
15. Not permanent, to Septimius Severus
16. Canadian musicians' company: _____ North Records
17. Has a cheatin' heart
19. Debate position
20. Big hockey event in '72: _____ Series
21. Closer to the head
23. Street, in Sept-Îles
25. Turkey moistening tools
26. Spouse
30. Might, in the Elizabethan era
32. February 2010 venue: Richmond Olympic _____
33. Pen end
34. Orange-coloured antiseptic
39. Renter's upfront payment
42. Embrace a new hobby
43. Bro's opposite
44. Arm bone
45. Foam
47. Angler's carrier
48. Swimmer's kick type
52. Hit from Vancouver's Doug and the Slugs: "_____ Bad"
54. Canadian _____ Exhibition
56. Small firearm
61. Not written
62. Some pots, say
64. Wheat farmer's bundle
65. _____ Fraser University
66. Rainbow shapes
67. "Come Sail Away" band
68. Relaxes restrictions, say
69. Without ice

DOWN

1. Swindles
2. Honolulu locale
3. Slightly built
4. Vessel's steering mechanism
5. African ethnic group
6. Hyperactivity disorder (abbr.)
7. Mr. T's squad (with "Team")
8. BC island
9. States of bliss
10. Onset
11. Order of Canada curler Richardson
12. Student's aide
13. Legatees
18. Intangible
22. Bar a barrister?
24. Time anagram
26. RSVP recipient
27. Eye layer
28. Sponsor a candidate
29. National health insurance provider: _____ Cross
31. Old-style chasm
33. Like Edo residents
35. Sullen
36. Land form
37. *Star Trek: Deep Space* _____
38. And others, in Latin
40. *Ransom* actress Rene
41. Scale down?
46. Greek Muse of astronomy
47. Helical shaped item
48. Elitists
49. Gemstone weight
50. Rome home
51. Proctor _____
53. Unlocks
55. Ewes' escapes?
57. SK/MB river named for a bird
58. Biblical weed
59. Shamu, for one
60. For fear that
63. *SCTV* station manager Green

Shining in Sochi

Canadian athletes excelled at the 2014 Games

ACROSS

1. Not glossy
6. Abbreviated Canadian infantry unit: Princess _____
10. Accidental occurrences
14. 1989 Meryl Streep movie: _____-Devil
17. Not silently
18. Aid and _____
19. Fairy tale blackguard
20. Barrel for beer
21. **Canada won three medals in this inaugural genre**
23. Red Skelton's Kadiddlehopper
24. RRSP equivalent, in the US
25. They use stopwatches
26. Roused from sleep
28. Jackfish
29. Volcano's emission
31. Odour
33. Like a handsome man in Montréal?
34. Uniform Resource Locator (abbr.)
35. Contend with
37. Blemish
38. Armpit gland
41. Wooden box
43. Crime scenes, for example
45. Touch and taste
46. Scores, say
49. Canadian Winter Olympian Samuel Edney, for example
52. Blunder
53. Final threats (var.)
55. Make a change to text
57. 1983 Juno-winning single: "_____ of a Stranger"
58. **Our closing ceremony flag-bearers won gold in this**
60. Hindu god (var.)
64. Cell centres
65. Unbuttoned, say
67. Priest's shoulder cloth
71. Former Showcase show: _____ vs. Spenny
73. Did in draft
74. Spiny-skinned Chinese fruit (var.)
76. Matures
78. Condition to
79. Completely sincere
82. State of need
85. Sign of future events
86. Rather unusual
87. Detective's lead
88. More refined
90. Tally up
91. Important ages
92. Slip in concentration
94. Palestine, previously
96. Roar of the crowd, say?
97. Learning style
98. **Our total medal count**
102. And more, for short
103. Manipulative person
104. Mac's middle
105. Western, say
106. TV's "science guy" Bill
107. Atlantic ice mass
108. *Bonanza* brother
109. Hot fat pan: Deep _____

DOWN

1. Mothers, for short
2. Every bit
3. Crest or Colgate product
4. Brazil Native group
5. Cause of bodily puffiness
6. Canadian Ski _____
7. Awful
8. It precedes Aviv
9. Goulash, for example
10. **Our men's and women's teams scored gold in this**
11. Shining, old style
12. Fiancés' contracts, for short
13. Theology students' school (abbr.)
14. **Thompson and Serwa took gold and silver in this**
15. Announced a new newspaper?
16. "Yikes," old style
22. Middle Ages slave
27. One bound by an official agreement
28. Like some religious Iraqis
29. Build in value, like assets
30. "You'll be _____ missed"
32. Illegally out of the barracks
36. Mesdames' cases
39. Blood compound containing iron
40. Early Paul Anka hit: "_____ Beso"
42. Nightmarish street?
44. **See 10-D**
47. Indian *Life of Pi* star
48. TSE word
50. Malevolent
51. _____ mortis
54. Completely competent
56. "Scram!"
59. Parliament Hill's Red Chamber, et al.
60. Repeat sign, in music
61. Lack of compassion for people?
62. Swerved
63. Number next to a plus sign
64. _____-do-well
66. _____ *generis*
67. Famed boxer Muhammad
68. Description of Canada's 2006–08 federal government
69. **Virtue/Moir silver skating discipline**
70. Nickelback singer Kroeger, et al.
72. High-pitched dog sound
75. Pen up

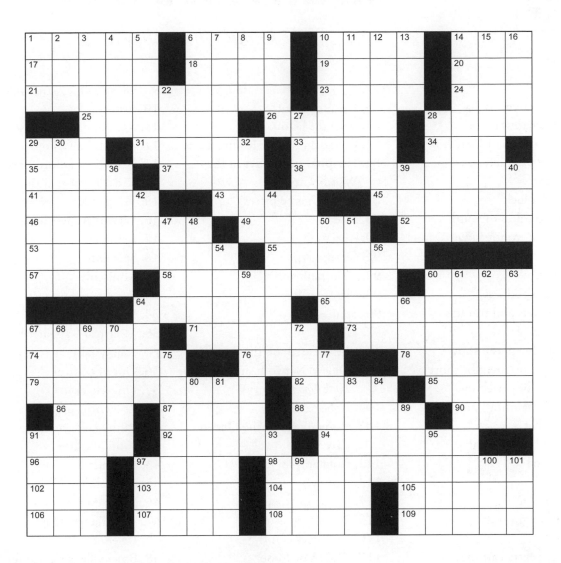

77. UFO crafts
80. Merrymaker?
81. **Jan Hudec won bronze in this skiing event**
83. Some birds

84. Ontario municipality: Chatham-_____
89. _____ sunshine
91. Canadian *Monkey Beach* author Robinson
93. _____ A Sketch

95. In the distance
97. Canadian-made topical product: _____ A535
99. Entice, romantically
100. Canada geese flying formation
101. Miscue

20 On with the Shows

. . . if you know where they're set

ACROSS

1. BC community: Bella _____
6. Scandinavian war god
10. Former centre of French tapestry production
15. Epithet
19. Farrier's block
20. Greek goddess of youth
21. American frontiersman Daniel
22. Saint's circle
23. Plant stem
24. Egyptian goddess
25. Trumpeters and tundras
26. Choir singer
27. **Tic-tac-toe game show**
30. Old-style teacher, for short
31. Concept of perfection
32. Still-life paintings jugs
33. Somewhat
35. Stringed instrument
38. Legislated
41. Thug
42. Love, in Laval
44. Asian weight unit
45. Tripod
47. Waiter's extra earnings
50. **Beantown law dramedy**
53. Crone
54. Crop up
56. Where stars shine
57. Canada _____
58. Vim or vigour
59. Andean animals
60. Wise teacher
61. Capital of Georgia
64. _____ moss
65. **Malden/Douglas police drama (with "*The*")**
71. Advil target
72. Fire _____
73. Oriole or owl
74. Jellied dishes
76. Always, poetically

77. _____ apparent reason
79. Pasture parent
82. Take the helm
83. Canadian flautist Koffman
84. **Hospital drama set in the Windy City**
87. Fellow's game pieces?
88. Alter
90. Airy tune
91. Orange type
92. "You can bank _____"
93. Plants again
96. Split
97. Holy
100. Bewildered, on the Bering?
102. Old W Network show: *How to Look Good _____*
104. Abbey area
105. **Comedy set in the Queen City**
112. Colorado ski resort
113. Red dye
114. Group of troops
115. Asset's opposite
116. Sea eagles (var.)
117. RONA or Roots
118. _____ of execution
119. Common practice, say
120. Eye redness cause
121. Buff
122. Gallup's yardstick?
123. Fruity-smelling chemical compound

DOWN

1. Discovery program: _____ *Cab*
2. "I'm _____ your tricks!"
3. Humpty Dumpty-shaped
4. *Gulliver's Travels* locale
5. Oil-based paint
6. Cleveland resident, for example
7. Leaves neglected
8. Footnote abbr.

9. 1987 Kevin Costner role
10. Just silly
11. *Mr. Bean* star Atkinson
12. Sounds like a lion?
13. Nova Scotia-born singer Murray
14. Red Chamber sitting
15. Witch doctor's relative
16. **City of Angels legal drama**
17. Extreme
18. Spacious
28. Miniscule
29. Put down a protest
34. Knobby
35. Montréal Canadiens, colloquially
36. Out of control
37. Pink-cheeked
39. Zoo enclosure
40. Palin's favourite kind of party?
41. Kind of order
43. Scoundrel
45. Mantelpiece
46. South American forest mammal
47. Victoria newspaper: _____ *Colonist*
48. Brockville is named for him
49. Garlic/basil sauce
51. Some bridge seats
52. Wretched
55. Swift
58. Ale amount
59. Coat's inner layer
60. Long-time Canadian film award name
61. Old Russian ruler
62. Excommunicate, say
63. Nazareth native, for example
65. Throe
66. Sample
67. Turn red, like a green tomato
68. Canadian theatre chain: Cineplex _____
69. Unleashed?

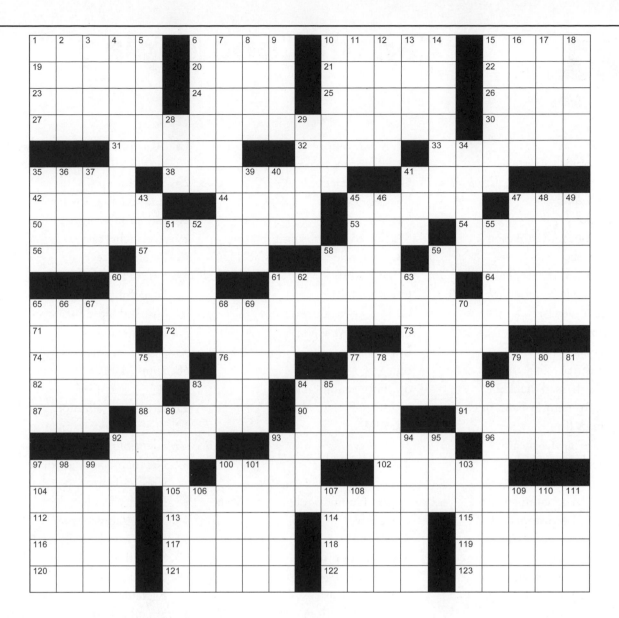

70. Sing like Sinatra?
75. Construction site machine
77. Folder for papers
78. Occurring every eight years
79. Inlet
80. Ready for business
81. Fuse metal
83. Intersected
84. Vacuum or dust
85. Short greetings

86. Austerity
89. US geographic region
92. Ultimatum words
93. Held back (with "in")
94. Three-syllable metrical foot
95. Schuss
97. Puts away for a rainy day
98. Separated
99. Big Apple crime drama
100. Felonious fire

101. Temple tower
103. Provide with powers, say
106. Japanese stringed instrument
107. Precipice
108. 1996 Céline Dion hit: "Falling _____ You"
109. Like _____ out of hell
110. *The Mod Squad* actor Andrews
111. Old Roman road

21 Canada Cornucopia 7

ACROSS

1. Helicopter spinner
6. CBC comedy: _____ *Hour Has 22 Minutes*
10. To-do
14. Caribbean destination
15. Boorish
16. Montréal movie venue
17. Constellation for a toy poodle?
19. Tat-tat lead-in
20. Frozen surface
21. Grimace
22. Censured
24. Gets dressed quickly
26. Escarpment or Falls, in Ontario
27. Chef's list
28. Move, at the theatre
30. Agent, for short
31. Regret
33. Karl Marx compatriot?
35. Okay, by custom
38. ON-born actor Carrey
39. Billy's kids?
40. Bewitched by Samantha Stephens?
42. Cornwall crag
43. Cleanser brand
44. Old coin, in Barcelona
46. Marlo Thomas sitcom: _____ *Girl*
50. Make your mark?
52. Historical record
54. Leg segments
55. Besides
56. Silver metal
57. Served to perfection?
58. Song title from Rita MacNeil and Rush
61. Narrative
62. _____-lock brakes
63. Expensive violin
64. Annexes
65. _____-*majesté*
66. Fifth canonical hour

DOWN

1. Bigotry
2. Delphi diviner
3. Listen to music?
4. Alec Guinness role: _____-Wan Kenobi
5. Files
6. Group of three
7. Look for big game
8. Altar vow
9. Novi Sad citizen
10. Mutton neck, say
11. Liqueur type
12. Scotiabank pays this
13. Adjusts again
18. Two-time Governor General's fiction award winner Brian
23. Saddle strap
25. Adar celebratory day
26. Indian subcontinent tree
29. Avalanche, say
32. Perfect place
34. Saskatchewan city: _____ Battleford
35. Suspend like a magician
36. Not friendly
37. Mulroney's successor
38. 1966 Margaret Laurence novel: *A _____ of God*
41. Urban revitalization
42. They connect to 54-A
45. Silent film follower, colloquially
47. Nickname for Canadian wrestler Hart
48. Fly Air Canada?
49. Milos Raonic's sport
51. Ferris wheel, et al.
53. Sir Arthur _____ Doyle
55. Canadians Linkletter and Eggleton
59. Singular song from *A Chorus Line*?
60. Genetically Modified Organism (abbr.)

ID this Canadian music icon

ACROSS

1. Choleric
6. **She is . . . (with 73-D)**
10. Delt neighbour
13. Cried
17. Spent
18. River in Russia
19. Actresses Alicia or Ortiz
20. Eclectic group
21. What the OPP fights
22. Small, medium or large
23. Climb Kidd, in Kananaskis?
25. **Her biggest single (1974)**
27. Type of office machine
28. Foot levers
29. On the move
31. Spends time in front of a mirror
32. Dire fate
36. Purple shade
37. Adding water
41. Remove sails
43. Like vintage clothing
45. Nighttime noisemaker
46. Public approval
48. Sharpens
51. Ticks, for example
52. Like most gasoline
54. Canadian pianist Frank
56. Tie off
57. **Her Alberta birthplace**
60. Thick chunk
64. Sheer fabric
65. Silt, say
70. Three-dimensional
72. Ricochet
74. Remedy for all ills
75. Spotted wildcat
77. French navy sloop
79. Old operating room liquid
80. Oil field surface structures
83. Goon

85. Rockies' ruminant: Big _____ sheep
86. Some drums
87. Lists one's references
89. Raised, like a cameo
92. When repeated, a dance
93. **University that granted her an honorary doctorate (2004)**
98. Treating the lawn
99. No longer working (abbr.)
101. CBC _____ One
102. Sizzle a steak
103. Pindar poem, for example
104. Ingrid's *Casablanca* role
105. Writer's rep
106. Scraped by with little
107. US VP who served with GRF
108. **Her fourth album (1971)**
109. Costume components

DOWN

1. Chicken pox annoyance
2. To laugh, in Longueuil
3. Seed covering
4. Take on a contract job
5. Swelling symptom
6. Morning beverage in Bécancour
7. Hole in the head?
8. **Group that covered her "This Flight Tonight"**
9. Holly genus
10. Quiche dough
11. Acclimatized (var.)
12. Professional pursuits
13. **Famed festival song she wrote**
14. Twelfth Jewish month
15. Common tree in Canada
16. Little taters?
24. Spanish "tomorrow"
26. Clairvoyance, e.g.
30. Curry spice
31. Speech-related

32. Twofold
33. Children's story opener
34. Georgia Strait mammal
35. Cheddar cheese flavour
38. Middle Eastern country
39. Roman emperor
40. Parliament Hill politician, colloquially
42. Fishing hook
44. Tsar clan
47. Canadian engineers wear rings made of this
49. Building wings
50. Spend a night under the stars
53. European volcano
55. Pop
58. Murky entanglement
59. Eat
60. Flat-bottomed boat
61. Clare Boothe _____
62. 2012 Olympics Canadian diving medal winner Jennifer
63. **Music magazine that honoured her with a Century Award (1995)**
66. Subject that adds up?
67. 1980 Juno single of the year: "_____ Beach"
68. Poet's contraction
69. Lake Louise, for example
71. Steven, to Chris, on CBC
73. **See 6-A**
76. Stress or strife
78. Massage technique
81. Order of business
82. Los Angeles MLBer
84. Garnet or amethyst
88. "Beat it!"
89. Lighten up?
90. Humble
91. Highlands hillside
92. Nursery bed

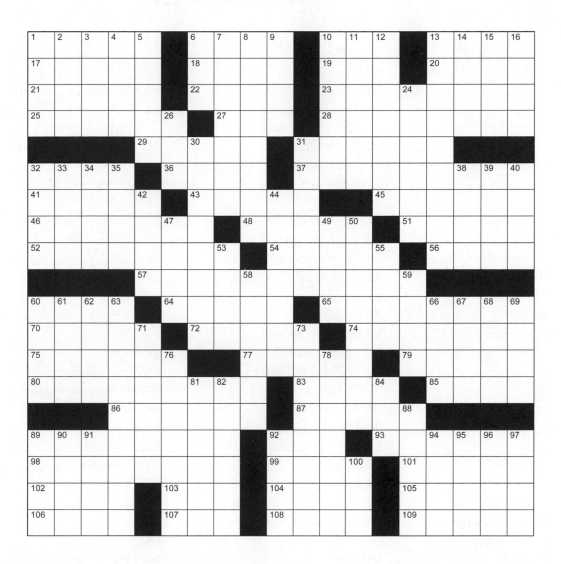

94. Pop singer: Lady _____

95. Caesar's bad day

96. Part of a chain

97. Plenty of properties?

100. *Hawaii Five-0* star: Daniel _____ Kim

Cattle Call

Fun with breeds

ACROSS

1. 1960s Canadian band: _____ Allan and the Expressions
5. Green spaces, in Gatineau
10. Youth Criminal Justice _____
13. Stratford-_____-Avon
17. Top-rated
18. Sparkling headgear
19. Pi follower
20. Tropical palm stem
21. **Conrad's cattle?**
23. Planted petunias, say
25. Blackthorn fruit
26. Highlanders' toppers
27. Got one's bearings
28. Forever, old style
30. Bingo kin
32. Like Oscar Madison
33. Mo. when winter begins
34. _____ play
37. Steals the spoils
39. Pose for an artist
40. Vancouver area: North _____
41. "Ode on a Grecian Urn" poet
43. Expression of disgust
46. Drug-induced stupor
48. Ceramics component
49. Liver secretion
50. Sign of the ram
51. Long snakes
52. Bit of info
53. Outdoor meal
56. *Hockey Night in Canada* post-game show: *After _____*
58. Tenant
59. 1777 Sheridan play: _____ *to Scarborough*
60. Overly complacent
61. Savoury taste, in Japanese cuisine
63. Honolulu greetings
64. Order of the court

65. Code of conduct
68. Meditation chant syllables
69. Rhett Butler's expletives?
70. Varnish ingredient
71. American crooner Damone
73. Cook a plum pudding
75. Discharges
77. Bird that lays big eggs
78. Ghanaian capital
80. Prevent, in law
82. Frightening film genre
85. Infected
87. Prohibits
90. Maori art symbol
91. _____ gland
92. **William Tell's type?**
95. Tip like a sinking ship
96. Author Amy
97. Eastern Québec city
98. *Nurse Jackie* star Falco
99. Effortless
100. _____-mo
101. Greek Muse of poetry
102. Arctic Native group

DOWN

1. Calloway's taxi?
2. **Oktoberfest celebrant's breed?**
3. Collection of writings
4. Interior designer's design
5. Harper Valley org.
6. "_____ Too Proud to Beg"
7. Indian music
8. Collapses like a cookie?
9. Mouthed off
10. Atmospheric gas
11. **"Cuchi-cuchi" singer's breed?**
12. She wrote *Spelling It Like It Is*
13. Online discussion group
14. Ladies' clothing options (var.)
15. S-shaped mouldings
16. Enid Blyton children's character

22. Canadian artist Danby
24. Trade show presentations, for short
28. Former premiers Stelmach and Schreyer
29. Onomatopoeic
31. Request
35. Fire truck equipment
36. Dublin dude
38. Canada's capital (abbr.)
40. Canadian Tire money, for example
42. Tape gaps, in Nixon's White House
44. Paste
45. Blood pigment
47. Sari-wearing royals
49. Fundamental
51. Pester
52. Evil spirit
53. California place: _____ Alto
54. Gossip tidbit
55. Enlace
57. Commencement
58. Not timely
60. **Psychologist's preference?**
62. Just about all
64. US airline regulator (abbr.)
65. Tax return pro, say
66. Countermand a carousel operator?
67. **Chauffeur's favourite?**
69. Distributed cards
72. Mongrel
74. Dependable
76. Eat lots of turkey?
78. Granny Smith or Gala
79. Papal court
81. Courtroom clerk, for short
83. Approves
84. Paddled
86. Dines

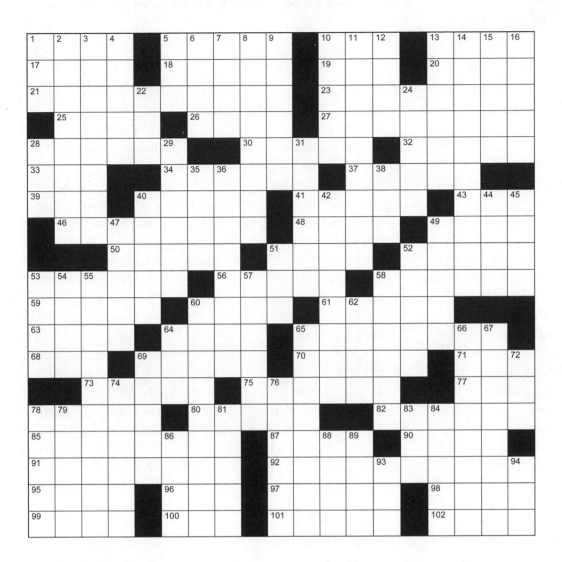

88. Half of a province's name
89. *M*A*S*H* actress Loretta

93. Newfoundland Symphony
Orchestra (abbr.)

94. _____ the light

ACROSS

1. Canadian retirement income vehicle (abbr.)
4. Silicon bit
8. Actor's role
12. Long-time Manitoba MP/MPP Blaikie
13. *Twenty Thousand Leagues Under the Sea* captain
14. Canadian _____ Company
16. 1997 Sarah McLachlan song
17. Ornate wall hangings
19. Edge of the Atlantic, say
21. Jails, colloquially
22. Shuns
23. Barbecue briquettes
24. Farewell syllable
25. Not open
26. Big jerk?
29. Hindu courtesy title
32. Buy back
35. Mature
37. *Nota bene*, say (abbr.)
38. Empress or Bessborough
39. Québec Ski-Doo inventor
42. Cincinnati MLB team
43. Cleopatra's snake
44. Eager
45. Canadianese expressions
47. OPEC VIP (var.)
49. US catalogue retailer since 1865
53. House of Commons session: Question _____
55. Having tender tootsies
56. Omissions
58. Extremely large
59. Long-time CBC kids' show: *The Friendly* _____
60. Viking's letter
61. Incense causes this in Chicago
62. Very, in Val-d'Or
63. English historical mysteries author Clare
64. Have supper

DOWN

1. Takes transit
2. Pelvic bone-related
3. Photographer's light source
4. Top Toronto building?
5. Listens to
6. American televangelist Jack Van _____
7. Early detective story writer
8. Ceremonial feast, for Pacific NW Natives
9. Fourth month
10. Put back
11. Long journey
12. Diamond corner
15. Aesop fable: *The* _____ *and the Pig*
18. Use an S.O.S. pad
20. Street greeting
23. Slide
25. Barcelona country
27. Previously owned
28. Sets, like aspic
29. Ali _____
30. Disturbances
31. Dodgem vehicle
33. Esteemed First Nations person
34. Niagara River attraction: _____ Falls
36. Some curling shots
40. Marsh plants
41. Takes a rest
46. Canadian Top 40 smash, say
48. Writer who fictionalized a beloved Winnipeg bear
49. Cher's ex
50. Edam alternative
51. Farm fungus
52. Ogle
53. Cribbage playing piece
54. Public door sign
55. Blue Jay's mis-hit
57. Irish nationalist grp.

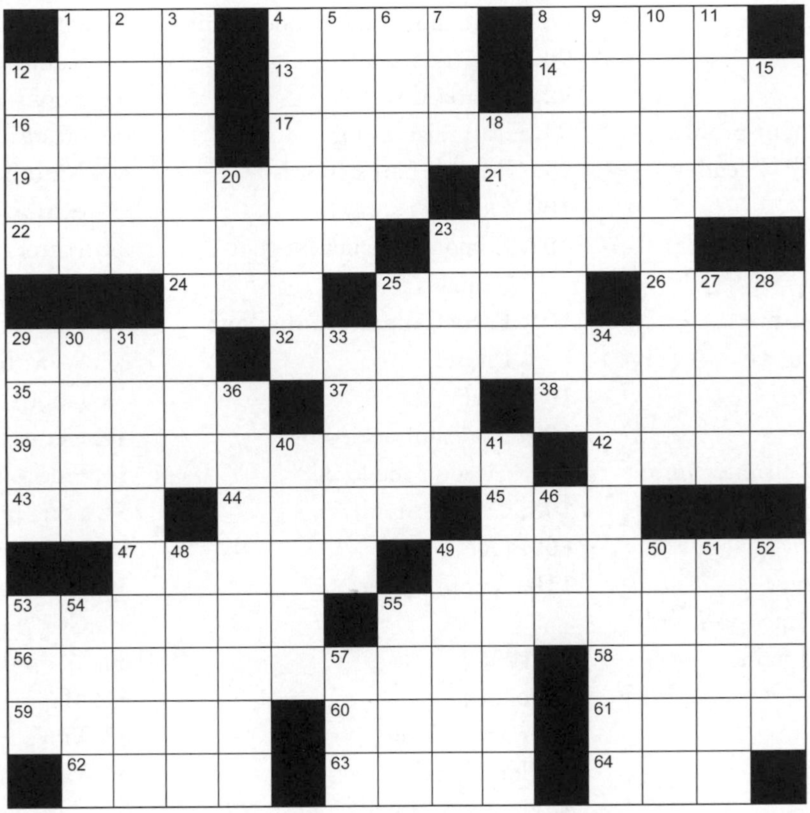

Solution on page 181

Meet the Flockers

Famous Canadians' avian names

ACROSS

1. Clobbers
7. Famed 1930s lawman Eliot
11. Decorate a plate
18. Geological era
19. Imperfection
20. Speech impairment problem
21. **Long-time CUPW leader Jean-Claude**
22. Greek letter
23. Wound up film
24. Where to rock-a-bye baby?
26. Toast with caviar, say
28. Wizard, old style
29. Guarantee
31. Decimal-based currency units
33. Nova Scotia-born Oscar nominee Ellen
37. Tex-Mex shell type
38. Fatty northern Italy pork dish?
39. Sucralose brand name
41. Lethargic
43. Enjoys a cigarette
48. Morning glory?
50. At any point
52. **18th-C. Mohawk leader Joseph**
53. 19th-C. sharpshooter Annie
54. Attacked like killer bees
57. *Bob & Carol & Ted & Alice* star Cannon
58. Not noticed
61. State that faces Canada
65. Interesting books?
66. Search for sustenance
71. **Governor General's Award-winning poet Robert**
73. Architect's detail, say
74. Pessimistic about people
75. Steepled one's fingers
77. Edmonton CFLer
80. South Seas nation
81. Don't exist
83. Toiletry powder
85. Justin Bieber, when he broke big
86. International travel document
90. Dangers
92. X marks this
93. East Indian sailor
95. Old-style harpsichords
100. Heats glass, say
102. Edmonton Oiler Nugent-Hopkins
104. **Early Canada troubadour Pierre**
105. Heir
106. Not bamboozled by
107. Most on the level?
108. Caped crusaders?
109. Hoe
110. Record player

DOWN

1. Sobbed
2. Frosty coating
3. Plot of land
4. Prepare for burial, old style
5. Gets tied up?
6. Start a journey
7. Oscar-winning federal film org.
8. MP chooser
9. Skewered meat dish
10. **P.T. Barnum performer Anna**
11. Cigarette, in Chelsea
12. Tacks on
13. See 22-A
14. Wynonna Judd's mom
15. Muhammad's faith
16. Blockade
17. Helluva place?
25. Speak vapidly
27. McGill, say
30. *The Name of the Rose* writer Umberto
32. Grant's grave?
33. Mexican money
34. Watery colour?
35. Engine crud
36. Former *The National* anchor Cameron
38. Books, in Saint-Bonaventure
40. Stead
42. **National Gallery of Canada exhibitor Graham**
44. Former California fort
45. Steppenwolf lead singer John
46. Bambi's aunt
47. Score Television Network (abbr.)
49. Get in tune
51. Press on the gas
54. Long biblical reptiles
55. Most amusing (var.)
56. Resist authority
59. Cyst liquid
60. "Stop that!"
61. Many a time, for short
62. Move apace
63. Vacation stop
64. Canadian holiday mo.
67. Demonstrators' donnybrook
68. Skin outbreak
69. Canadian educational publishing company
70. Vivacity
72. Uriah's pile?
74. Infant's tummy trouble
76. More whimsical
78. Restate
79. It follows Feb.
82. Rubs out
84. Chin indentations
86. Hymn
87. Sleep disorder
88. "O Canada" and "Our Dominion"
89. T-bone or porterhouse
90. "Band of Gold" vocalist Freda

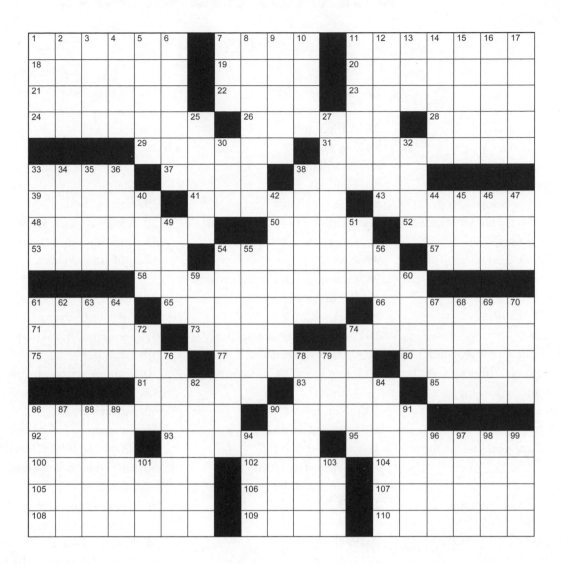

91. Canadian poet/novelist Elizabeth
94. 1990s Bank of Canada governor John
96. John Labatt's favourite colour?
97. Tennis serving whiz
98. Misplace
99. Wild about division?
101. Munched on
103. Give a sign of assent

26

Get Into the Groove

A musical medley

ACROSS

1. Get a pooch from the pound
6. Pretentious parvenu
10. Deciduous tree
13. Dalai _____
17. Combat gear (var.)
18. Tiny skin opening
19. Like Santa's workshop workers?
21. **Miner's music?**
23. **Hoodlum's genre?**
24. Supreme Court of Canada sitting
25. Jazzy lady Laine
27. Stretcher
28. Walked like a two-year-old?
30. Secure a rock climbing rope
31. Renaissance era stringed instrument
35. Produce progeny
36. ABC morning show, for short
38. The sky's the _____
41. Native
43. South African antelope
45. Cairo river
46. Utah city
47. Checkers or chess
49. Pleasing, artistically (var.)
51. Most painful
53. Just cut
55. Cassius Clay, today
56. Colloquial affirmative
57. MI5 operative
58. Rats' domain
60. It follows Mar.
62. US crime-fighting grp.
65. Computer key, for short
67. Church section
68. Long-time official religion of Japan
72. Rent collector
75. Three-piece suit component
77. Egg-shaped
78. *Commedia dell'_____*
79. Snow, in Sorel-Tracy
81. Amigo
83. See 10-A
85. Javier's uncle
86. Havana's country
87. Wine sediment
88. Help save the environment?
90. Proved, to a miner?
93. Easy
95. Grammy-winning Canadian band: Arcade _____
96. Peek
101. **Otis employee's option?**
103. **Mafioso's music?**
105. Iconic 1971 Carole King album
106. Not in port
107. Type of acid
108. Aardvark's meal
109. Salem state (abbr.)
110. Broadway light type
111. Dubs

DOWN

1. Long sighs?
2. _____ one's weird
3. Grandmas, in Germany
4. Opinions, for short
5. _____ on for size
6. What you're doing while shopping
7. Negative word
8. Whether forecaster?
9. Lake St. Clair community: _____ River
10. Phil's '70s hockey line nickname
11. Bucharest buck
12. Animal's skin disease
13. Parachute Club lead vocalist Segato
14. Namelessness
15. Nutmeg spice
16. Sot
20. Cranium
22. Common Canadian mammal
26. Jittery
29. Sleep visions
30. Model airplane wood
31. Important guests, for short
32. Obi attachment
33. Scent, in Seattle
34. Alice Munro book: _____ *of Girls and Women*
37. *She Done Him Wrong* star West
39. Pelvis parts
40. Training school, for short
42. **Preacher's preference?**
43. **Surfer's style?**
44. Geography buff's book
48. SK-born NHLer Travis
50. **Cool dancer's option?**
52. Canadian singer Sylvia
54. Guelph-born *Party of Five* actress Campbell
59. Save from harm
61. Maple Leaf to a Hab
62. Extra flesh
63. Stripped down?
64. Head off at the pass, say
66. Island in the Aegean
69. Bodily bump
70. Radial
71. Some poems
73. Tricks
74. 502, to Tiberius
76. Sled for winter fun
80. Mongolian desert
82. Manhandles
84. Maui dances
86. Fold
89. Tussle
91. Church instrument

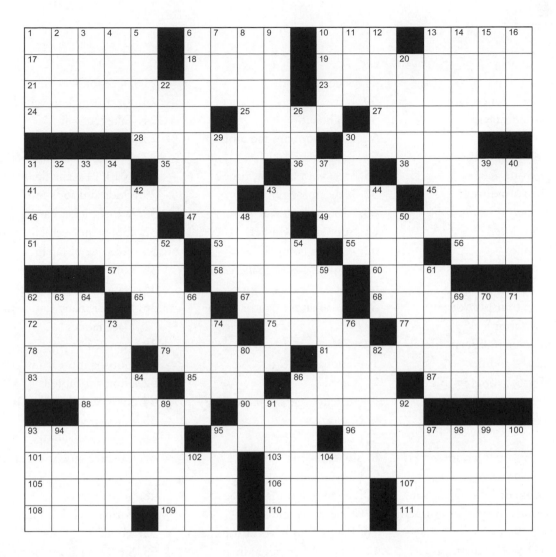

92. Magnate of industry

93. Greek cheese

94. Canada's Walk of Fame inductee Thicke

95. Canadian literary theorist Northrop

97. Papa's spouse

98. Dainty

99. Not off one's rocker

100. Narrative poem form

102. Famous hockey surname

104. Part of *The Matrix*

Solution on page 182

27 Canada Cornucopia 9

ACROSS
1. Shaped like a dunce cap
6. Golf course obstacle
10. Impoverished area
14. Silent films star Bara
15. Emerge from sleep
16. It parallels a radius
17. Oath taker
18. Not quite closed
19. Gullible ones
20. Ontario city
22. Calgary NHLers
24. Société de transport de Montréal (abbr.)
26. Romanian ex politician Iliescu
27. Toonies and loonies
28. Like 57 crosswords in this book
30. Shape
31. Completed a task again
32. Shores
37. Ancient Egyptian goddess
38. Chop finely
39. Home state of Johnny Carson
40. International border monument at Surrey/Blaine
42. Like the Quechuan empire
43. Leg part
44. Narrow look
45. Introduce gradually
49. Sheep's sound
50. I, to Augustus
51. Highfalutin
52. Band worn around a bicep
54. Large trees
55. Deal with difficult times
57. New York city
60. "Too bad, so sad"
61. Support a swindler?
62. Paths to Pompeii
63. Summit Series goalie Esposito
64. In case
65. Canadian ice dancer Virtue

DOWN
1. National network
2. "Gosh!"
3. Current events documenters
4. Notion
5. Borne
6. Singer Shania
7. East Indian royal title
8. Pseudonym initials
9. Of necessity, old style
10. Poppy Family vocalist Jacks
11. South American animal
12. Take clothes off the line
13. Mulroney-era cabinet minister Marcel
21. Doze (off)
23. Airport pickup vehicle
24. Take it all off
25. Plural pronoun
27. Michel Therrien was this for the 2013/14 Canadiens
29. Odds and sods category (abbr.)
30. White picket barrier
32. Emergency vehicle sound
33. Indigene of Japan
34. Non-profits, often
35. Nasal sounding accent
36. Start of many Latin American place names
38. Frenzied
41. Got the most from
42. Nunavut capital
44. Juno Award winner Roberts
45. Curtain fold
46. German greeting
47. Creative guy on Madison Avenue
48. Scaredy-cat
49. Former NHLer Hull
52. Mimics
53. Smallish suffix?
56. UK merit award (abbr.)
58. Catholic Relief Services (abbr.)
59. Simile's centre

28

Leading Canadian Men

You know their names – what were their shows?

ACROSS

1. North American shrub
6. Murder
10. Pronoun for that woman
13. Not at all certain
17. Use to one's advantage
18. Overdo the ouzo
19. It displays art in Ontario (abbr.)
20. Nettle
21. **Raymond Burr**
23. Spoil
24. Big responsibility
25. Calendar abbr.
26. Most urgent
27. Cowtown, for example
29. Iron Age tribe member
30. Breaks a wild horse
32. May and Man
33. William and Harry play this sport
36. Spoken
38. Unstable, in physics
40. Maui greeting
42. Greek god of darkness
44. Draw a conclusion
47. Realistic
49. Mountain nymph, in mythology
51. Hot spot in Sicily?
52. Canada's Rick Hansen: Man in _____
53. Evil
56. National ladies clothing chain: Smart _____
57. JFK's mom
59. Ottawa performing arts venue, for short
60. Bit of a glitch
62. Ben, to Brian Mulroney
65. Billionaires' lots?
68. Used a rotary phone (var.)
72. Deafening

74. *American Pickers* star Frank
75. Worship service activity
77. Nigerian tribe
79. Get ready to go camping?
81. RCMP uniform: Red _____
82. Yorkshire or Airedale
84. Amend
86. Layer
87. West African ethnic group
89. Rum-based libations
91. Alaska city
93. Hot-air balloonist, say
95. Thorny shrub
97. PC component (abbr.)
100. Leipzig lady
101. Former Ontario premier Bob
102. **Michael J. Fox**
104. Hue
105. One _____ million
106. Dart about
107. With it
108. Cain and Abel's brother
109. Beavers' construction project
110. Mysterious (var.)
111. Kitchen bays

DOWN

1. Weakens
2. Eye part
3. Canadian financial services retailer: Money _____
4. Oxygen
5. Former Newfoundland premier Wells
6. **William Shatner**
7. Come in second
8. Judas or John, in the bible
9. Yiddish gossipmonger
10. Skydivers' equipment
11. Narcissistic one
12. US campus org.
13. **See 21-A**

14. You see these at the cinema
15. Log ride slide
16. Affirmative responses
22. Venus de _____
28. Toy for a windy day
29. Will proceeds recipient who shares
31. Hockey's "The Rocket" Richard
33. One side of a hand
34. Medley
35. Garret
37. Greek mythology name
39. Textual extras
41. Cool in mood
43. **Lorne Greene**
45. Annual Toronto fair (abbr.)
46. Nosh
48. To such an extent
50. Automated Tracking System (abbr.)
54. Unborn, as yet
55. VIA tracks
58. Slip up
61. Reproductive cell
62. Crafty
63. Winning tic-tac-toe row
64. Providing TLC
66. Technical problem solving group
67. PEI nickname: _____ Island
69. 1984 Olympics Canadian gold winner Fung
70. Precipice
71. Canadian international affairs columnist Gwynne
73. **Paul Gross**
76. **See 102-A**
78. _____ muffin
80. Amend an architectural drawing
83. American lizard
85. Strenuous work
87. Hilts and handles

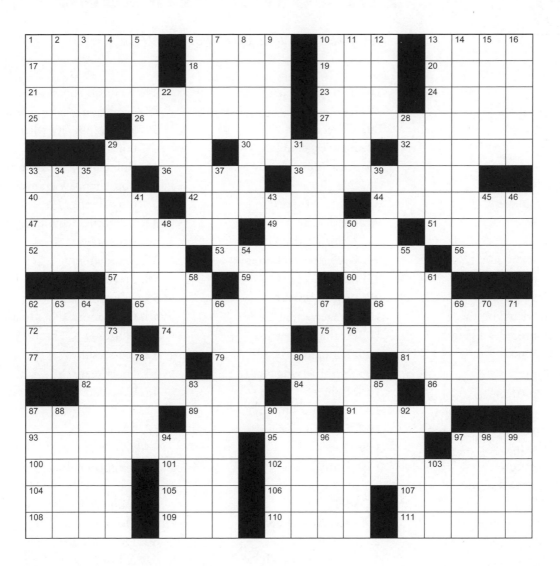

88. Birds' nesting spot

90. Embarrassing blunder

92. Central American Native language

94. Dry

96. Important Arab

97. "Later!" in Lombardy

98. Brew coffee

99. Plays for a fool

103. Hugh MacLennan classic: _____ *Solitudes*

For Posterior's Sake

A puzzle you can get behind . . .

ACROSS

1. Baby's apron
4. Tuck away
8. Flower type
12. Frost
16. Aroma (var.)
18. Square footage
19. Zero
20. Diabolical
21. Bone marrow storage spot: _____ cavity
23. **Traveller's pouch?**
25. Fragrant rice type
26. It often precedes a verb
28. Steam rooms
29. Experts' tips?
31. Coyote's cry
32. Cold War country initials
35. Long-legged bird
36. Saved the trees?
41. Star's signature
44. Ex-Reform MP Grey
45. Skin layer
46. Reaction to a pun
47. Inert gas
49. 1990s CTV drama
51. Thailand, at one time
52. US College Board exam (abbr.)
54. Diana Krall album: *When I _____ in Your Eyes*
56. It's shaped like a circle
58. Step on it
59. **Worst choice?**
63. PBS documentary show
64. Hot spring
65. Marine mammal
66. Launched a civil court action
67. Colbie Caillat song: "Before _____ You Go"
69. Where films are filmed
71. Dieter's milk
73. Canadian Christmas song: "Huron _____"

76. Irish "Breathless" band
78. ". . . see hide _____ hair of"
80. Travel plan
82. Business contacts, say
85. Tokyo's early name
86. Delight
87. Magician's stick
88. Heidelberg homebody?
91. Eyeball membrane
94. Coffee bean grinder
95. Stalemate
99. **Last to finish?**
101. Stagecraft, at La Scala?
103. Cathedral section
104. Naturalness
105. Sushi serving
106. Plunge
107. Necklace bit
108. Swedish carpets
109. Totals
110. Farm pen

DOWN

1. Destructive weapon
2. Creative concept
3. Figures, informally
4. More tangy to the tongue
5. Railroad employee
6. Poetic contraction
7. Hockey's Gretzky
8. Made tea, say
9. Soft leather
10. 1948 film: *No Room at the _____*
11. Motion detector, for example
12. Disgusts
13. Terrible tsar's name
14. Dam north of Revelstoke
15. Charitable organization: _____ of Canada
17. **Butcher's offering?**
22. Tony Randall movie: *7 Faces of Dr. _____*

24. Went off course at sea
27. Canadian aviator Marion
30. Mississippi city where Elvis was born
31. Rub elbows with the rich
32. Top Utah law enforcement official (abbr.)
33. California region: Big _____
34. Brief stays
37. Retainer, say
38. Having three surfaces
39. Inbox message
40. Old Montréal landmark: Notre-_____ Basilica
42. No-see-ums
43. Foals' feet
48. Canadian students' aid: Coles _____
50. Mardi _____
53. Toys that spin
55. Uniform colour?
57. Canadian Music Hall of Fame inductee Cockburn
59. Decorative ties
60. Dionysus devotee
61. A-listers
62. **Troop group?**
63. Typographic unit
68. Laid it on thick, in Tennessee?
70. Small child
72. Space on a soccer pitch
74. It sometimes requires refinement
75. Cleaning supplies item
77. Intimidate
79. Brings back to the firm
81. Usual temperatures, say
83. More goofy
84. *Dog Day Afternoon* character
89. Part of UHF
90. Pertinent
91. Bayonet
92. _____ Breton

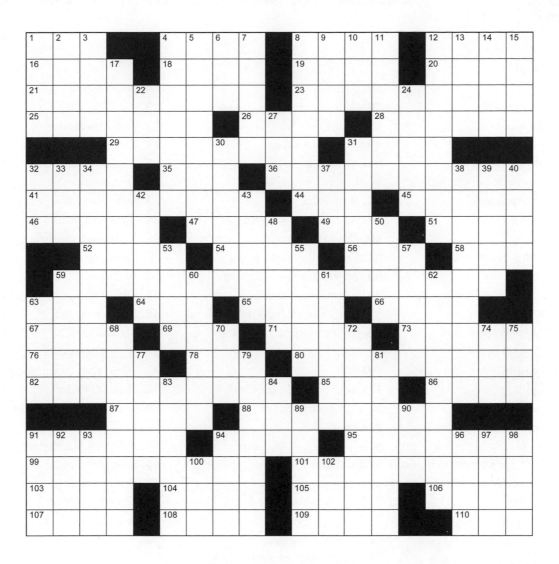

93. Giller nominee Moore
94. Flat hill
96. Knights' titles

97. Aberdeen resident
98. Catch sight of, old style
100. July event: Canada _____

102. Coal carrying trough

ACROSS

1. Sin city, in the bible
6. Accuse of wrong
11. With 17-A, board game invented in Canada
14. Escorts for ladies of the knight?
16. Lack of attendance?
17. See 11-A
18. Demeanour
19. Hong Kong-based airline: _____ Pacific
21. Former Portuguese colony in India
22. Grp. that meets at school
23. Able-_____
24. Oxide coating
25. Shrub trellis
27. Misrepresent
28. Mulroney's US contemporary
29. Causes of bodily puffiness
31. Canadian band: Tom Cochrane and _____ Rider
32. Anger, in Athlone?
33. Canadian dining chain: Swiss _____
36. National _____ of Canada
39. Eschews
40. Sword with a curved blade
42. Bit of zest
43. Muffle sound
44. Aquamarine, for example
46. Baseball great Mel
47. Birdbrain
48. As well
49. "Funny" cigarettes
51. Originality, say
53. Nightclub entertainment
54. Recipient of largess
55. Canadian poet Musgrave
56. Smart-mouthed

DOWN

1. Calgary CFLer, for short
2. It circles the earth
3. Illness
4. Microwaving appliance
5. Sixty seconds (abbr.)
6. Inter
7. Cape Breton scenic route: Fleur-de-_____ Trail
8. Peppery salad green
9. Cell division process
10. Lord's land
12. Public praise
13. Prefix, perhaps?
14. Orb
15. Patrick Chan jump
20. Don an ascot?
23. Deli "donuts"
24. Thaw out again
26. Malaysian machete
27. German city
30. Width of 14-D, say
33. Ottawa hotel: _____ Laurier
34. They chase prey
35. African insect
36. _____ one's time
37. Some aerie nestlings
38. Flowing locks
39. Long-legged birds
41. Harsh crow cry
43. *A Bridge Too Far* star Bogarde
45. Saunter
47. Bright colour description
48. Canadian folksinger McGarrigle
50. It monitors Delta (abbr.)
52. Existed

31

An American in Canada

Yanks who made good here

ACROSS

1. Oompah instruments
6. Some House of Commons legislation
10. Campus guys' grp.
14. Hockey star-turned-MPP Apps
17. Burst
18. **Wisconsin-born Kessel, Toronto Maple Leafs star**
19. It wasn't built in a day
20. Second-person French pronoun
21. Type in data
22. Yearn for a Christmas tree?
23. **Atlanta-born Olson, Food Network Canada host**
24. Supply with weapons
25. Odysseus dreamed up this horse
27. Dried plum
29. Process component
30. Perfect tennis serve
32. Italian porridge
34. Any *Time*?
36. It follows Shoppers Drug, in Canada
38. *Bell, Book and Candle* co-star Lanchester
39. False fronts
43. **Maine-born Coombs, a.k.a. Mr. Dressup**
45. Parliament Hill body
47. Washington city
48. With an energetic step
50. Legal action initiator
52. Military doctor
53. Changed states?
55. Sack cloth
57. They cross tennis courts
58. Removed a bridle
61. Whales' groups
65. Some appetizers
66. Like ready-made concrete pieces
71. Cavell with a Rocky Mountain named for her

73. Not pre-recorded
74. Develop over time
75. 1984 Parachute Club Juno single of the year
77. Stroke
81. **Brooklyn-born CBC news name Abel**
82. Like an idle fiancé?
84. Strikebreaker
86. Dye
87. Game's outcome
88. Six-by-nine-inch books
91. Commercials
92. Alongside
94. Bone cavity
96. Tripoli citizen
98. Aquatic eggs
99. **Brooklyn-born Jordan, "Marina del Rey" singer**
100. Tack component
102. Filthy money?
105. Little Bo Peep might have lost one
106. Latvian capital
107. **Oregon-born high jumper Joy, 1976 Olympics silver medallist**
108. Before surgery lingo
109. *Platoon* setting, for short
110. Big ticket thing?
111. Canada's women's eight blades
112. Schwarzenegger catchphase starter

DOWN

1. Golfer's peg
2. Large vase
3. Squash type
4. Jungle impressionist?
5. Sharpen shaving equipment
6. Disgusts
7. These labourers helped build the CPR

8. Some roofs are made of this
9. Got some shut-eye
10. Munich madam
11. **Arkansas-born Hawkins, Canadian music trailblazer**
12. General pardon
13. Victoria's Fairmont Empress has its own blend of this
14. South of the 49th, say
15. Olden days description
16. Like a wet noodle?
26. **Pittsburgh-born Flaherty, *SCTV* star**
28. States of bliss
29. Like divers' treasure
30. Tiny organism (var.)
31. **Illinois-born Shields, award-winning writer**
33. Thailand river
35. A-line line
37. Trident prong
40. Staggers
41. Give off
42. Ova pouches
44. Neutral colour
46. Let no man put it like this?
49. Hankerings
51. Speak hoarsely
54. East Indian foodstuff (var.)
55. 1958 Gregory Peck film (with "*The*")
56. Papa, in Papineau
59. 1987 Order of Canada inductee Parizeau
60. Hindu spirit
61. Neighbour of Chile
62. VIP at Valhalla
63. Low regard
64. Fetid smell
67. Corral delivery
68. Pacts
69. **Minneapolis-born Robinson, former Burnaby MP**

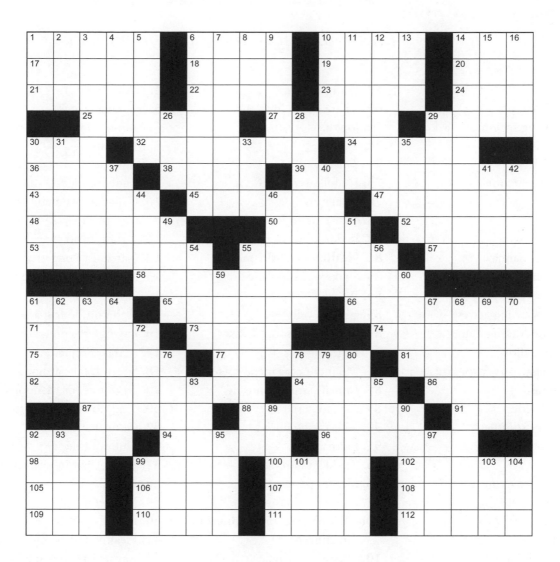

70. Outdoor shelters
72. 1989 Eastern Canada hurricane moniker
76. Ice cream treat
78. Compass point, in Prévost
79. More reptilian?
80. CSB word

83. Mississippi-born Reed, '60s CFL star
85. Wisconsin-born Homme, *The Friendly Giant* host
89. Freight
90. Air spirit
92. Famed English architect

93. Cedar Rapids state
95. Fraud
97. That certain glow
99. Medical scan (abbr.)
101. Important historical time
103. Decay
104. US environmental org.

32

Mass Confusion?

Praise the puns and pass the humour

ACROSS

1. Old-style charity
5. Tea-growing region, in 98-D
10. _____ Nostra
14. Lots
19. Canadian Dennis Lee, for example
20. Old-style
21. Actor Baldwin
22. *Frida* star Salma
23. Greek letter
24. Judge, perhaps
25. Emmy-winning actress Ward
26. Like a doddering dame
27. Grey in pallor
28. **Congregation's favourite operetta?**
31. _____-Georgian
32. Shades of summer?
33. Car rental giant
34. Tense
35. Window covering
37. "I cannot tell _____"
38. Be excessively sweet
39. Indolent
41. Narrow fissure
42. National convenience store name
43. Unknown spaceships (abbr.)
47. Annoy
48. **Best buddy, at the basilica?**
50. Garlic bulb
51. _____ alia
52. Occupied
53. Lemony drink suffix
54. Page one headline
55. See 23-A
56. Any moment now
58. Six-Day War gun
59. Orangutans' home island
60. Alberta Cancer Board (abbr.)
62. **Church clairvoyant?**
66. Erode

67. Put in motion
69. Charged bit, in science
70. Joplin's cloths?
72. The _____ Four
74. Tings
75. He followed FDR
76. Skier's tow
78. First-rate, to Rudyard Kipling
80. Reddish brown colouring
81. **Healthy Catholic mom?**
83. Shakespearean verse
84. Wired
85. Golfer's yell
86. Cole Porter song: "Miss _____ Regrets"
87. Mountaineer's metal spikes
88. Famed statue: Venus de _____
89. Sack material
90. Give the go-ahead
91. Eternal
95. Presidential rejection
96. Miner's passage
97. Lily, in Laval
100. **"Don't even think about it," in church?**
103. Lessee's payment
104. Beloved public figures
105. Geological time spans
106. Burrard _____ BC
107. Scandinavian myth source
108. Upbraid
109. Womanizer
110. Copy Sidney Crosby
111. Opposed to, colloquially
112. Colas
113. Proofreader's reversal
114. CN _____
115. Result of a tire puncture

DOWN

1. Bee-related
2. Like pocket change
3. **Nativity play technique?**

4. "Don't go!"
5. Sketcher's stock
6. Amino acid found in proteins
7. Mixes up
8. Rug type
9. Deadly thought?
10. Canadian women's hockey star Campbell
11. Yellow bread spreads
12. Narcissist's preferred person
13. Mexican vacation destination
14. Crude cabin
15. Oahu outdoor space
16. Laying orbs on (var.)
17. Actress Raquel
18. Sport to take a shot at?
29. 1996 role for Madonna
30. Traditional poem form
32. Guns that stun
36. Dull routine
37. "_____ fair in love and war"
38. Pen up
39. Mayberry kid
40. Like a squid
41. Health club room
42. Journalists' milieux
43. Arm bone adjective
44. **Source of the rite information?**
45. Passed by
46. Transfusion fluids
49. Demolish
50. *Canada's Worst Driver Ever* legal expert Woolley
52. Audio equipment brand name
54. Hamlet, say
57. Decides on
58. Coffee container
59. Cook quickly
61. Little rabbit
63. Fine thread
64. Speck of dust
65. Heavy carts
67. Sore spot?

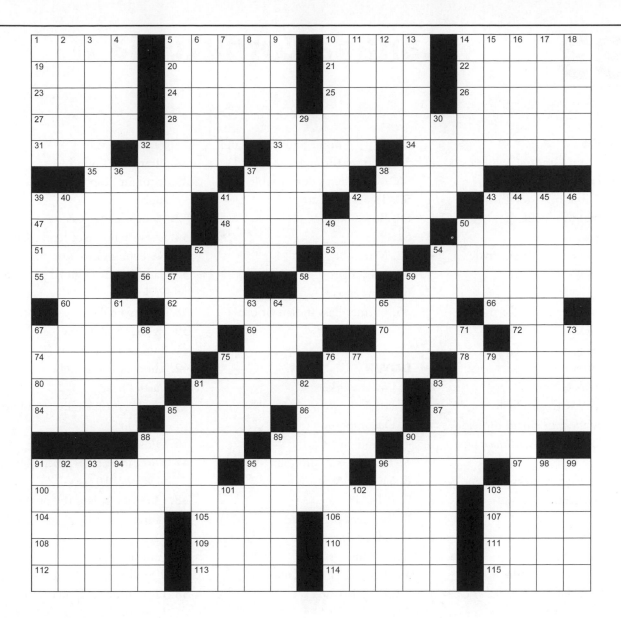

68. Wanted poster abbr.

71. Gone mouldy, say

73. Swats flies?

75. Strait separating BC and WA

76. Inking artist

77. Soft cheese

79. "For _____ us a child is born"

81. Gunslingers' gear

82. Face part

83. Electrical current routing device

85. Trawl

88. Disorderly conducts?

89. They're high on travelling?

90. Stick

91. Heroic tales

92. Dorito, say

93. Bot

94. Griffiths who's won five Dora Mavor Moore awards

95. Calgary's Jack Singer Concert Hall, for example

96. Radiant

98. New Delhi nation

99. Smelled really bad

101. Holler's mate

102. Extraordinary, in Edinburgh

103. _____ Canadian Superstore

ACROSS

1. Juno and Grammy winner McLachlan
6. Ex-prime minister Turner
10. Email to block
14. Jagged
15. It precedes formaldehyde
16. *Frasier* star Gilpin
17. RRSP word
19. Some retrievers, for short
20. Quick
21. Desert garment (var.)
22. Knitted fabric
24. Earth's elites?
27. Pacify with goodwill
30. *Thunderball* villain Blofeld
31. Global's *The West Block* host Tom
32. Insect repellent ingredient
33. Not 'neath
36. All the vogue?
37. Swiss _____
39. Child's boo-boo
40. Hurricane's middle
41. *The Wonderful Wizard of Oz* writer L. Frank
42. Avoid trouble
43. Peterborough university
45. Showed scorn
47. Ontario ski resort
50. They precede pupae
51. "_____ home and native land"
52. Saunter through the surf
56. Adolescent's skin trouble
57. Treats some crops
60. Boat's bottom
61. Film _____
62. March heavily
63. Misjudges
64. Tiny insect
65. Former East Indian British army soldier

DOWN

1. Lowly worker
2. Local _____ network
3. Decomposes
4. Seemingly
5. Third-person pronoun
6. Mix-up
7. Pal of Pan
8. Rooster's partner
9. Talked, informally
10. Gymnast's feat
11. Parliament Hill landmark
12. Pergola (var.)
13. Fine sprays
18. They grow on stalks
23. Blistering diatribe
25. Treasure hunting island off Nova Scotia
26. Labatt or Molson brew
27. Farm field unit
28. Dramatist's offering
29. It might keep you awake at night
32. Hydroelectric facility
34. Literary home of leprechauns
35. Receiving OAS, say
37. Paddling through Algonquin Park, say
38. Rwanda tribe
39. Pyrex, for example
41. Sanctuary platform
42. Three of five vowels
44. Parties hearty
45. *The Vinyl Cafe* CBC radio host McLean
46. Old-style ointment
47. Ontario-born NHLer Rob (1989–2010)
48. One who spikes the punch
49. Water wheel
53. Over
54. Audition tape, say
55. US cable sports award
58. Long-time CFL quarterback Lancaster
59. Bryan Adams song: "_____ Only Love"

34 For a Song

A selection of Canada's musical colours

ACROSS

1. Abandon a plan
6. Amphetamine, say
13. Long-time Stratford Festival actress Henry
19. Weeps
20. 1940 Disney film
21. 1930s leading lady Merle
22. **Manitoba love song**
24. Canadian political journalist Ezra
25. "What's the big _____?"
26. Bird's lofty home (var.)
27. Nunavut island
29. Nephew of Cain
30. One way to be wounded
32. Canadian actors Green and Jackson
33. Cleaning cloth
35. Painful sounds
36. Luau necklace
37. _____ *en scène*
38. **Irish immigration song (with "The")**
47. Long-time quintet: Canadian _____
49. Some limbs
50. Crafty, like a coyote?
51. 1985 Kim Mitchell hit: "_____ Soda"
52. United
53. Vancouver Canuck Henrik Sedin, to teammate Daniel
54. Bygone time
55. Voiced, phonetically
56. Like a monarch's residence?
59. Word in a Doris Day hit
60. Princesses' crowns
61. **Northern Ontario classic**
65. *Citizen Kane* co-star Joseph
68. Southeast Asian country
69. Decorative shelving units
73. Soft palate lobes (var.)
74. Hefty reading?
75. Congeal
76. Conquistador's find
77. Appraiser
78. Minestrone
79. Performers' lone moments (var.)
80. Deep gulf
82. **Hank Snow recording**
86. Hurried
87. Grey or Flying follower
88. Plugs, say
89. 1979 Broadway show: _____ *Playing Our Song*
92. Arrogant person
94. Keeps at it
99. Palindromic ladies' title
100. Camera stand
102. Unadulterated
103. French needle case
104. Eight-legged sea creatures (var.)
106. **New Brunswick traditional song**
109. *Obiter* _____
110. Bluish skin discolouration
111. Part of a poem
112. Colourless gas
113. Agrees, in the House of Commons?
114. Severe fear

DOWN

1. Theatrical backdrop
2. Personal motto
3. 1970 Guess Who hit: "Bus _____"
4. Lawn care machines
5. Letter before omega
6. _____ Sound ON
7. Jealousy
8. "Harper Valley _____"
9. Saturated fat source
10. Quran faith
11. Mortgages
12. Puts down the chips?
13. Snail or slug
14. *Barney Miller* actor Vigoda
15. Face with masonry
16. Global HVAC company
17. Sly Cooper video game: _____ *Among Thieves*
18. Aardvark's meal
20. Experience
23. French composer's dance composition
28. Provide enlightenment
31. Astonishes
32. Some shirts, for short
34. Like liners and tankers
36. Delineate
37. Shed (var.)
38. Highlander, old style
39. Mogul's underling
40. Ruffle
41. Overshadows Snow White?
42. Carpet style
43. Minority, historically
44. Quite distant
45. Spanish lady
46. Ottawa venue: National _____ Centre
47. Knock on the head
48. Hospital helper (abbr.)
53. "Listen up," in Laval
54. Black tea
55. Brown furred animal
57. 1940s British prime minister Clement
58. Divine sovereignty, old style
59. Seafood dish
62. Not quietly
63. Coca-Cola product: Mello _____
64. Zeno follower
65. Suppress an appetite
66. Egg shape

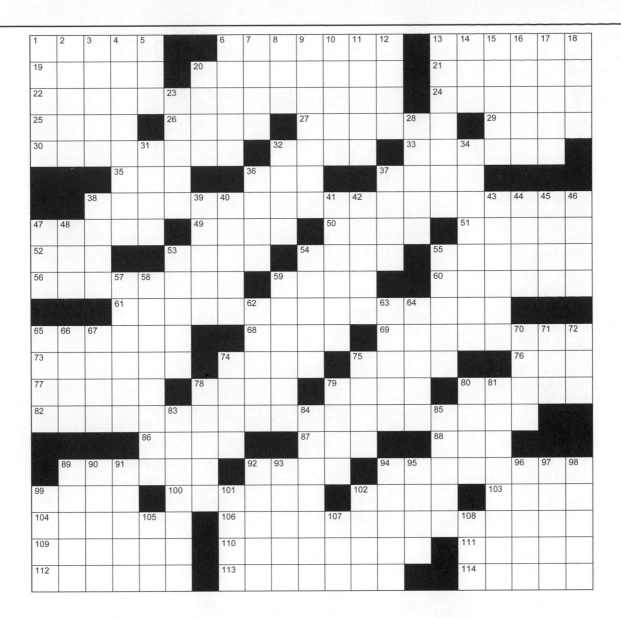

67. Ballerina's costume
70. French-Canadian author Gabrielle, et al.
71. Vocal hesitations
72. Ship's distress call
74. Bumpy amphibian
75. Maize
78. Scornful expression
79. Rebuff, socially
80. Abets

81. Ottoman Empire, at 1453 Constantinople
83. Lisa LaFlamme's moment?
84. Pain alleviator
85. 1970s Canadian figure skater Magnussen
89. Silently understood
90. Submarine opening
91. Overdramatize
92. Neuters
93. Starbursts (var.)

94. Hungarian sheepdogs
95. Mesozoic and Paleozoic
96. Mark's, in Canada
97. Oklahoma city
98. Allied with
99. Methodology
101. Early Andeans
102. Quiet interjection
105. Wordplay
107. Charged particle
108. Optical disc, for short

Around the World

Travel for some fun

ACROSS

1. Maybelline products
9. United Farmers of Alberta (abbr.)
12. Cardiac test, for short
15. Some Greek letters
19. Post-burp phrase
20. Never-ending
22. _____ the crack of dawn
23. _____ Alberta Institute of Technology
24. **You might display this in Amsterdam**
26. No ifs, _____ or buts
27. Funny car propellant
29. Hawaiian "bro"
30. Mexicali mister
31. Ravel contemporary
32. Green or yellow veggie
33. Wilfred Owen poem line: "Pro patria _____"
34. **You might aspire to this in Arkansas**
39. Title for Wilfrid Laurier
40. Swedish air carrier
43. Romp
44. Former Manitoba premier Gary
45. 2008 Meryl Streep movie: *Mamma _____*!
46. Via, in West Virginia
47. Gwich'in or Mi'kmaq
48. Storage trunk
50. Sleeping pill, say
52. Suncor produces this
53. Contact lens cleaner
55. Money roll
56. Jazz great Fats
57. Space shuttle org.
59. Small state in India
60. Tendon
62. Manipulate an environmentalist again?
63. **You might pet this in Edinburgh**
68. WWI French private
71. Peevish
72. Broadcast
73. Watering holes?
77. Scour
79. Hearst's abductors (abbr.)
80. Kill the _____ calf
83. iPod download
84. Gets additional coverage from Intact
86. Embankment
87. Vietnamese capital
89. Sunrise compass point
90. Notes after dos
91. 2002 Bryan Adams single: "_____ I Am"
92. Former prime minister Borden
93. "Be quiet!"
94. Laureen Harper, to Benjamin and Rachel
95. **You might dance this in Salzburg**
98. "_____ the night before . . ."
100. Wee weapon
101. Holds on tight
102. Canadian "Moonlight Desires" singer
104. Beaufort and Bering
105. Trudeau cabinet member Joyal
106. Opposite of 91-D
110. **You might need this in London**
113. Like a cuckoo clock (var.)
115. Ain't correct?
116. Wear out one's welcome
117. Inorganic chemical compound
118. Pitch a horseshoe
119. Math class ordinal
120. Flock female
121. Responded

DOWN

1. Flat hill near Phoenix
2. Nerve cell thread
3. Missile developed by the Soviet Union
4. Slices
5. Volcanoes spew this
6. Dramatize a Civil War battle, say
7. Hindu nectar of the gods
8. Remitted
9. Annul
10. Crazy, in Québec
11. Aardvark a.k.a.
12. Eleven-year Edmonton Oiler Moreau
13. Former NYC mayor Ed
14. Mail depot (abbr.)
15. More pristine
16. **You might catch this in Madrid**
17. Othello villain
18. Suffix for young or old
21. "Get out of here!"
25. "You're either with _____ against . . ."
28. Blush
31. Fathers
32. Borscht bit
33. Cat's call (var.)
34. Follow advice, say
35. Opera great Callas
36. Bad doings of men
37. 2013 newsmaker Ford
38. Wooer's flower
39. Drink a little
41. Pisces follower
42. Sweet stuff, in Shawinigan
45. Temper a Conservative?
46. They install ceramics
48. Blood masses
49. Respites
50. On one's rocker
51. Not common
54. Way back then
55. Bon mot, say

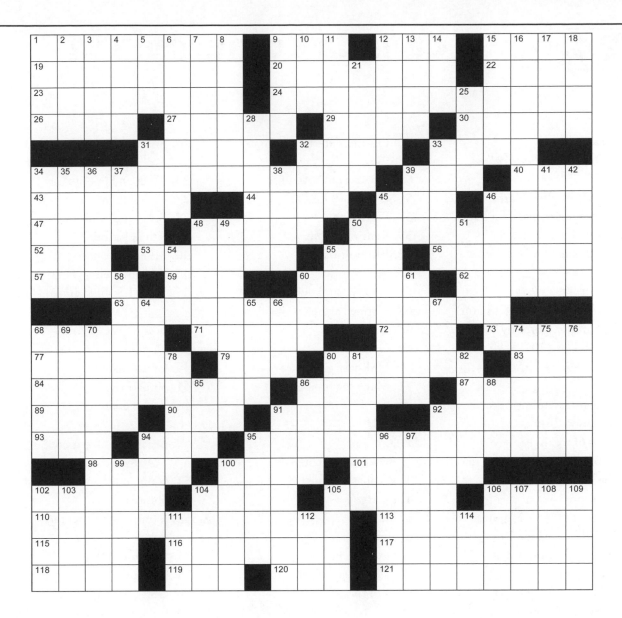

58. Not level
60. Timid
61. Emulate Atwood
64. Cows chew these
65. Measles and mumps?
66. Reggae relative
67. Boiling point?
68. Cuts back on potatoes?
69. West Indies witches' practice
70. **You might see these in Dublin**
74. Electrical box board
75. To the left, at sea
76. 1972 Olympics swimming star Mark
78. Milan money

80. Popular plant in Boston?
81. Pay back
82. Arabian coastal vessels
85. Sleep stage
86. Vichyssoise ingredient
88. US lawyers' org.
91. Hairy
92. Previously shown shows
94. Gershwin composition: "The _____ Love"
95. Little perfume bottles
96. Lists of printer's goofs
97. Register at the desk, say
99. Light bulb strengths
100. Not length or width

102. Computing storage unit symbol
103. Estimate phrase
104. Close
105. Hebrides island
106. Fido's treat
107. Cooking thickener
108. Guitar kin
109. Feat
111. Ex-Toronto Maple Leaf Brian Conacher, to Lionel
112. Crow's cry
114. The _____ Society of Upper Canada

ACROSS

1. Reality show: *Undercover _____ Canada*
5. 17th-C. English diarist Samuel
10. Aussie marsupials, for short
14. Before long, old style
15. 1970s sitcom: *One Day at _____*
16. Parrot, say
17. Toronto food market named best in the world by *National Geographic* (2012)
19. 2012 Alice Munro book: *_____ Life*
20. Bulgarian capital
21. Machine disk
22. Cost of a cab
23. MB MLA Harper who rejected the Meech Lake Accord
26. Rainforest vines
28. Sirius, in Canis Major
30. 1990s boy band: 'N _____
31. You might boil one for breakfast
32. Nosy snob?
34. Like *The National*, say
38. Grey, in Gatineau
40. Ancient Africa kingdom
42. *China Beach* star Delany
43. South Korean capital
45. Drops to the bottom
47. Formal address for him
48. Labatt Bass _____ Ale
50. Québec entertainer Reno
52. Eked
55. One way to sort a list
56. Not near
57. Peace sign
59. Rent out again
62. Petite British car
63. Vex
66. US oil company
67. Happen again
68. Wildebeests
69. Oracle
70. Ordinary guy
71. Make the final cut?

DOWN

1. Fish type
2. Aware of shenanigans
3. Vocalist's exercise (var.)
4. Escargots
5. Links average
6. Summer, to a Quebecer
7. Dash of salt
8. 1978 Village People hit
9. Appropriate
10. Visibly embarrassed
11. Big body of water
12. Toronto-born *SCTV* star Catherine
13. Cold spots?
18. Serves restaurant patrons (with "on")
24. Juno-winning female artist Arden
25. Whet an appetite, say
27. Hostel
28. B.A.s and M.A.s
29. Shrek, for one
30. Miserly
33. Kimono belt
35. 1922 T.S. Eliot poem: "The _____"
36. Tizzy
37. Nimble
39. Great Lake
41. Similar to
44. Young chap
46. Trap
49. Bruce Cockburn hit: "_____ in a Dangerous Time"
51. Come out from a cocoon
52. Some parents
53. John Ritter TV comedy: *Hearts _____*
54. Samba or salsa
55. Seashore
58. Corp. bigwig
60. Case for Colette
61. Canadian band: Crash _____ Dummies
64. Total
65. Not amateur

37 Only in Canada, Eh?

Things unique to us

ACROSS

1. You don't wash these with lights
6. Tibetan priests
11. Canadian flag colour
14. Hagen of Broadway
17. Cyber message
18. Pass into law, in parliament
19. Madness?
20. _____ *de plume*
21. **Annual May event**
23. **CFL trophy**
25. Clytemnestra's killer
26. Rich tapestry
28. Needy
29. More rundown, like a neighbourhood
31. Utter impulsively
32. BC-born *Knocked Up* star Rogen
36. Eye part
37. Overly curious (var.)
39. Conk out
41. Shrub with yellow flowers
43. Seed coat
44. Canadian history Louis
45. Cause embarrassment
46. Sketched
48. Always, in old verse
49. *SCTV* news anchor Camembert
50. Iran, in the past
52. Lennon's in-laws
54. Winter eavestrough adjunct
56. **National honour**
59. Have a spat
61. RBC transaction, say
62. Not straight up
66. Skinny
67. _____ Democratic Party
69. Islamabad language
71. Dionne quintuplets' papa
72. Treads the boards
73. Reddish yellow, in Rochester

75. Cloisonné artisan (var.)
77. Mamie's mate, at the White House
78. 1960s protest type
79. Float on air
80. Mar a car
81. Make a good impression at the ranch?
83. Felix Unger's obsession
86. Niche in Notre-Dame
87. To the manor born?
88. Nickered
93. **Newfoundland rum**
95. **RCMP offering**
97. 2002 Giller Prize winner: *The Polished* _____
98. Calgary _____
99. Domicile
100. Ontario's motto: "_____ she began . . ."
101. Formic acid secretor
102. USNA graduate (abbr.)
103. Ecclesiastical assembly
104. Hindu teacher

DOWN

1. 1980s New Wave band
2. Arabic VIP
3. CTV show: *The Amazing* _____ *Canada*
4. They go with caboodles?
5. Openings at Caesars Palace?
6. Like the idle rich?
7. Women's tennis player Ivanovic
8. Shady ladies?
9. Mites
10. Liquid hydrocarbon for plastics
11. Oil field structures
12. Go astray
13. With great intensity
14. Not welcoming
15. **Québec meat pie**

16. PA system component
22. Kindled anew
24. Lightfoot hit: "If _____ Could Read My Mind"
27. Got up for the day
30. It reflects on you?
31. Asian mammal
32. Shower bar?
33. European river
34. Eye drop
35. Church cushions
38. Oktoberfest mug
40. Architectural annex
42. Dodge one's duties
43. **Case of beer**
44. Summoned a memory
47. Carbon compound
51. Lump in one's throat
53. Identifying mark
55. Local colour, in speech
57. Build
58. Like llamas and condors
59. **Peameal product**
60. Make sense of Swedish?
63. Carpet alternative
64. Equally distributed
65. Pub patron's projectile
66. Long-time Chinese premier: Chou En-_____
68. _____ Rock BC
70. Like a yard yet to be landscaped
74. Mysteries
76. Not on land
78. "Gesundheit" preceder
79. First female Supreme Court of Canada justice Bertha
82. *Peer Gynt* character
84. Glutinous, old style
85. Houseplant ledges
87. Greek letters
89. Mature
90. Colloquial hello

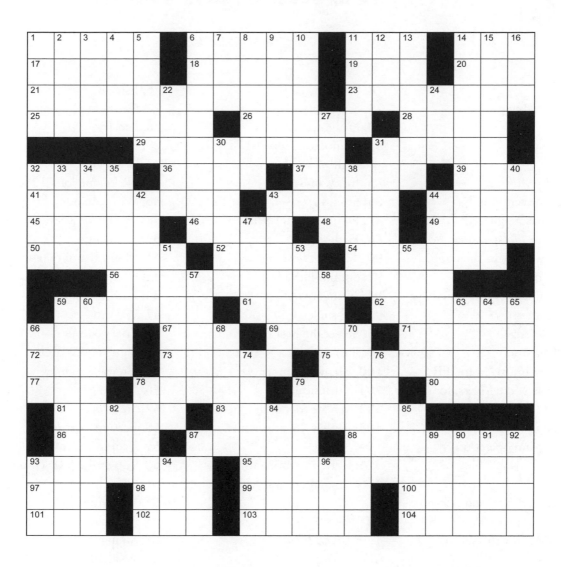

91. Gouda kin

92. Cold cuts shop

93. _____ Na Na

94. Fool a felon?

96. 1996 hit from Alberta's Paul Brandt

38 Say It with Food

Eat this one up

ACROSS

1. Stay up studying
5. Sup
9. Mooring post
13. "Psst!"
16. Town in Muskoka
17. Social conventions
18. Soothsayer's sign
19. *Canadian Idol* 4 winner Avila
20. Lose courage, in the coop?
22. Lovers' quarrel
23. Metric thickness measurement
24. Trigonometric ratio
25. Sidewalk edge
26. Small channel
27. Shooting injury, in the ER
30. Toronto's Mike Myers, for example
31. Left on the plate
33. SWAT team operation
35. Treat the lawn
37. Foot soldier?
40. *To Hell and Back* star Murphy
42. Strike out instruction
43. Put aside, for the sailor?
44. Fortifies oneself
46. Good taste?
48. Wipe a hard drive
49. Ideal cigar?
52. Piece of history?
54. Colourants
55. Ingratiate oneself, in India?
58. Bert who played the Cowardly Lion
62. Tintin's chien
63. Heralds one's husband?
68. Assortments
70. Super football games?
72. Canada's Group of Seven, for example
73. Flatter a dairy farmer?
75. Shakespearean king
78. Rueful
79. Seat a jury
80. Daughters of Atlas
82. Edmonton's top 2012 NHL draft pick Yakupov
83. Risky, in Reno?
85. Frolics
87. Diminutive for Willie Winkie
88. Had on
90. Tabloid twosome, say
91. Sounds like a frog?
93. "Caught you!"
94. Big smile
95. Select the best fruit?
99. Purge of
100. Many millennia (var.)
101. Intrinsically
102. Female friend, in Québec
103. Author Edgar Allan
104. Say no
105. Butt, on a Britcom
106. Like an optimist's cheeks?

DOWN

1. *The Fifth Estate* network
2. Cheering syllable
3. *Arabian Nights* Baba
4. Some apples, for short
5. Gave at the office?
6. Mined substance
7. Muted colours
8. Toronto clock setting (abbr.)
9. Merchant ship officer
10. Concert promoters
11. Brewing gadget
12. Explosive abbreviation?
13. Author Ernest
14. Nefarious
15. Everybody, in Alabama
17. Saudi Arabian city
21. New Zealand parrot
25. Billiards stick
26. Esteem
27. Get hold of a concept?
28. Pan-fry
29. More broad
32. Carry all?
34. Nickname for a 1960s PM
36. With copious crying
38. The life of Riley, say
39. Some liquor
41. Monthly utility (abbr.)
43. Complete a crossword
45. Lowlife, colloquially
47. Pod orb
50. Trial's partner
51. Ship's lowest deck
53. Grey and Stanley
56. "Ouch!"
57. Some deer
58. Earring location
59. Reunion goer, for short
60. Top of the pops countdown
61. Spin
64. Well versed in
65. Scarecrow's stuffing
66. Strange
67. Fashion
69. Ottawa NHLers, for short
71. Rescue team member
74. CPP recipient
76. Fans
77. Penitence
80. Shorten one's pants
81. Extra tire
84. "The Gambler" singer Rogers
86. Shade of blue
88. Distort
89. State with 18 Electoral College votes in 2012
92. Former Canadian aerospace company
94. Roam
95. Accounting expert (abbr.)

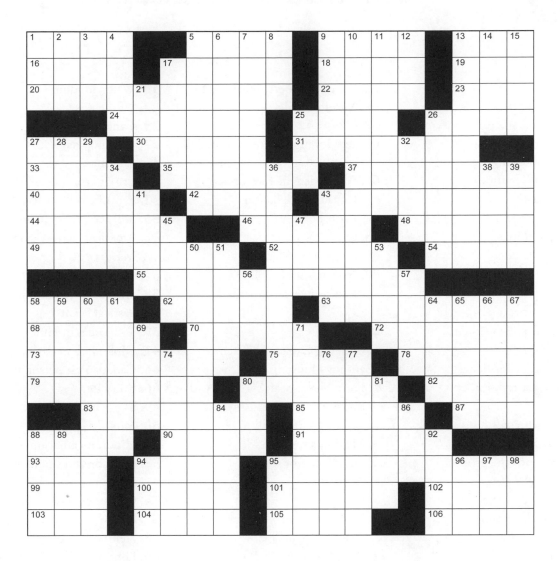

96. 1917 Halifax explosion ship

97. Org. that includes Kazakhstan and Kyrgyzstan

98. Door opening device

ACROSS

1. Acts of subterfuge
6. Clumsy person's exclamation
10. Rabbit's rear end
14. *Aida*, for example
15. House of Commons chair?
16. Vocal quality
17. _____ Creek AB
18. Irksome things
20. Dusk, to a poet
21. Goof
23. One way to get around
24. Relay or sprint
26. Old-style stereo system
28. Slog through
29. Latticework for lianas
31. Middle Eastern leader
33. Clan
34. Some farmers
37. Busy mo. for the CRA
40. She got into the groove, musically
42. Ball diamond stat
43. Earthquake, colloquially
45. Myanmar cash
47. It comes after alpha
48. National symbol
53. Primary
55. Perplexed, out of port?
56. Money to spend in Sofia
57. More feminine
59. Statue of Liberty locale (abbr.)
61. Meadow male
62. Ottawa CFLers as of 2014
64. Ex-Governor General Jean hails from here
66. Formaldehyde forerunner
67. Canadian ice dancer: _____-Lynn Bourne
68. Of an eye part
69. Ocean travel hazard
70. Noggin, in Neuville
71. Like a cheery Christmas?

DOWN

1. Order of Canada children's author Munsch
2. From Shakespeare's 49th: "And this my hand against myself _____"
3. Medium's session
4. Physics energy unit
5. Wise
6. Isis' spouse
7. Contraction in "The Star-Spangled Banner"
8. Biased advocate
9. Mix batter
10. Famed Vancouver park
11. Clear soup
12. More messy
13. Experiment with
19. Water conduit
22. Of the nose
25. Canadian mammal
27. Hats popular with '40s gangsters
30. Leg or arm
32. Part of a cell nucleus (abbr.)
35. Still active, on the field
36. American actress/comedienne Martha
37. Alberta bank (abbr.)
38. Toronto International Film Festival event
39. To hinder, in Hull
41. Diplomat's manoeuvre
44. Canada Post person's tote
46. Every iota
49. Thought, to Thierry
50. More creepy
51. Hindu incarnation
52. Cape Breton singing group: Rankin _____
54. Goose egg, say
57. Chow
58. Steinbeck book: _____ *of Eden*
60. Long-time Toronto radio station name
63. Chocolate bar: Kit _____
65. "_____ Maria"

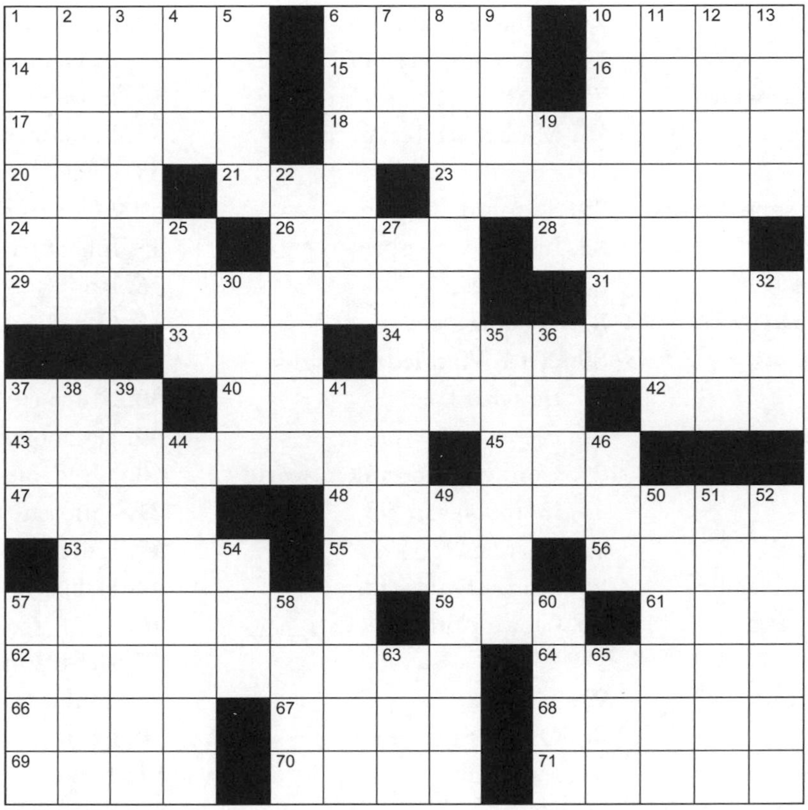

Solution on page 184

40

Tennis, Anyone? 1

For true-blue tennis lovers

ACROSS

1. Temporary, to Tiberius
6. Dubai VIPs
11. For lack of _____ word
18. Motto
19. Former Governor General LeBlanc
20. Complains
21. **2014 Wimbledon semi-finalist Raonic**
22. Mature on the vine
23. **Marino who reached WTA #38 in 2011**
24. Turns turtle
26. Blue jeans manufacturer Strauss
27. Make _____ of
28. Follows
30. Solved a cipher
32. Dixie Chicks singer Natalie
34. Crazy Eights or canasta
39. Pantyhose shade
43. *Deliverance* actor Beatty
44. Paid off to retire
45. Sidekick
47. Nine-_____ battery
48. Elbow
49. Pertaining to a policy's paragraphs
50. Astronomer Sagan
51. _____ *Pepper's Lonely Hearts Club Band*
52. Laugher's sound
53. **Lareau who won Olympic doubles gold in 2000**
56. Film starring 37-D: *Agnes of _____*
59. _____ bull terrier
61. Bard's output
62. Buddhist's blissful place
65. Director Polanski
68. '92 Olympics golden Canadian swimmer Tewksbury

69. For real
70. Occur
72. Through
73. Remains behind
74. Like some NHL plays
75. Heat
77. More miserable, to the exterminator?
79. Seasoned rice dishes
83. Insurance salesperson
85. Pitt's brad?
87. Looking glass
89. **2014 Wimbledon finalist Bouchard**
91. Feeble
93. **Connell who ranked world #1 in doubles in '93**
94. Positions
95. Classical music form
96. Clorox cloths brand: _____ Wipes
97. Most brief
98. On pins and needles
99. Little kids

DOWN

1. Wile E. Coyote's product supplier
2. Canadian country band: Emerson _____
3. **Kelesi who reached WTA #13 in 1989**
4. Scents, in Sausalito
5. Theatrical clothing designers
6. Airport posting (abbr.)
7. Drudgery
8. Blocked progress
9. Canadian actor Keanu
10. _____ boom
11. Sandpaper, for example
12. BMWs, colloquially
13. Affixing securely

14. Opposite of fingers
15. Some mints: Tic _____
16. Contained herein (abbr.)
17. ANC country
25. Black or Yellow body of water
29. Just one
31. Butterfly wing spots
33. Character played by 9-D in *Matrix* movies
35. Inflammatory illness
36. Ian _____ Sylvia
37. Canadian–American actress Tilly
38. Dutch city
39. Dashboard gauge, for short
40. _____ breve
41. 45th state to join the Union
42. Little bit, in Beaupré
44. Halifax and Québec City
46. _____ Coast
47. **2014 Wimbledon men's doubles co-winner Pospisil**
50. Exclusive group
51. Tizzy
54. Pucks carom off these
55. Live outdoors
56. Charity event, say
57. Canadian restaurant chain's former name: Joey's _____
58. Calendar components
59. Gasp
60. Rudeness
63. Old-style candle, in England
64. Wine tub
65. Highway 66, for short
66. Ontario Renal Network (abbr.)
67. Irate
68. Most teensy
69. Yukon carrier: _____ North
71. Showy flowers
72. A little difference
75. Grate against

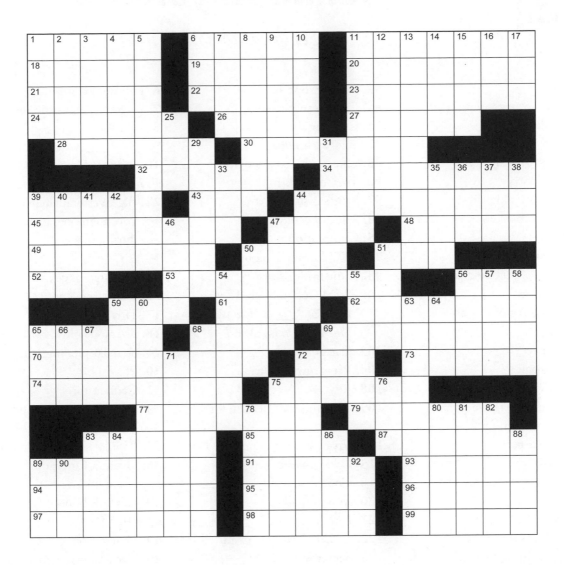

76. Tiny Dickens character
78. Under, to Augustus
80. Set out in order
81. Davis Cup team member since 2002 Dancevic

82. Atmospheric assessment device
83. Laboratory gel
84. Army bigwigs, briefly
86. Eyeball coverings

88. Remote Traffic Information System (abbr.)
89. Trenton time setting (abbr.)
90. American Native
92. Powell's *Thin Man* co-star

41

Tennis Anyone? 2

Serving up some fun

ACROSS

1. Medieval security deposits
6. Start a blaze
12. To and _____
15. Alberta MP Ambrose
19. Concur with
20. Kicked out a kicker?
21. Suffix for musket
22. Level
23. **Criticism?**
25. Emergency services acronym
26. Tropical tree
27. Old-style cry of disgust
28. Borders
29. Et cetera
32. New recruit
35. Window seat site
36. NS World Heritage site: _____ Town Lunenburg
37. **Easy victory?**
40. Not post
41. Two-time NL batting champ Lefty
44. Humiliation
47. Silent films star Theda
49. Transmit by cellphone
51. Sneaky
52. Sculler's stick
53. Frontier felon
58. *Tosca* composer
60. Move quickly
62. Take one's time
63. Food colouring
65. Reagan's "slipped the bonds of surly earth" speechwriter Peggy
66. Church exclamation
68. Agenda entries
70. Prod
71. **Ultimate commitment?**
75. Chicken _____
77. 1980s Canadian hit: "_____ Are Not Enough"
78. Sensory organ
82. Release rope
84. Caribbean music
85. Comedy sketches
87. Sandwich filling
88. Like earthquake activity
90. They embellish
93. Yang's counterpart
94. Antiquity, old style
95. Commotions
97. 1977 Robin Cook book
98. Some bridge seats
100. 2004 Cohen book: *While Canada _____: How We Lost Our Place in the World*
102. Catcall?
104. **Pre-game boost?**
108. Jiffy
109. Working class person, for short
111. Viva voce, for example
115. Overly sweet
118. Counsels, old style
120. Move rapidly
121. LAN part
122. *Golden Girls* star Arthur
123. **Secret weapon?**
127. Huckleberry _____
128. New Canadian's course (abbr.)
129. Private party
130. Attack
131. Has lunch
132. Slalom bend
133. Sweet liquids
134. Canadian NHLers Richards and Richardson

DOWN

1. Blooper
2. 1990 Blue Rodeo hit: "Til I Am Myself _____"
3. Thin porridge
4. Long fish
5. Matching group
6. Footnote word
7. Played a percussion instrument
8. Lymphatic knot
9. "So _____ written"
10. John A. Macdonald bill
11. Bronfman family son
12. Big river branches
13. You might perchance to dream during this
14. Ish
15. Narrated once more
16. Exceeding a prescribed amount
17. Tidy
18. Pharaoh's cross
24. Spanakopita ingredient
30. Playful bite
31. **Grub stop?**
33. School of thought suffix
34. Toboggan
35. Popular southwest US veggie
38. Over, in Otterndorf
39. None, to a Scot
42. Forearm bones
43. 1975 Eagles hit: "_____ Eyes"
44. Living room piece
45. Canadian comedy group: The Kids in the _____
46. Seed's sheath
48. Supplement
50. Convent resident
54. Paulette's petite purse
55. Québec city: _____-Georges
56. Speaks too quickly
57. _____ and terminer
59. Brass instrument
61. Tall tents (var.)
64. Syrup of ipecac, for example
67. **Perfect romance?**
68. MPPs and MPs, say
69. Provincial neighbour?
72. *Hockey Night in Canada* commentator Scott
73. Former currency in Cannes

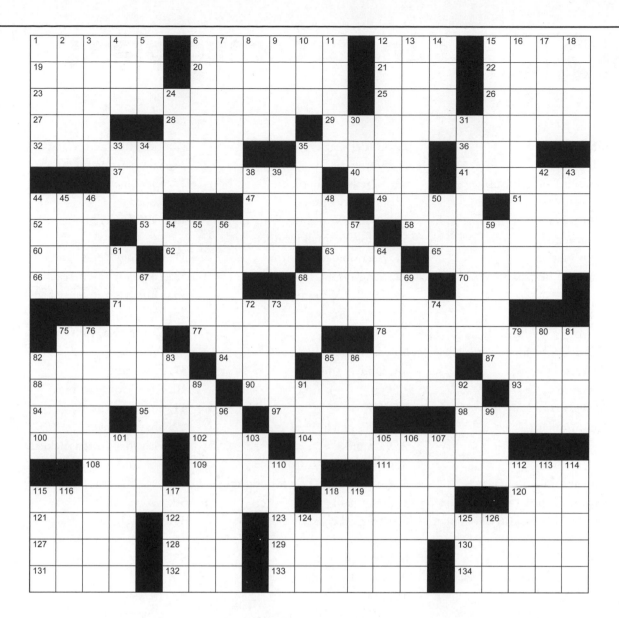

74. Konstantin Chernenko's country (abbr.)
75. Unappealing bell sound?
76. Gleaming
79. Makes a purchase
80. Segment of study
81. Canadian actors Aykroyd and George
82. Purposes
83. You might flip this
85. Not any different
86. Hill crest

89. Ice bag, for example
91. Optimism
92. Vend
96. Soap operas
99. "Yes, admiral!"
101. Nut-bearing trees
103. Took first
105. Nova Scotia premier MacDonald (2006–09)
106. Rocky ridges
107. Eyelid hair
110. Dog handler's tether

112. Southeast Africans
113. Had the flu
114. Gets acquainted
115. Secure
116. Opera solo
117. As busy as _____
118. Rider's strap
119. Old name for Ireland
124. Dove's murmur
125. Wane
126. Genie-winning film: *Away from _____*

Solution on page 184

42

Canada Cornucopia 14

ACROSS

1. Small blister
5. Vegetarian's protein substitute
9. Dieter's friend or foe?
14. Vishnu avatar
15. Parliament Hill party disciplinarian
16. American newspaper: *USA* _____
17. Oversights
19. "Have _____ day!"
20. Mulroney-era finance minister Michael
21. Portrayed
23. Adages
25. Colour quality
26. Leaks
28. St. Lawrence _____
32. Tiny amphibians
34. Area in the heart of Manitoba
36. Jim Bakker's ministry, for short
37. Suspicious
38. Family
39. Vancouver shopping mecca: _____ Island
42. Storage building
44. Sea near Greece
45. Machine in a carpenter's shop
47. Slanderous comment
49. Underwear type for a Canadian winter
53. Scheduling book
57. Not very often
58. Santa's Workshop workers
59. Smoker's small product
61. Accustomed practice
62. Sang-froid?
63. 1990s TV drama set in BC: _____ *Rider*
64. Ditties
65. Footnote abbr.
66. Understands

DOWN

1. Ladies pluck these
2. Vampiress
3. Canadian artist Carr
4. Rush's Geddy Lee, for example
5. Sharp pain
6. Surprised cry
7. Locate
8. Top seed's loss
9. Furniture worker
10. Hide
11. Mine shaft entrance
12. String for a shoe
13. Ogled
18. Sound units
22. Indie film actress Parker
24. Salesperson's pitch
27. Short fishing line
29. Rouse
30. 1995 Leslie Nielsen film: *Rent-_____*
31. Craving
32. To be, in Taschereau
33. Ours has a maple leaf
35. Trick-or-_____
36. Sports assn. for Canada's Mike Weir
37. Flax genus
40. RRSP, for example
41. Small suitcases
42. Shave a sheep
43. Fish that's often pickled
46. Servitude
48. Case the place
50. Crowd clash
51. Fairly share
52. Southeastern France city (var.)
53. _____ *ex machina*
54. _____-ran
55. 1970s Montréal Canadiens star Cournoyer
56. See 50-D
60. Former Portuguese colony in India

43 Let's Talk TV

Canadian chat show hosts

ACROSS

1. A bit wet
5. Business tycoon (var.)
9. Dirty rats, say
14. Biden and Gore, for short
19. Coloured eye part
20. City near Lake Tahoe
21. Buddhist who attains Nirvana
22. OB/GYN test
23. Her eponymous show aired from 1989–1997
25. Google competitor
26. _____ Charlotte Islands BC
27. Eccentric
28. Beetle sacred to ancient Egyptians
30. Irate
32. Sigh of satisfaction
33. Actor who hosted '80s Canadian and American talk shows
35. National TV network
38. Grins
41. Land in *The Iliad*
42. Crossbow pro
44. Fire warning bell
45. They share a womb
47. Sachet contents
50. Attire
51. Challenges
52. Zoroastrian
53. Neckwear
54. Makes a Martian hostile?
56. Rude soup-eating sound
57. Catalogues
58. Former Eastern European region
59. Some Labatt products
60. Hiking trail
61. Canadian singer Sky
62. She hosted a '90s CTV show
66. Ornamental shrub
69. Rejections
71. Own
72. What a black sheep might do to his family
74. Final musical passages
76. Horn sound
78. Greek mythology prophetess
79. Zeus' offspring
80. Canadian clothing store
81. Orderly display
82. Reverend's exclamation
83. Ready to be fired?
85. Foe
86. Blind boards
87. Brought up Cain?
88. Z _____ "zebra"
89. Faints
91. Some switch settings
92. She hosts *The Morning Show* on Global
97. Embrace
98. Fruity alcohol
99. Draw out
101. Unlock, poetically
104. Japanese menu offering
107. Lead guitarists' shining moments
109. He hosted a '70s CTV afternoon show
111. Celestial hunter
112. Beginning of a musical refrain
113. Seashore bird
114. Hair products
115. Take in the laundry
116. Football field measurements
117. "Indian Love Call" singer Nelson
118. Poker word

DOWN

1. Carthage founder
2. Dry like a desert
3. It's a terrible thing to waste
4. Greek letter
5. Nativity scene
6. See 4-D
7. Sinus cavities
8. Writers' payments
9. Utter
10. Like a sly artisan?
11. "Yeah"
12. New Zealand Native
13. Unemotional
14. Catalonia cowboy
15. Flightless birds
16. Toronto-to-Oshawa dir.
17. Chart type
18. Justin Trudeau, to Pierre
24. "The Lord is my shepherd," for one
29. Farm buildings
31. Congo creature
32. Inflatable mattress
34. French pronoun
35. He co-hosts with Steven Sabados
36. Mademoiselle's chapeau
37. American magician Angel
38. Canada's Kathy Kreiner won gold in this "giant" Olympic event
39. CTV show host since 2011
40. _____ cling
43. "_____ out!"
44. Colourful lizard
46. Cause havoc
47. Wait for it?
48. Boston Bruins great Bobby
49. Baking soda amt.
51. Former Ontario premier Bill
52. United States Naval Academy freshman
55. Church sections
56. Great _____ Lake

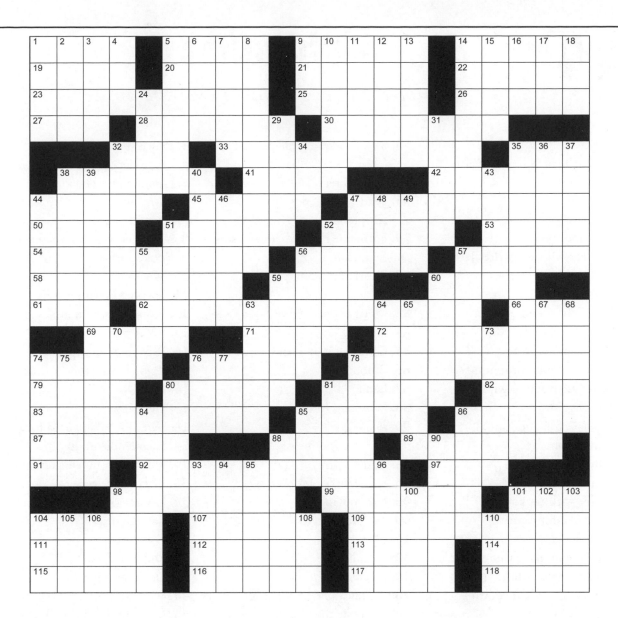

57. Mrs. Bush
59. Chefs' thickening agents
60. "Sweet Dreams" singer Cline
63. Joan Jett hit: "_____ Myself for Loving You"
64. Get more guns
65. Students' writing assignments
67. Some herons
68. Withdraws, gradually
70. Sahara spring
73. Not digital
74. Ontario town or Egyptian city
75. Keyboard instrument

76. Hockey Hall of Fame inductee Gainey
77. "That's funny," in texting
78. Build a battlement (var.)
80. _____-Canada
81. Japanese cartoon genre
84. Significant
85. Edmonton Symphony Orchestra (abbr.)
86. Saskatoon river: _____ Saskatchewan
88. The Governator Schwarzenegger
90. Horse's communication
93. Teeming with tang

94. Plaza for Pericles
95. Made with fine threads
96. Exasperated
98. Loafer, e.g.
100. Jack or five
101. Sign of things to come
102. Hide
103. Otherwise
104. Old French coin
105. Mantel vase
106. Bit of a quaff
108. Airline with Scandinavian hubs
110. Cotswolds cooker

Alphanumeric

Solve these "equations" to get the answers

ACROSS

1. CODCO comedienne Walsh
5. Nightclubs
9. Iraqi port city
14. Pigpens
19. Classroom quiz
20. Pulitzer-winning writer James
21. Some Greek letters
22. Article of faith
23. Honestly, it ends a letter?
25. Sheepish sounds
26. Actor without lines
27. Water-soluble compound
28. First Oscar acting winner Jannings
30. "_____, foh and fum . . ."
31. Dined at home
32. **G8**
36. Sunburned, say
37. Melee with the media
41. State of confusion
42. Long lock
44. Chefs who make things clear?
46. Media events: Photo _____
49. No charge, in Chicoutimi
52. Slow down gradually, on a score (abbr.)
53. Directed
54. Northern Italy city/province name
56. Hindu royal
57. Engine lubricant
58. _____ of 1812
59. Excitedly, to Elgar
61. Twirler's stick
62. Laundry appliances
64. Haggis ingredient
65. Adult male sheep
66. PGA tournament: RBC Canadian _____
67. **N9**
71. Talk with a French feline?

73. Saskatchewan Walleye Trail (abbr.)
74. Spice Girls B and C
75. Lead yourself not into temptation
79. Former CTV talk-show hostess Davidson
80. WestJet, for example
82. Deface
83. Oslo's country (abbr.)
84. Stuck in _____
85. Group of islands in Greece
86. Blubber
87. Fool
88. Fame and fortune
90. *Enola* _____
91. Artisan who rocks?
94. Rough copy
96. "Ave Maria," for example
98. Not moving
99. Tax prep pro
101. **N3**
105. Adjust wheels, say
107. *China Beach* country, for short
108. Guinea pigs and goldfish
109. Out for the evening?
114. Mother-of-pearl
115. 1994 Rankin Family single: "_____ Miner"
117. Scarcely detectable amount
119. Step up?
120. Just right for her majesty
121. Deserve
122. Tousle hair
123. _____ and conditions
124. *Skyfall* theme song singer
125. Fix the pooch
126. Woeful word

DOWN

1. Arizona land form
2. Botanical angle

3. Like a smelly sergeant?
4. Disco-era dance floor favourite
5. Containing element #56
6. Grow up
7. Gave in to pressure
8. Mrs. Henry VIII #3 Jane
9. Book lover's prefix
10. WWW giant
11. Shepherd's workforce?
12. Proportion, in math
13. Say it is so
14. Rice cooking appliance
15. iPhone message
16. **I-75**
17. Uncanny
18. "We _____ on guard for thee"
24. Lacquer oleoresin
29. Folklore troublemakers
33. Willow tree type
34. Dubrovnik resident
35. Basic desire
37. Fish entree
38. Ontario's Lake St. _____
39. Stock market bounce back
40. Web browser acronym
43. Mexican shawls (var.)
45. Thermos
47. Give the gift of the gab?
48. Arrangements
50. Wise to
51. Pride or lust
54. **B$_{12}$**
55. Second-yr. high-schooler
58. Composed
59. Vienna country
60. Jewel
61. Orthopaedist's error?
63. Law-making thespian?
64. Making the cut?
68. World Golf Hall of Fame member Aoki
69. Stimpy's cartoon pal

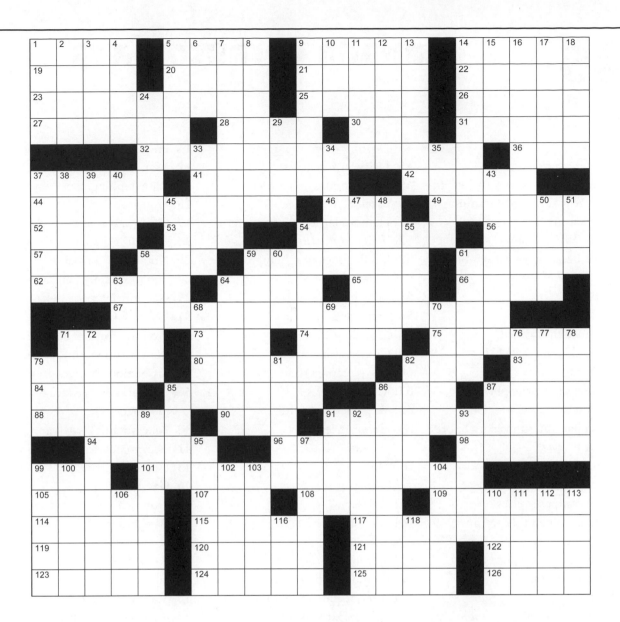

70. Give a pompous presentation
71. CANDU reactor centre
72. **i-10**
76. Unavailable
77. Lethargy
78. Ontario river
79. Cookie container
81. Directive to Macduff
82. Heavenly food?
85. Just the facts, ma'am?
86. Lined paper

87. Ottawa-born NHLer Boyle
89. Actors David and Jack
91. King's address
92. Sleeping sickness carriers
93. Centre of things
95. Mystical Buddhist writings
97. Potato chip ridge
99. Art able to
100. Canadian horse race: Queen's
_____
102. Issued a challenge

103. Public persona
104. Children's caregiver
106. Like a poor prognosis
110. Name of a bean or a city
111. Jewish month
112. Coco Chanel rival Schiaparelli
113. Rockies landmark: Crowsnest
_____
116. _____ de mer
118. International Reading
Association (abbr.)

ACROSS

1. *Dr. Zhivago* character
5. Canadian Faith who won Record of the Year at the '61 Grammys
10. Artery issue
14. Ayatollah's domain
15. 1972 Leacock Medal-winning book: *The Night We _____ the Mountie's Car*
16. Yorkshire river
17. Province that joined Confederation in 1871
20. Split into two
21. Hunter's favourite plover?
22. Each one
23. Canadian Interuniversity Sport (abbr.)
24. Gull's kin
25. Change
26. They compose verses
28. Canada joined this org. in 1949
30. Manages
33. Gregory Hines' dance milieu
34. Like richer soil
37. Fixes shoes
39. Aesop fable: *The _____ and the Grasshopper*
40. Rules the roost, say
42. Temporary beds
44. Doctors' diagnostic tools
45. Dairy farm females
49. Most winning Super Bowl coach Chuck
51. Halifax Harbour boat
52. Virile, in Puerto Vallarta
53. Sea that separates Italy from the Balkans
55. Like some peanuts
56. Large land mass in 17-A
58. Moulding style
59. Conservatory plants
60. _____ upon a time
61. Methodologies
62. Very, to Monteverdi
63. Hammer segment

DOWN

1. Women's _____
2. Land, say
3. Early Joni Mitchell hit: "_____ on Robbery"
4. Foyer for five-card stud?
5. Attention-getting murmur
6. Eritrea neighbour (abbr.)
7. Jasper or Banff locale
8. Getting thee to the nunnery?
9. Shout
10. New Jersey city
11. Free
12. Monopoly game avenue
13. Rip wrapping paper, say
18. Frigid
19. Of the last month (abbr.)
23. Casts or glasses
26. Nobility, in England
27. Top tournament entrants
29. CIA missions, for short
31. PM or GG
32. Pronoun for that lady?
34. Body of water, in Québec
35. Six Nations Natives
36. Canadian Bar Association member
38. Bake potatoes, say (var.)
41. They match teacups
43. Pieces of pizza
46. Gas pump word
47. From what place, old style
48. Wet through
50. Southeast Asian ethnic group
52. Some York University degrees (abbr.)
53. Make a promise
54. Rock garden rock
55. Emphatic "yes," in Spain
57. Hospital nursing worker (abbr.)

46 — Best of the West

Canadian prairie writers

ACROSS

1. Like a famed piper
5. Calgary-based oil company
10. Cabbie's customer
14. Early hour
17. Ethnic group in Japan
18. _____ non grata
19. Great Big Sea singer Doyle
20. *Stars Wars* character Solo
21. Odds and sods
23. **W.O. who wrote *Who Has Seen the Wind***
25. Basements
26. At what price?
27. Quite pretentious
28. Psychoanalysis subject
30. English empiricist John
31. Silhouette
33. Large coffee dispensers
35. *Pink Panther* movies star Peter
37. Last a long time
40. Maniacs, in Mexico
42. Iconic American singer Bob
43. Number type
44. Happenings
46. Tapestry
48. Himalayan creatures of legend
49. Cultural Revolution radical group
52. Layered cake
54. Canadian DIY chain
55. **Max who wrote *Why Shoot the Teacher?***
58. Delicacy
62. Block for a blacksmith
63. Woodworking tools
68. Boise state
70. Pesto herb
72. European wildflower
73. Erode
75. Minor obstacles
78. More severe
79. Petite decorative items
80. Foretold
82. Canadian Brass horn
83. Huge
85. Weddings and baptisms
87. Vitality
88. Early IBM database technology (abbr.)
90. Some cards
91. Put faith in
93. **Arthur who created a "prairie trilogy"**
95. Dogbane
98. Beaufort, for example
99. Without any give
100. Sniffer dog's trail
101. Biblical twin
102. Oprah's network
103. Ilia
104. Traffic sign
105. "_____ on it!"

DOWN

1. BC-born actress Anderson, for short
2. Three, to Tiberius
3. Firmly affixed
4. Mussolini title component
5. Greetings
6. Took off one's shoes
7. Barely?
8. **W.P. whose stories were set in Hobbema**
9. Excited exclamation
10. National cinema chain: _____ Players
11. Best guests?
12. Noisy snake
13. Business letter abbr.
14. Old-style adverb
15. Disney or Whitman
16. Shania Twain tune: "It _____ Hurts When I'm Breathing"
22. Building extension
24. Easier to reach
26. Braid style
28. 18th-C. Swiss calculus genius
29. **Abe Spalding's creator Frederick Philip**
32. Harrison Ford film character, for short
34. Early Anne Murray hit: "Danny's _____"
36. Inhabitant of our planet
38. BC's Hartley Bay gets the most of this annually
39. *Bride of Frankenstein* actress Lanchester
41. Ticket bit
43. Central Italy city
45. Gilbert of *The Talk*
47. Saudi or Kuwaiti
50. Checked with first
51. Old Canadian specialty channel: Showcase _____
53. Carve
56. Kleenex box contents
57. Got by on a bit
58. Sports stalemates
59. Canadian kayaker van Koeverden
60. Two-hulled boat
61. Grey matter masses
64. Fit of fury
65. Most brusque
66. **Rudy who wrote *The Temptations of Big Bear***
67. Suitcase handle
69. They give a hoot?
71. **Margaret who wrote about Manawaka**
74. African spear (var.)
76. Coffee bean crusher
77. Novel's "where"
80. Forestalls a fiasco
81. Lower electrical capability
84. Get slick on the streets

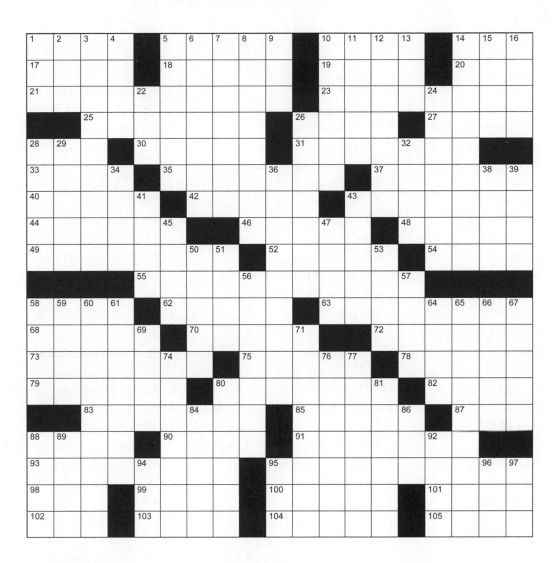

86. Toronto or Winnipeg newspaper name

88. "This _____ unfair!"

89. Crock-Pot creation

92. Sows and cows

94. To the _____ degree

95. Theology, say

96. Hollywood West

97. Newborn Newfoundland?

Repetitious

There's an echo in here . . .

ACROSS

1. Placid
6. 1969 Max Braithwaite book: *Never Sleep Three in* _____
10. Climbing vine
15. Provoke
19. Vietnamese city
20. Ex-Toronto Maple Leaf Tie
21. _____ a high note
22. Pot for paella
23. **Magician's phrase**
25. **Stuffed shirt**
27. *Iron Chef America* chef Cat
28. Those voting "no"
30. Contradicts
31. Cosa Nostra members
35. Poisonous snake
36. Contemplate
37. _____ *Well That Ends Well*
38. Bivouacs
40. Lend a hand
41. Go rotten
43. Pierce the matador
44. **Monkey business**
51. Nautical rope
53. Mecca journey (var.)
55. "_____ whiz!"
56. Mme. Chrétien
57. Early Childhood Education (abbr.)
58. Canadian territory
60. Bit of brio
62. She wrote *Pride and Prejudice*
63. Flit
65. _____-boom-bah
66. Used a broom
67. Lists of electoral candidates
68. Brightly coloured Aussie bird
70. Cook's strainer
71. Like hot tamales?
72. Lacking limbs
74. Foolish action
75. Legal Aid Ontario (abbr.)
76. Ova
79. Update an electrical system
80. Mandolin's relative
81. Indonesian island
83. Modern music genre
84. Principles
85. Canadian's gov. ID
86. Roald or Arlene
88. Emend
90. **Barrel organ**
93. Shaft of light
95. Mountaineering spike
96. Allow
97. Old-style ointments
100. Auricular
101. Ontario river
105. Despise
106. Scottish philosopher Thomas
108. Greeting in Jerusalem
109. Michigan locale: Ann _____
110. Apple variety
111. **Jumble**
113. **Gibberish**
119. *Magic Flute* component
120. Scrub
121. Many kilometres away
122. Romance, in Rimouski
123. Canadian-born PGA pro Mike
124. Ebbs off
125. *The* _____ *Ranger*
126. Sam's shovel?

DOWN

1. "Hush!"
2. Chinese principle
3. South African political group (abbr.)
4. Debtor's promise to pay
5. 1970s music style
6. Crazy about
7. _____ Raton FL
8. Australian bird
9. Removed rifles?
10. Like a Liberal?
11. Indigenous Canadian people
12. Interjects
13. Cain fled to this land
14. Someone
15. Canadian pianist Glenn
16. Retro gold?
17. Birch tree kin
18. Week components
24. Sit for a sculptor
26. CBC show: *Dragons'* _____
29. Snooze
31. Prepared potatoes
32. Animal found in 73-D
33. **1960s movement**
34. Egyptian goddess
35. DKNY designer Donna
36. Jackfish
39. Some salmon
40. With regard to, old style
42. Grassland, in Greenwich
45. Open-mouthed
46. Catherine the Great's successor
47. Region in France
48. **Practical details**
49. Joint in the leg
50. Cravings
52. Leaves' noise
54. Decorated with diamonds (var.)
59. South Korean carmaker
61. Tax
62. _____ as a church mouse
64. Cleaned up
66. Riverbed muck
69. Late
70. Owen _____ ON
71. Gagner drafted by the Oilers in 2007
72. Foot part
73. Andes land
74. Make eyes at
75. Purple hue
77. Petroleum distillate

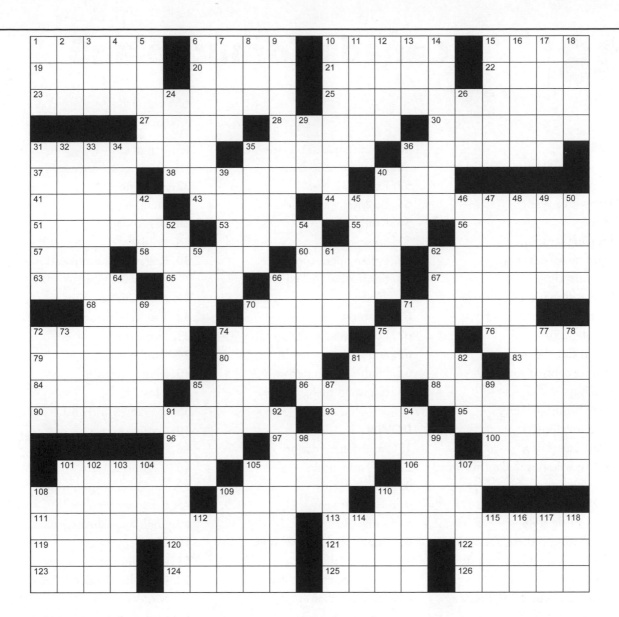

78. Canadian diamond retailer
81. Third-person pronoun
82. Agt.
85. Beef fat
87. Not quite right
89. Baroque era instrument
91. Quick look
92. Chats in the Outback
94. Gruesome
98. 17th Greek letter

99. Former Vancouver Canuck Sami
101. Task
102. Arm bones
103. "Pomp and Circumstance" composer
104. John or Jane surname?
105. Debate
107. Hindu royals

108. Canadian telecommunications company
109. Brouhahas
110. Fellow FBI employee?
112. Wood sorrel
114. Aliens' ship
115. Baseball arbiter
116. Extinct bird
117. Beginning of a bloom
118. Discontinued Swedish coin

Solution on page 185

ACROSS

1. Former Israeli prime minister Sharon
6. African tree (var.)
10. Wan
14. Jousting weapon
15. Love, to a Latino
16. Eye infection
17. Cause of marital impurities?
19. Mama's man
20. To laugh, in Laval
21. Baffin Bay danger
22. Harper cabinet minister MacKay
23. New Brunswick city
25. River in Bonn
27. Wine barrel
28. Indian bakeries make this bread
29. Put down turf
32. Orbital point
35. Soul music style
36. Bombs and bullets, for short
37. Flowery Vancouver Island attraction
40. Conscious minds, to Freud
41. Mislay
42. *Sesame Street* Muppet
43. Computing key that lets you get out
44. Pooch on *The Flintstones*
45. Long-time Chinese leader
46. Gold standard measurement
48. Large Ontario lake
52. Expensive (var.)
54. Business transaction
56. Kind of list
57. Sty sound
58. Italian opera composer
60. Former Barenaked Ladies singer Steven
61. Starburst
62. Letters that make plurals
63. Something different
64. Hydrocarbon derivative
65. Firewood delivery unit

DOWN

1. Cause consternation
2. CBC milieu
3. Inter cremains
4. Broad thinkers
5. Tennis court call
6. Canada's Baldwin who was Miss Universe 1982
7. *Funny Girl* co-star Sharif
8. Mountain chain in Newfoundland
9. The National Gallery of Canada displays this
10. Popular Colorado skiing area
11. International affairs fellows
12. Hoopla
13. Vintage
18. Black, to a bard
22. ATM no.
24. Heinie
26. Maori dance
28. Bonkers
30. Rogers Communications multicultural network
31. Medicinal amount
32. You might be as busy as this
33. Small dogs
34. Pantyhose
35. Main entrance
36. Most skilful
38. It follows *inter* in Latin
39. Gather what you sow?
44. Sere
45. 5,280 feet
47. Jamaican cuisine fruit
48. Birth-related
49. Highlands shrub
50. More strange
51. Cacophony
52. Catholics' leader
53. Mideast currency
55. One of the deadly sins
58. Québec legislature member (abbr.)
59. Visual Effects Society (abbr.)

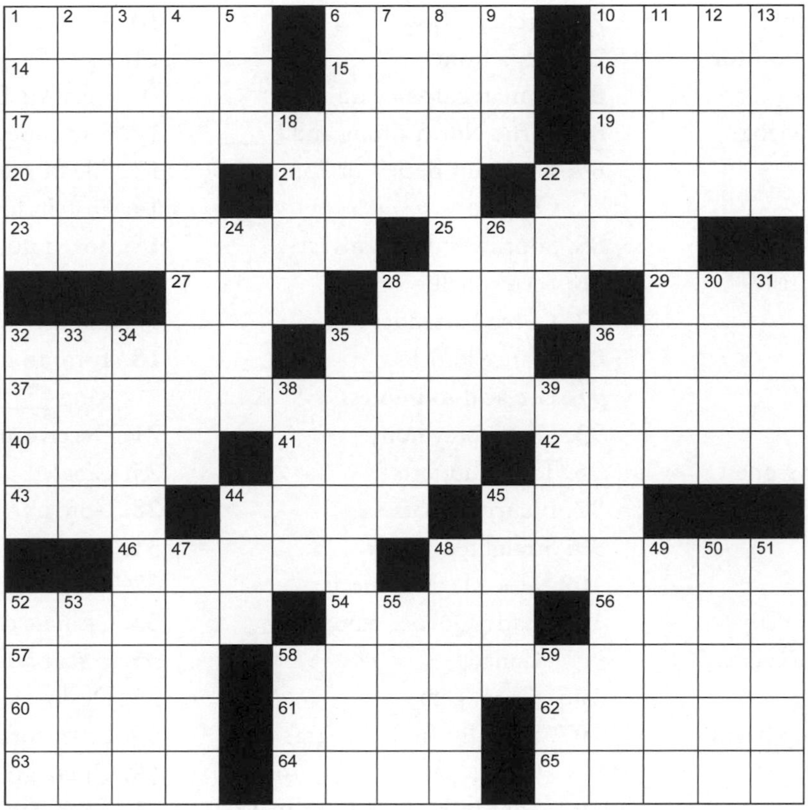

Solution on page 185

49 Going to Gatineau

Top attractions in this beautiful park

ACROSS

1. They suit knights? (var.)
7. Royal Conservatory of Music teaching diploma (abbr.)
11. **Geological attraction for spelunkers**
19. Expand one's knowledge
20. Wife of Jacob
21. Worried about
22. Beyond measure?
24. Praised too generously
25. And so on abbr.
26. Jewish month
27. Fad
29. Deli or diner
30. Escorted a wedding guest
32. Glove fabric
33. Dole out
34. Soup serving
36. _____ bitten, twice shy
38. Dangerous day for Caesar
41. Stylish
43. Middle Eastern rice-based alcohols (var.)
45. Trace a shape
47. Edge
49. Slow
50. US/USSR arms agreement
51. US gossip columnist Barrett
52. It stores what you reap
53. 1995 Giller nominee: *The _____ of Longing*
54. European Business Association (abbr.)
56. Gossips in the Bronx?
58. Christmas tree decoration
60. Magical incantation
62. Family tree expert
64. **View from King Mountain**
67. Industrialized livestock operation
69. Winter Olympics racers
70. Cellular protein
71. Houndstooth, et al.
74. Ones, in French
75. CTV *etalk* host Mulroney
78. Pitcher
79. Tibia front
81. Iranian currency units
83. "True North strong and _____"
84. Sir Adam Beck 1 or 2 in Ontario
85. Southwest US Natives
86. Seed's shell
87. *Cheers* bartender Sam
89. Seance knocks
91. Use acid to impress
93. One-storey house
95. Table supports
97. Incurred debts
99. Straightens out
102. Hot Mexican meal?
105. Early Québec name: _____ Canada
106. Green gem
107. 2004 hit from Alberta's Terri Clark: "Girls _____ Too"
108. Your bishops and cardinals?
110. Alias
113. Scrapes
114. Cheerleaders' encouraging words
115. Beautiful observer?
116. **Tea room cottage**
117. Board under a bed
118. Take stock of

DOWN

1. French farewell
2. Gets a tenant
3. **Site of a 1977 constitutional meeting**
4. Roman harvest goddess
5. Slows down the pace
6. Dudley Do-Right's foe: _____ Whiplash
7. Winged, biologically
8. US Civil War soldier, for short
9. Do some math
10. At that place
11. 1997 Shania Twain hit: "_____ Gets Me Every Time"
12. Feminine article, in Frontenac
13. Pile of rocks
14. Protein found in hair
15. Boxed up
16. Poker game opener
17. Careen
18. Toronto hotel, colloquially: King _____
21. Deceive an Elizabethan?
23. Created
28. Uproars
31. Simplistic
32. Nasty natured
33. Chinese dish: Chow _____
35. US air safety org.
37. Deal sealers
39. Draw forth
40. Opera great Beverly
41. Canadian Payroll Association (abbr.)
42. Ship's record
44. **Original name of a prime minister's park estate**
46. Fellow posties?
48. Verse writer
50. *The Flying Nun* star Field
51. _____ close second
52. They tell drivers where to go
54. Read-only memory chip
55. Doctor's order to stay off your feet
57. Shamus, for short
59. Campus kids
60. Sylvan deity
61. NDPer, say
63. Top mark
64. Itchy skin condition

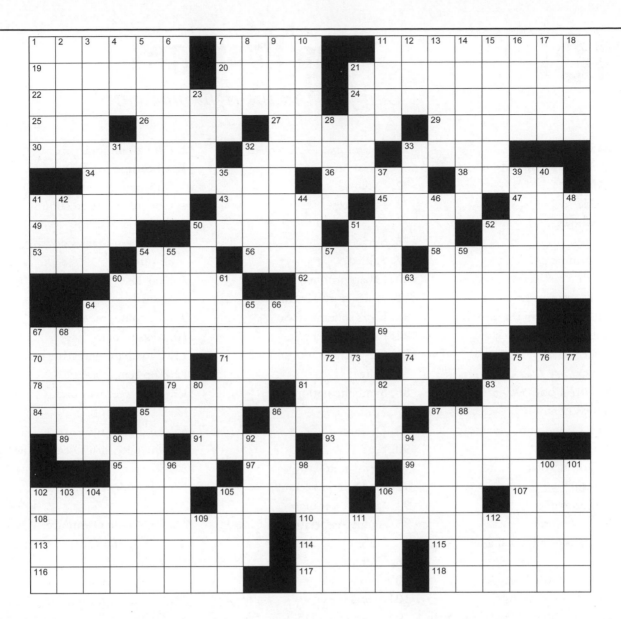

65. Sign of sleepiness
66. Previously, to a sonneteer
67. Put dinner on the table, say
68. Former Egyptian president Sadat
72. Payment
73. Took notice, say
75. **Body of water**
76. Dusk, to Donne
77. Margaret Thatcher, _____ Roberts
80. 1960s Tory MP George

82. PC connection network
83. It might be near a berg
85. Of no benefit
86. Melt
87. South African icon Nelson
88. Light reflection ratios
90. Two-dimensional
92. Church topper
94. US island in Micronesia
96. Exceptionally smart people (var.)
98. Closes in on

100. Bluenose coins
101. Prognosticators
102. Ottawa Senators, say
103. Old-style pulpit
104. Surrealist painter Joan
105. "Lucky Number" singer Lovich
106. Fair
109. _____ liver oil
111. Saskatchewan Hockey Association (abbr.)
112. French pronoun

50 Time Passages

Can you find the right moment?

ACROSS

1. Hill in the Highlands
5. Sickly
8. A buck, say
11. Cowboy's scarf
18. Greasy
19. Subatomic particles
22. South American country
23. Look amorously at
24. **Shopper's bargain bonanza?**
26. Rolaids rival
27. Egg cell
28. *Canterbury Tales* character
29. Montréal-born *Night Court* actress Diamond
30. James Bond's door gizmos?
32. In favour of
33. QC or NS place name: Presqu'_____
35. Get brown?
36. Nauru capital
37. Psychologically unstable: _____ up
39. Title, in Trois-Lacs
42. Stockholm citizens
44. German philosopher Immanuel
45. WWII aid program
50. Doesn't win
51. Canadian-born Hollywood actor Glenn
52. Canadian author Urquhart
53. Hair _____
54. Liberal university pursuits?
55. Angel's glow
56. Group of seven
58. The whole kit and caboodle?
59. Compass pt.
60. Blue Jays complement
61. Word of woe
62. Ready-to-assemble furniture giant
64. **In the blink of an eye?**

71. *Charlie and the Chocolate Factory* author
72. "My bad!"
73. Divorcees
74. _____ *Got a Secret*
75. Singe
77. Sullied
80. Labatt product
81. Hoity-toity person
82. Jury's statement: So _____ all
84. Rum-infused cake
85. University Park campus: _____ State
86. Symbolic national tree
87. Hint at
89. Deceives
90. Fear
91. Agate or amethyst
92. Had a yen to scratch?
94. _____ Domingo
95. Agility Association of Canada (abbr.)
98. Mimic
100. Ewe's mister
101. Soft leather
104. Former Indian honorific
107. Dark
109. Went to ground?
110. Country singer McEntire
111. **Future trip for singers Cetera and Grant?**
114. "Put a sock _____!"
115. House of Lancaster king
116. ". . . partridge in a _____"
117. Field size
118. Sidles
119. Arctic bird
120. NA alarm system co.
121. Energy efficient lights, for short

DOWN

1. Winter footwear
2. Find a temporary fix
3. **A lifetime for Edward G. Robinson?**
4. Golfers' sun protection
5. Orthotic cushions
6. Robertson Davies novel: _____ of Malice
7. Doozies
8. Spanish gold
9. Like some freezers
10. Keys in data
11. Canadian margarine brand
12. Top tennis serve?
13. They wear wimples
14. Couple's outing
15. All grown-up
16. Québec-born Oscar winner Shearer
17. Old Indo-European race
20. Pro _____
21. 1997 Giller nominee: *Where _____ Has Gone*
25. Plain to see
31. Mining extracts
32. Get along for oneself?
34. Finale
37. *The Girl with the Dragon Tattoo* star Rooney
38. Go by, as time
40. Not young
41. Corporate union
42. / or \
43. Not as good
44. Seoul country
46. Maiden name preceder
47. **Annual vacation for author Peter Mayle?**
48. South China _____
49. Stumble
51. Provide capital
52. Denim duds
55. Garlic-based mayonnaise
56. Grade

57. Race track official
60. Utmost degree
61. Ancient Athens assembly area
63. Powerful punches, in the ring
65. Insect with pincers
66. "Yes siree," to a gambler?
67. High school students
68. Bovine beasts
69. Moulding type
70. BC-born NHLer Shea
75. CBS drama since 2000
76. Chewbacca's co-pilot
78. Graduate student's degree (abbr.)

79. Imperturbable invalid?
80. Curve in the road
81. Tailoring-related
83. Compass reading (abbr.)
85. "Alligator Pie," for example
86. Fix a broken heart?
88. Thurman of *Pulp Fiction*
89. Québec City hotel: _____ Frontenac
90. Petite quiche
93. Ukrainian peninsula
94. Dirty
95. _____ *World Turns*
96. Obeyed a doctor's request?

97. Canadian concert pianist Angela
99. Russian leader Vladimir
101. *The Nutcracker* girl
102. Margaret Laurence book: _____ in the House
103. Designer Berkus and basketballer Archibald
105. Concerning
106. Ottoman Empire governors
108. Rim
109. At the back of the ship
112. Louis who got the chop
113. Aggravate

Solution on page 186

O Canada Crosswords Book 15 ■ *107*

ACROSS

1. Spouses' squabble
5. MuchMusic show: _____ *and Icons*
9. Sheds skin (var.)
14. SW US critter
16. Cognizant
17. School sports events
18. 1960s Toronto Maple Leaf Bob
19. Diplomat's HQ
20. Loan period
21. _____ split
22. Mining vein
24. Settle debts
26. Sexy skirt feature
27. Cherry and cedar
29. Royal fathers?
31. *Much _____ About Nothing*
32. Atlantic City resort: Trump _____ Mahal
34. Selectively bred plant
36. Changed, like cells
40. Dionysian devotees
41. Argos and Lions, say
43. Roll of dough
44. End in a draw
45. Hit the sack
47. *Melancholia* actress Kirsten
51. Clerics' coverings
53. Alberta motor coach transporter: Red _____
55. Sibyl or swami
56. Type of freeze
58. Arabian bigwig
60. Hemingway classic: *The Old Man and the _____*
61. Nitrogen compound
62. Unyielding
64. Reconnoitre, briefly
65. TELUS provides this type of service
66. Vexed
67. Greek god
68. Some grps.

DOWN

1. Least dangerous
2. Painter's first coat
3. Microscopic organisms (var.)
4. 2000 Juno best new artist Bachman
5. Duck to get down with?
6. Harsh sun reflections
7. Calgary winter sports venue: Canada _____ Park
8. Pot scrubbing pad brand
9. "Give that _____ cigar!"
10. BC-born *Sayonara* co-star Patricia
11. Samoan skirt
12. Birth country of CBC's Ian Hanomansing
13. Ottawa's NHL team
15. Banned pesticide
21. Local ordinance, in Oxford
23. Tin or titanium
25. Lily plant type
28. Hits the spot
30. Position
33. Traveller's malady
35. Pakistan river
36. WWI dancer/spy
37. Practical person?
38. Canadian furniture retailer
39. Alberta city: Red _____
42. More Zen
46. Large citrus fruit
48. Canadian Daniel with multiple tennis doubles grand slam titles
49. _____ is believing
50. Vestiges
52. From that time on
54. Canadian *30 Rock* actor Arnett, et al.
57. "All You _____ Is Love"
59. Eminem's music style
62. Decorate a cake
63. *Dexter* network (abbr.)

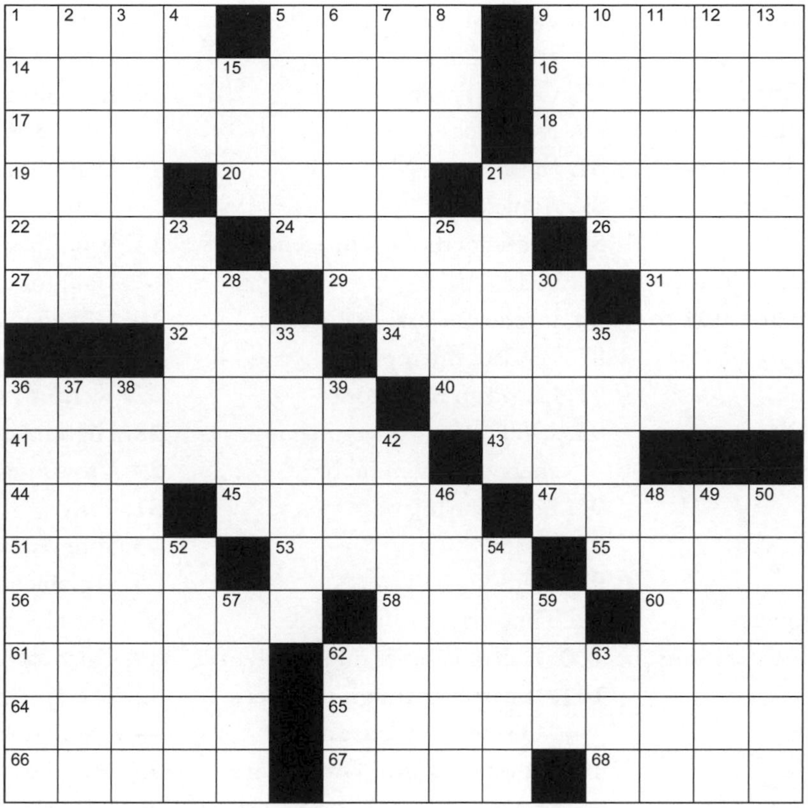

Solution on page 186

52

Going with the Flow

Canadian rivers

ACROSS

1. Star in Aries
6. Get ready
10. The Grinch even took the last can of "Who" this
14. Breakfast food for Brutus
17. Anoint, in olden days
18. NHLer Bourque who's played for the Flames and Habs
19. Sax type
20. It empties into Lake Winnipeg
21. It connects the Great Lakes to the Atlantic
23. Footnote note (abbr.)
24. *Ugly Betty* actress Ortiz
25. Most simple
26. Like farm country
28. Former schoolmate, say
29. Fellow male?
30. Cowboy boots adjuncts
32. Chemical compound creations
34. Perched on
36. Peanut butter type
38. January 1–December 31
39. Second-to-last rounds
41. Singer Goulding, et al.
43. Gibberish
47. Limned
49. Openly express one's opinion
51. It crosses from BC into Alberta
52. Oil cartel acronym
54. Long-winded list?
56. Pierce Brosnan's homeland (abbr.)
57. Canadian Arthur who hosted *History's Mysteries*
60. It's Canada's longest river
63. Nasty racial remark
64. He was coming, in a Three Dog Night hit
65. Like some bees
66. Bang a bumper

68. It shares its name with a territory
70. Japanese floor mattresses
73. Good wishes to the bride and groom
77. Carved the roast
79. French pastry
81. Morning, in Montréal
82. Adolescent
84. Greek mythology messenger god
86. It follows Casa, in Toronto
87. Pendant microphone
91. Canadian bookstore
93. 1980s federal government energy program (abbr.)
94. Like the Mojave
95. Nearby
97. Finds
99. Time for morning coffee
100. Harper cabinet minister Raitt
101. It passes through northern Québec to Hudson Bay
104. It empties into Great Slave Lake
105. Smell, in Salem
106. Well-behaved, say
107. Wheat disease
108. Course for an Alberta immigrant (abbr.)
109. Canadian tenor Heppner, et al.
110. Possesses
111. Third-person biblical verb

DOWN

1. See 110-A
2. Aardvark
3. Cancerous growth
4. Regrettable word
5. Former Ontario politician Stephen
6. Make an assumption

7. Landlord's list
8. Letter abbr.
9. Look at a lord?
10. Hirsute
11. One of Ontario's longest rivers
12. Excessively formal
13. Coal carrier
14. Exams that are spoken, not written
15. Winnipeg's Centennial Concert Hall, for example
16. Canadian singer Bryan
22. Sales force employees, for short
27. Welcome the New Year
28. High habitation spot
29. Crow's nest pole
31. Only
33. Shrewish woman
35. Ornamental lace loop
37. Star turn, say
40. Calendar mo.
42. Therapeutic bath type
44. Colorado skiers' town
45. Pantyhose colour
46. Salacious stare
48. *G.I. Jane* actress Moore
50. Picked up the tab
53. Young bovine
55. Depilatory brand name
57. Piano's ivories
58. Month on a Jewish calendar
59. Churchill, Manitoba's MP Ashton
61. Professor Plum board game
62. Some sailing vessels
63. Thunder Bay-born NHLers Jared or Jordan
65. Prepare to pray
67. It precedes *de guerre*
69. Group of eight
71. Law enforcement drug officer
72. Slang for a buck, in the US
74. Fred and Wilma's epoch

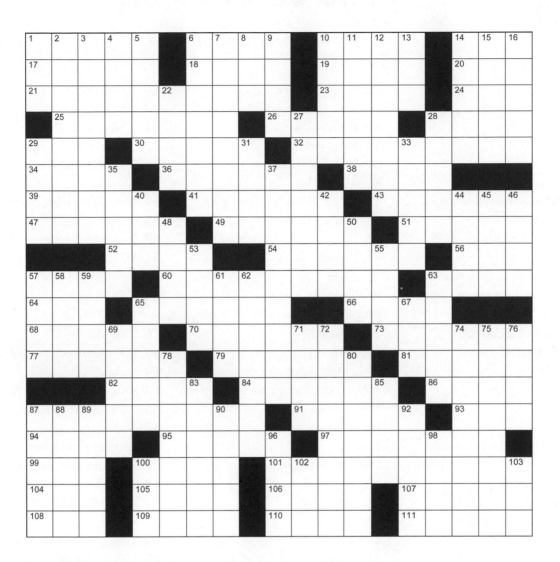

75. TV schedule segment
76. Break from the cold?
78. Murder of a god
80. Gets ready to shoot again
83. **It flows into Hudson Bay in Manitoba**

85. Clannish group
87. Carpenter's shaping machine
88. Vicinities
89. Flooring option
90. Serengeti sounds
92. Cut wood

96. Frozen waffle brand
98. Robert Burns preposition
100. High ball, on the tennis court
102. Use oars
103. Djibouti neighbour (abbr.)

53

The Colour Purple

A spectrum of shades

ACROSS

1. Toronto pro player
5. _____-masochism
9. _____ Level AB
13. _____ Network Canada
17. See 1-A
18. Sound of a well-oiled engine
19. Actress Skye
20. Strange, in Scotland
21. Swerve sharply
22. Auditory
23. Over study, at Oxford
24. Familial affiliation
25. Lyric poem section
28. **For February?**
30. Little leaguer's adjective
33. Powdered candy treat: _____ Stix
35. Cupid a.k.a.
36. Canadian media personality Charles
37. Perennial grass
39. Morphine, for example
43. Charmed a gunslinger?
45. Streets of Saguenay
47. Montréal _____ Centre
48. Banned sports pill
49. Gunwale adjunct
51. _____ for tat
52. Bother
53. Blood-typing system letters
54. Explosive
56. Created candy floss
59. **At the greengrocer's?**
62. Laptop brand
63. In a bombastic manner
65. US author: John _____ Passos
66. See 52-A
68. Grp.
69. Safe surface description
71. Earthquake-related (var.)
75. Former Toronto Raptor Sonny
77. Ugandan dictator Idi

78. Ocean liner's opening
79. First order angel
81. Born in Bosnia, say
83. Bank job?
84. Pace of a pacer
86. Math subj.
87. Yo-Yo Ma has many of these
88. **In a sachet?**
92. Dairy aisle purchase (var.)
94. Russian "John"
95. Barge _____
97. Gape like Groucho?
98. Sun News Network's Levant
102. Mailed
103. Proboscis
104. Memorable past periods
105. Crazy Canuck Ken
106. Domain
107. Sudden seizure?
108. Sort
109. Patches together

DOWN

1. Loo a.k.a.
2. Afore
3. Bio info
4. Renouncing
5. Plant reproductive cell
6. Lexus or Lincoln
7. Fell, like candle wax
8. **In a conservatory?**
9. Belonging to that guy
10. 29th state to join the Union
11. Munchkin kin
12. Attracted to the opposite sex
13. **In the garden?**
14. Just
15. Wood sorrels
16. Aerosmith song: "I _____ Want to Miss a Thing"
26. French Revolution event: Reign of _____
27. Super special

29. Kansas capital
30. Writing tablets
31. Tinker with text
32. Something _____ altogether
34. *Global National* segment: _____ Canada
37. Mountie's jacket colour
38. Presley gyrated his
40. Room in the rafters
41. Fabric with a scenic pattern
42. Do not _____
44. Gilbert and Sullivan opera (with "*The*")
46. Imminently
49. UK meritorious award (abbr.)
50. Smart
53. Pits, in poetry
55. Accountants' havens?
56. Packs cargo
57. Blender setting button
58. Someone who exhorts
60. Neighbour of a radius
61. 1977 George Burns comedy: *Oh, _____!*
64. Yoke up the oxen
67. One or the other
70. Highlander's skirt
71. Liberal Arts area of study (abbr.)
72. Hard work
73. Plus
74. Marilyn Monroe movie: _____ *Make Love*
76. **In a Crayola box?**
78. Sty
80. Not in plain sight
82. **Under the lights?**
85. Male choir member
87. Put a hex on
88. LaFlamme of CTV news
89. State with certainty
90. Weather _____
91. Parks of US civil rights fame
93. Pile

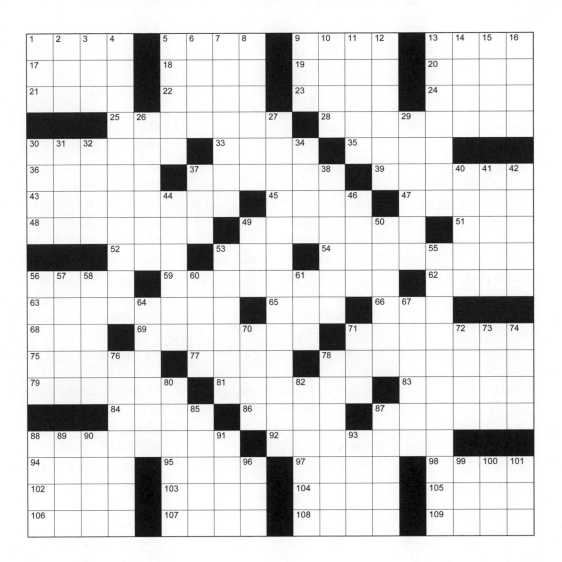

96. Canadian energy agency since 1959 (abbr.)

99. Last letter, in Louisiana

100. Chafed, say

101. Marketers' promotions

54 Canada Cornucopia 18

ACROSS

1. Momma's partner
6. Clarion sound
10. Welcoming rugs
14. Trial and _____
15. Stephen Leacock book: *Arcadian Adventures With the Idle _____*
16. Gothic arch
17. SW US lizard
18. Decongestant ingredient
20. Newman who hosts an eponymous CTV News Channel show
21. Pregnancy period
22. Raise the roof?
23. Farmyard female
24. Ray of light
25. Physics unit
26. Boasts
28. Yours, in Québec
30. Like Christmas cake fruit
32. Rhythmical
35. Recess the court
38. Castro overthrew him
39. Swiss luxury watch brand
40. Not as diluted
41. Former Canadian music industry magazine
42. Owls' sounds
44. Demonstrative pronoun
48. It's sometimes more?
51. Lop
52. Sportsnet 360's former name: The _____
53. Grand piano's middle pedal
55. _____ Apso
56. Like a moron
57. Encouraging endorsement
58. Canaanite god
59. Thin
60. New Brunswick neighbour
61. Eyelid affliction
62. 1970s Spanish language hit: "_____ Tú"
63. Calgary Olympic Oval sport: _____ skating

DOWN

1. Ill, in the Rockies?
2. Contrary, in mood
3. Shown to be true
4. OPP canine, say
5. Sinatra song: "_____ You Glad You're You"
6. Church flock members
7. Interpret for the deaf
8. Persistently painful
9. Those folks
10. _____ code
11. Stirs up strife?
12. Rundown urban area
13. Prophet
19. Cotillion girl, for short
26. Newborn's arrival
27. Surgery reminders
29. Italian greeting: *Come ___*
31. Montréal street name?
33. Consumed food
34. Inexpensive, to a gardener?
35. Canadian Cancer Society daffodil mo.
36. Manitoba's Gary Doer, since 2009
37. ON/QC body of water
38. Nates
40. Canadian cheese curds serving
43. Vision-related
45. Submarine sandwich a.k.a.
46. Poisonous gas
47. Razzed
49. Plant part
50. Dry, like wine
52. Bangs a drawer
53. Sis and bro, say
54. Longest river in the world

55

It's Outta Here

Canadian exports

ACROSS

1. German military subs
7. _____-leaf beetle
10. Inexperienced one
14. Bit of medicine (abbr.)
17. Shamrock Summit attendee
18. Moo _____ gai pan
19. Early Peruvian
20. _____ de France
21. **Fossil fuel export**
23. **See 21-A**
24. Cape Breton choir: _____ of the Deeps
25. They hypothesize
26. *Fallopia japonica*
28. Red Chamber pol.
29. Media mania
31. A Canadian coast
32. Getting up there
36. Canadian Native group
38. Native leader's office
42. Spoils (with "on")
44. Rides the waves
46. "Okay"
47. Forever, to an old poet
48. **Metallic element export**
50. Insurrection participant
52. Arizona city
53. Call, old style
54. Whale constellation
55. Tattered, to a rodent?
56. "_____ a chance"
57. **Agricultural export**
58. Air mist
59. Grey and Stanley
62. Loamy soil
63. Crepe kin
66. Top guns
67. Language for some New Zealanders
68. **See 21-A**
70. Storm type

71. Former Toronto Maple Leaf Horton
72. Metrical feet (var.)
74. Rosetta _____
75. French streets?
78. Theories
80. Back then
81. End of a hammer
82. Units of resistance, in physics
84. Valentine's Day mo.
86. MLB catcher a.k.a.
89. Coat lining, for example
94. Banks pay this (abbr.)
95. **Forestry export**
96. **Sweet export**
98. Summer in Shawinigan
99. Stare at
100. Rod Hull's bird puppet
101. Famous Players, for example
102. 1960s drug
103. Old Russian royal
104. Cozy room
105. Minuscule

DOWN

1. Buffet appliance
2. Long-running game show: _____ the Clock
3. Swear words?
4. Fever, old style
5. Starchy tubers
6. Entrapped
7. Cake ingredients
8. One who abhors
9. Covered in lichen
10. **See 48-A**
11. Unknown, for a short time?
12. UN civil aviation agency (abbr.)
13. Hesitates
14. Hours worked record
15. Most dangerously slick
16. Hang in the balance
22. Forms a queue

27. Mordecai Richler book: *Solomon Gursky* _____ *Here*
30. Former Spanish currency units
32. Town in Oklahoma
33. **See 48-A**
34. Small case for notions
35. Bossy requests
37. Keyboard feature: _____ lock
39. Clairol products
40. Aquatic "snake"
41. What you do in church
43. Grain storage bins
45. Bouquet flower
49. Someone who's crazy for cashews?
51. "Close _____ no cigar"
52. Small generator
54. Hold dear
55. Banned sports drugs, for short
57. Romance
58. Recommended annual shot type
59. Not clerical
60. They live there?
61. Rewarded your MP?
62. Eastern priest
63. 2012 Canadian play: *A* _____ *of Asha*
64. Animated show, colloquially
65. **See 48-A**
67. Some scale notes
68. Truckers' radios, for short
69. Canadian poet Dennis
71. Wallet bill, colloquially
73. Assign the wrong title
76. Garage door product manufacturer: _____ Canada Inc.
77. **See 48-A**
79. Pick
83. Played charades
85. Jazz Count
86. 2012 *Total Recall* actress Jessica
87. Pulls a boat?

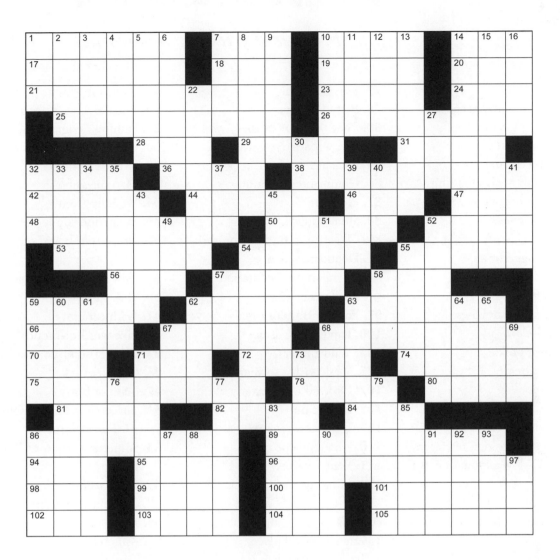

88. Earthenware pot
90. Turned

91. *Cagney & Lacey* star Daly
92. Hebrew Old Testament name

93. Some bottles behind bars
97. _____ it forward

56

A Puzzle for Anna

. . . because she likes palindromes

ACROSS

1. Shrub that blooms in spring
6. CTV _____ Channel
10. Coffee house staffers
18. Waikiki welcome
19. 1997 Sarah McLachlan hit
20. This often occurs on *Hockey Night in Canada*
21. More sad
22. Drop a suggestion
23. Clever chatter
24. **ERAs and RBIs**
26. These fit into mortises
28. Pig's noise
29. Periods of polka?
31. Pub libation
32. _____ mot
34. Still lifes and sculptures
37. 1980s music genre
40. Like a guilty golden retriever?
44. Where Old MacDonald had a house?
46. Belgian city
48. What a miner hopes to find
49. _____ *iacta est*
50. **Long stories**
52. *Raiders of the Lost* _____
53. Strait below Vancouver Island: _____ de Fuca
54. Ruler's domain
56. Temporary monarch
58. Empower
60. Spills the swill?
62. UN labour org.
63. Plot of land
64. See 28-A
66. To any extent, old style
68. Tooth type
71. St. John's _____
72. The conscious mind
74. **Guys and gals**
76. *Nota* _____

77. Jungle animal
78. Part of a biota
80. They take care of their own
82. Like a seductive voice
84. Elegant
86. Command to a canine
87. Pronoun
88. Small stinger
89. Old-style second-person verb
91. Debutantes' dance
94. Garrulous service station employee?
97. **Former Iranian royals**
100. Landlord's ouster
103. Wild and crazy
105. Wash with a solvent
107. Ordered into custody
108. Mosaic unit
109. Get a new tenant
110. Charitable people?
111. Water vortex
112. Lithe lady

DOWN

1. Chemist's workplace
2. Trials and tribulations
3. Oaf
4. Like the leader of the pack?
5. Boxes
6. Slangy refusal
7. Redact
8. "Weeping Widow" Canadian group: April _____
9. Geo-spatial guidance system
10. Carried by the wind
11. Caesar's hellos
12. Sales force agt.
13. A Gershwin brother
14. Alberta motto: _____ and free
15. Rhythmic syllables
16. #1 Randy Travis hit: "Forever and Ever, _____"

17. Hunt for
25. **Editors' corrections**
27. Fashion designer Cassini
30. Curses
32. CIBC employee
33. Man. neighbour
34. Worship from _____
35. Inhalation sound
36. Non-profit board officer
38. Hourly pay rate
39. Slow musical movement
40. That gal
41. With certainty
42. Like word-of-mouth, say?
43. Chromosome component
45. Croquet stick
47. Beret or bowler
51. **Three-time French Open winner Monica**
53. Sometime Stratford Festival star Derek
55. Extinct bird
57. Catholic devotion
59. 1960s war zone, for short
61. Kilt creases
63. Timid, old style
64. Police team type
65. Hebrew letter
66. Kiefer Sutherland, to Donald
67. CEO or VP
69. Voting "no"
70. Musician's respite?
73. Hockey great Lafleur
75. **Divas' arias**
78. Like a tub of lard?
79. Awfully long times
81. Confines a collie?
83. The Tin Man asks Dorothy for this
85. Manufacturer's refund
88. Arcade Fire and A Foot in Coldwater

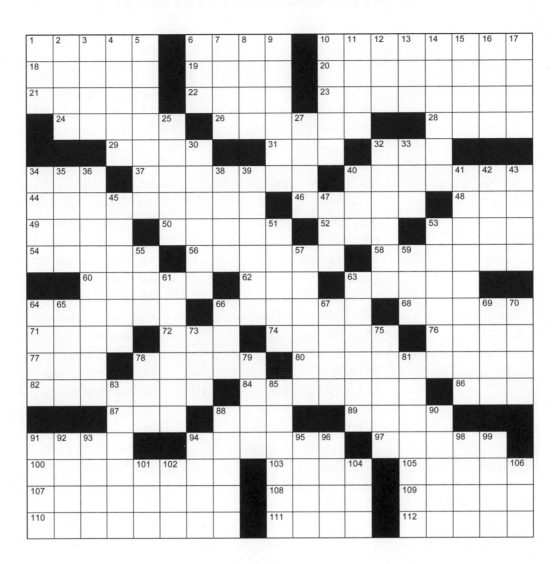

90. Bill who rocked around the clock

91. Canadian The Pursuit of Happiness singer Moe

92. Staunchly maintain

93. Mixed vegetables bean

94. Active person

95. In the thick of

96. 1975 Lightfoot album: *Gord's* _____

98. Québec place

99. Bit of choreography

101. Blasting substance (abbr.)

102. Wedding vow

104. Lock opener

106. African country (abbr.)

ACROSS

1. Israeli combat discipline: Krav _____
5. Touched the tabby?
10. Row
14. Missing from the barracks
15. Bell Centre in Montréal
16. Southern side dish
17. Yukon place
19. Makes a request
20. Golf great Palmer
21. New arrivals?
23. My, in Montmagny
24. Give permission
26. Network of nerves
27. HGTV interior designer Richardson
29. Kick out of Canada, say
33. Where boys will be boys?
36. Bard's black
38. *The Sound of Music* heroine
39. Queue
40. Showroom models, for short
42. National policing org.
43. Girl Guides founder Baden-Powell
45. Lively dance
46. Russian news agency: ITAR-_____
47. Spanish dish
49. Loses weight
51. Moistens
53. Where to enjoy hot springs
54. Network for *Nova*
57. Discard
61. Not singular
63. 1964–65 CTV game show: *Double _____ Money*
64. Peck or bushel, say
66. Street thug
67. Senegal city
68. Brink
69. Miners' finds
70. Cassoulet and chili con carne
71. Like a low voice

DOWN

1. Ethel Merman movie: *Call Me _____*
2. Informed
3. Dresses for debutantes
4. Further
5. Indulged, illicitly
6. Rainbow's crescent
7. 1960s Manitoba premier Walter
8. Go in
9. Sofa for a siesta?
10. Extra bits
11. First LPGA tour Canadian Sandra
12. Egyptian cross
13. _____ *of the D'Urbervilles*
18. _____ podrida
22. Thing
25. Alberta town known for its corn crop
27. Dofasco and Stelco
28. Canadian magazine: _____ & *Cottages*
30. Ocean predator
31. Wheel circles
32. Military bugle tune
33. Bird's wing movement
34. Latvia's primary city
35. Québec ski resort: Mont-Sainte-_____
37. Actor Coward, et al.
41. Indoor footwear
44. Bunch of killers?
48. Contrary, at the casino?
50. _____ fide
52. Indian city
54. Prim person
55. Boat with a flat bottom
56. REM _____
57. Keyboarding error
58. 1978 CBC series: *This Half _____*
59. Old Norse linguistic character
60. Child
62. Not brand new
65. Large mouth

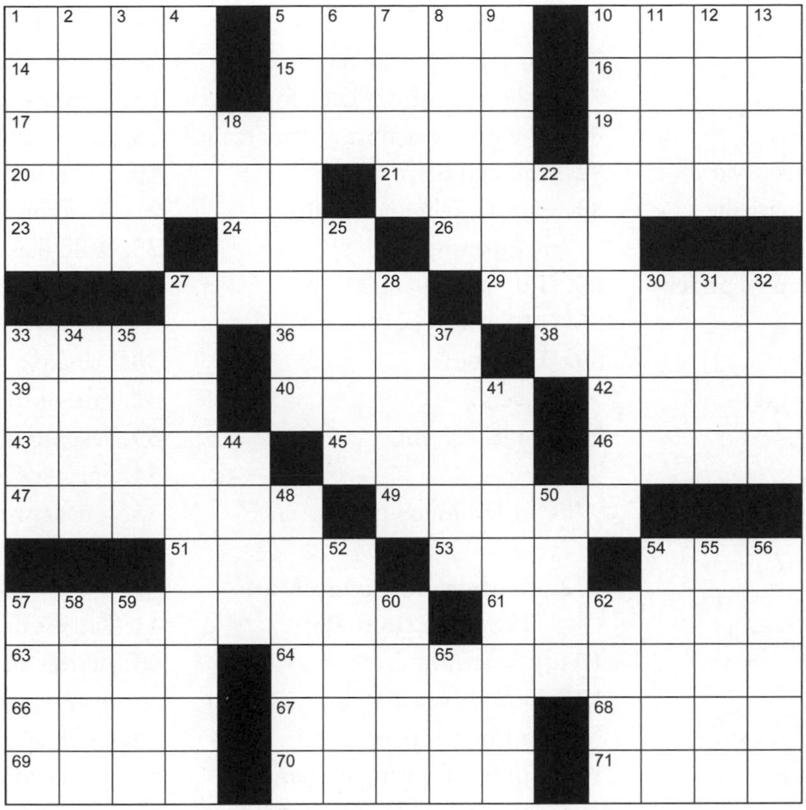

Solution on page 187

58 Playing for Keeps

Hockey stars who never left their teams

ACROSS

1. **Philadelphia Flyer Bobby (1969–84)**
7. Expression of contempt
10. Red Cross product
16. More sacred
17. Seth's sibling
19. Went out with a rush (var.)
20. Asian alternative medicine technique
22. **Montréal Canadien Maurice (1942–60)**
23. Less wild
24. Canadian Arctic route: Northwest _____
26. Door part
27. Ammonia compound
29. Greyish horses
31. Require
32. US anthropologist/author Margaret
36. Sluggishness
38. Something you might stub
40. Affected by illness, say
42. Nonet
44. Acronym for mad cow disease
47. Japanese floor mat
48. Yearly shareholders' mtg.
50. Glands near the kidneys
52. Pro _____
54. With rapidity
56. **Nordique/Avalanche Joe (1988–2009)**
57. Jai _____
60. **Toronto Maple Leaf George (1949–71)**
63. Canvas shoes brand since 1916
64. **New York Islander Mike (1977–87)**
66. Three-quarter pants style
67. Hit the spot, at supper
69. Tacit

71. Food Network Canada show: *You Gotta _____ Here!*
73. Welcome to the Order of Canada, say
77. *The Wizard of Oz* man metal
78. Saskatchewan CFLers, for short
80. Like games against a lesser team
82. Half and half?
83. 15th-C. religious group member
85. Gulf War missile
86. Golf club type
89. Wild guess
91. Salvers
93. Feudal servants
95. Iris site
97. Old-fashioned performance venue
102. **Pittsburgh Penguin Mario (1984–97/2000–06)**
104. Juicy fruit
106. Skreslet was the first Canadian to summit here
107. Suffix with gang or game
108. *Raging Bull* Oscar actor Robert
109. Tennis star Williams
110. Infomercials
111. **Montréal Canadien Ken (1970–79)**

DOWN

1. Words with friends?
2. Ricky Martin hit: "Livin' la Vida _____"
3. Reunion guest, for short
4. Finger pickin' good?
5. 1996 Olympics gymnastics star Strug
6. Up to, old style
7. California Rose Bowl city
8. Privilege usurper, say
9. Belonging to that woman

10. Samoan side dish
11. _____ Ness monster
12. Take _____ to
13. AB-born NHLer Doan
14. Get on the highway
15. Totalled
18. Introduction
19. Songbird
21. Backbone
25. Wild llama
28. **Chicago Blackhawk Stan (1958–80)**
30. Canada's Walk of Fame honour
32. Edmonton clock setting (abbr.)
33. Seventh Greek letter
34. Former Calgary MP Hanger
35. Journal writer
37. Alluring lady
39. Some Keats poems
41. Largest doctors' org. in Canada
43. Actress Barbara and prime minister Anthony
44. Cook at 350 degrees
45. Travelled on a toboggan
46. Some computer keys, for short
49. Huff or puff
51. _____ the day you were born
53. Produced an electrical charge
55. Sills' solo
57. Lie adjacent
58. Burt Reynolds' ex Anderson
59. Org.
61. Prospered, on the prairies?
62. **Montréal Canadien Bob (1973–89)**
65. Knitters' fibre
68. The Nashville Network (abbr.)
70. Michael J. Fox sitcom: *Family _____*
72. Majorettes, for example
74. University in Vancouver, for short

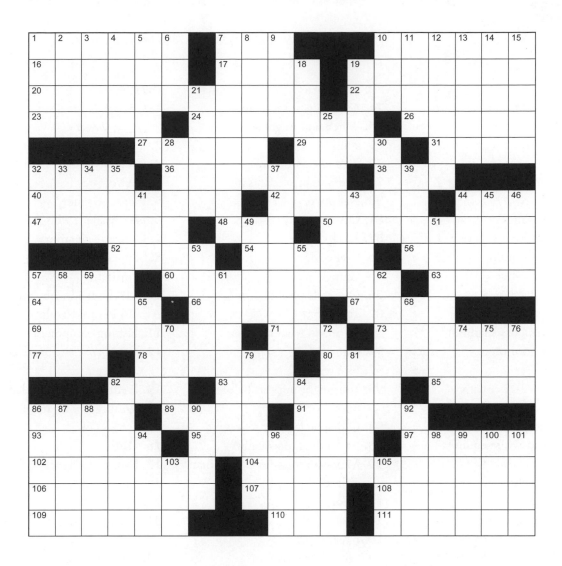

75. 1960s TV westerns actor Gulager
76. *The Apprenticeship of Duddy Kravitz* director Kotcheff
79. Flemish painter Peter Paul
81. Let _____ hang out
82. Enjoying a hot streak?
84. Averted: _____ off
86. British _____

87. Town council leader in some provinces
88. Mother-of-pearl source
90. Written words
92. More painful
94. Observed
96. Toronto tourist's stop: _____ Shoe Museum
98. Canadian NHLer Heatley

99. Bagnold or Blyton
100. Grimm baddy
101. Dodge make
103. American president's domain (abbr.)
105. Strange

59 The Face of Human Nature

Find the words that fit the feature

ACROSS

1. One of the former Navigator Islands
6. "Poppycock!"
10. Word on a gift tag
14. Tree trunks
19. Redact
20. Singular songs?
21. Where mother strikes it rich?
22. Type of moulding
23. Repaired a shoe
24. Small setback
25. American aroma?
26. Bolshevik boss Vladimir
27. ". . . the roof there _____ such a clatter"
28. They give 10 per cent
30. Fees
32. Repeated phrase
34. Black-and-white equine
35. Breakfast cereal
36. Alternatively
37. _____ Leone
39. Newfoundland artist Pratt
40. Canadian singer Paul
43. Cubism co-founder Pablo
45. None, at Loch Ness
46. Rock climbing spike
47. Old CBC entertainers: Wayne _____ Shuster
50. Famed diarist Anaïs
51. Go to _____ and ruin
53. WWI soldier's headgear
54. Push-up?
56. Wine description
59. Diving bird
60. Wine cask
61. Compass point (abbr.)
62. Self-directed
64. Regretting (var.)
66. Begin a trek
68. **Flustered?**

70. **Stubborn?**
74. Antiseptic for a scrape
75. When you might see an alligator
77. Like enclosed pools
78. Bed and breakfast, say
80. Neophyte newt
81. Otherworldly
82. Track circuit
84. "Take Me _____ the Ball Game"
85. Old-style phone
87. Trig abbr.
89. Thrilla in Manila boxer
91. Cut down
92. Fire residue
93. You might put this before the horse
94. Old-style legwear sellers
98. At no time, poetically
99. Max who founded a Canadian airline
100. Café
101. Adept
105. Team spirit
107. Smell or taste
108. Canadian _____ Awards
110. Descendants
112. Canadian-born actor Shatner
114. Adjust
115. Supreme _____ of Canada
116. Begged
118. Light beige
119. More friendly
120. Rose-scented oil
121. Peddle
122. Narrow opening
123. Make nighttime noise
124. Joe _____
125. Look like a creep?
126. Faction
127. Uptight

DOWN

1. Children's show since 1969: _____ *Street*
2. Without scruples
3. Crenshaws and cantaloupes
4. Foxtrot precursor
5. Hognose snake
6. Nearly silent whisper
7. Converts an atom
8. Some roofers
9. **Erudite?**
10. MacDonald who contested the '76 PC leadership
11. Fishing equipment
12. *Star Trek: Deep Space Nine* character
13. Freddie's favourite planet?
14. Weapon for a gaucho
15. On top of
16. **Old?**
17. Fashion designer Saab
18. Sacha and Justin, to Pierre
29. Notable years
31. Bachman-Turner Overdrive hit: "_____ You"
33. Botanical sacs
35. Canadian hockey great Messier
38. Canadian singers Tyson and Thomas
39. US big truck maker
41. Paradoxical Zen question
42. _____ *meridiem*
44. Illegal entrants
45. See 45-A
46. Red wine type
47. Somewhat
48. Nanette's taboo?
49. **Sad?**
52. Sought election
53. Rwandan people
55. Powdery starch
57. Great Lake

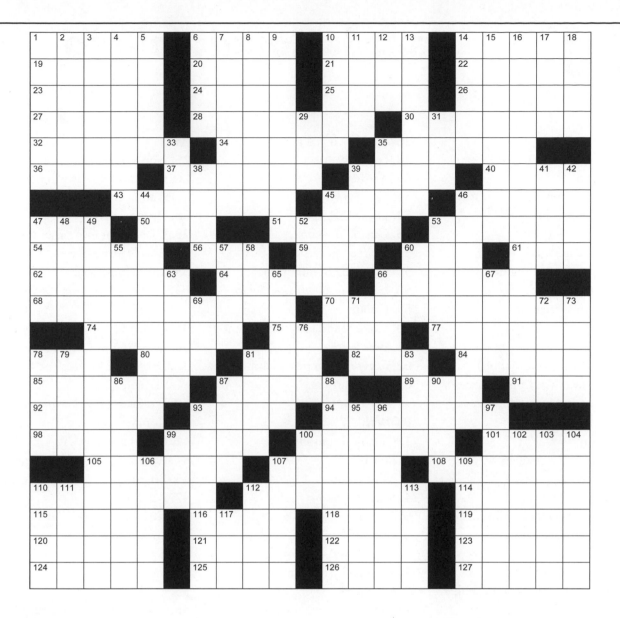

58. Pool stick
60. Canadian media magnate Rogers
63. Exalt
65. Most lazy
66. Vancouver-born *Water for Elephants* author Gruen
67. Language of Lahore
69. Dy-no-mite explosive?
71. Fish caught in a pot
72. Memo
73. Develop
76. Sailor's "yes"
78. Neighbour of Pakistan
79. Jet's front end

81. Oakville car manufacturer
83. Canada's Brasseur and Eisler, for example
86. Airmail letter
87. Show concern
88. **Cowardly?**
90. They can be born in July and August
93. Jacques Cousteau's ship
95. Middle ear bone
96. Kind of fatty acid
97. Fish in a can
99. Pasty-faced
100. _____ canto

102. Victoria attraction: _____ Hill Park
103. Pariahs
104. Supper serving
106. Canadian cable channel: MuchMore_____
107. Move laterally
109. "Thou _____ not then be false to any man"
110. Home care helpers (abbr.)
111. US college military grp.
112. Wishing _____
113. Mangy dog
117. Relay segment

60 Canada Cornucopia 20

ACROSS

1. Inclined to be creative?
6. Not pro
10. Tolkien creatures
14. C&W star Haggard
15. Horse colouring
16. Thunder sound
17. Large plant eating dinosaurs
19. It might erupt in Italy
20. Slimming regime
21. Trick
22. Antenna
24. Rank for a sailor (abbr.)
25. Poetic contraction that goes above and beyond?
26. Great Lake
27. In any way
29. Fertilizer ingredient
30. Tree type
31. Eagles' claws
33. Comes together, colloquially
34. PEI legislative assembly building
38. Kind of school
39. It's north of Richmond Hill ON
40. Ages and ages
41. Glass-making component
43. Cowboy Junkies vocalist Timmins
46. Top provincial job
48. Feel unwell
49. It's shaped like a circle
51. Skyscrapers, say
52. Grow
53. Gusto, in Genoa
54. Colloquial version of 6-A
55. Outshine in importance
58. Bergman role in *Casablanca*
59. Cooties
60. Coral Sea Islands component
61. Beer barrels
62. *Street Legal* actress Cynthia
63. DNA carriers

DOWN

1. Chemical compound
2. Prairie city
3. Most accurate
4. Strip of wood
5. Longing for
6. Love, in Louisiana
7. Twelve, say
8. Bronzed by the sun
9. Deranged
10. Musical drama form
11. RRSP funds recipients
12. Mob, in Les Misérables
13. Some ski courses
18. Butterfly wing markings
23. YYZ info
25. Norway's patron saint
26. Canada's 1987 world figure skating champ Brian
28. Sitting pretty?
29. Like a lawn in need of mowing
32. Broadcasting live
33. Thickening agent
34. Curtail a House of Commons sitting
35. Ordering more *Canadian Living*
36. Boys from the 'hood, say
37. Descriptor for hygiene or surgeon
38. Words to rally the troops
41. Coniferous tree
42. Posted on eBay, say
44. Canadian singer Lightfoot
45. Bright bird
47. Repairs
48. Go along with
50. Strikes out?
52. National nuclear technology org.
53. Moderate
56. Rail service crown corp.
57. Beldam

61

Ladies First

Trailblazing Canadian women

ACROSS

1. Empty spaces
6. Touch on
10. Canadian mining giant
14. _____-relief
17. Shenanigan
18. Clothing label info
19. Flue filth
20. Alberta teachers' grp.
21. **First federal party leader Audrey**
23. She taught in Siam
24. Bucharest buck
25. Helter-skelter
26. Jeer
28. Belgrade resident, say
29. South China Sea city
31. When the show must go on?
33. Rhino's relative
38. Long-tailed rodent
39. Beavers' kin
41. Parallel, in Pittsburgh
43. Canada's Breeders' Stakes, et al.
45. **Canada's first female lawyer Clara**
48. **First Canadian woman to win an Oscar Mary**
50. Lode finds
52. Left Bank river
53. Not aggressive
54. Red wine
56. Crusty skin spot
57. Best dog training student?
60. Sour
64. Like Nike or Adidas clothing
65. Walk aimlessly
70. Man _____ town
72. See a Dalmatian?
73. **Cassie who was the first female Hockey Hall of Fame inductee**
74. **First Canadian woman in space Roberta**

76. Middle Eastern mogul (var.)
78. Steeples
79. Former Global network newsman Rae
81. Filbert
83. Actor's comment to an audience
84. "Wrinkly" Chinese dog
86. Kidney trouble symptom
89. Prepares a hide
90. Canadian *No Logo* author Klein
92. Good Jewish guys
98. Reproduction necessities
99. Thor's father
100. **First woman in the federal cabinet Ellen**
102. Tie the knot
103. Prescription amount
104. Rankin Family hit: "Fare _____ Well Love"
105. 1980s Commodore computer
106. Portuguese pronoun
107. Ladies of the lea
108. Reddish brown gem
109. Two-time Juno vocalist winner Gallant

DOWN

1. Seductive Transylvanian?
2. Way back then
3. "_____ cost you!"
4. Rotary phone feature
5. Gunk on a pond
6. Stone building block
7. Hustler's ball, perhaps
8. Israeli submachine gun
9. It can be past, present or future
10. Jack Nicklaus contemporary Aoki
11. Like zero-calorie yogourt
12. Verify a hypothesis
13. Ontario Trucking Association (abbr.)
14. Spitting bullets?

15. Mr. T's squad (with "The")
16. **First female Governor General Jeanne**
22. Acquire
27. Cremation urn
28. Gawks at
30. School org.
32. Inlets
33. Canadian C&W star Gordie
34. *Inter* _____
35. Snapshots, for short
36. Signs a contract, say
37. Kit out again
40. Druggies
42. Birds of peace
44. *Gigi* scribe
46. Like two peas _____ pod
47. National energy regulation agency (abbr.)
49. Hauls in the harvest
51. Nasal dividers
54. Chemical element in stainless steel
55. Semesters
58. Varnish resin
59. Thin bark (var.)
60. Pop can opener
61. Blood classification letters
62. *The West Wing* actor who's not from our country?
63. 2010 Gemini-winning historical drama: *The* _____
66. Nile bird
67. TV actress Gilpin
68. Winter coaster
69. Ultimatum word
71. Infield cover
73. Of lesser quality
75. Give to your alma mater again
77. Moose Jaw-to-Regina dir.
80. Mediate
82. Layered

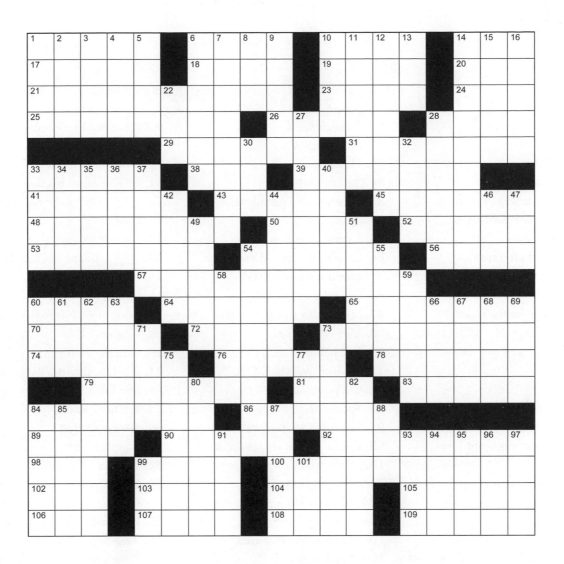

84. Canada's first woman doctor
Emily

85. Former Czech president Václav

87. Fissures

88. South African political grp.

91. Single units

93. Hit with an open hand

94. Prolonged sleep state

95. Eight, in Québec

96. Scrambled dish

97. Toronto-born *Pretty Little Liars*
star Mitchell

99. Provincial anthem: "_____ to
Newfoundland"

101. Kind of moment

62

OO!

Double your pleasure with this one

ACROSS

1. One of Adam's boys
5. Elementary particles
9. _____ and Span
13. Hail Mary, for example
17. Super stadiums?
19. *Peter Pan* reptile, for short
20. Can-Am writer Shields
22. Old-style prov. abbr.
23. **The old shell game**
25. Make amends for wrongdoing
26. Space to manoeuvre
27. Playwright/author Levin
28. Avid Parliament Hill tourists?
31. Stock market buys for a rainy day?
34. BC river
35. Alberta town off the QEII
36. Soak up liquid
37. Brussels nation (abbr.)
38. Snatch
39. Elizabeth's daughter
41. Celtic necklace
43. Riots
45. Ran like Roger Bannister?
47. "Deck the Halls" syllables
50. Spanish farewell word
52. First-class
53. Oppose
55. Bad luck at craps?
57. **Body art**
58. Actress Swenson of *Benson*
59. **Children's game**
60. So much, in Madrid
61. One who looks down one's nose?
62. Part of NA
63. **Hindu courtesy title**
64. The "M" in L.M. Montgomery
66. Snowboarder's run
69. Baseball icon Hank
70. **Australian marsupial**

74. Crosby, Stills, Nash & Young protest song
75. **Panda's food**
77. Smoke detector
78. Heart attacks
80. Table components
81. Former IOC president Jacques
82. Special _____
83. Corrosive substances
84. Governor General's writing award winner Toews
86. *Chocolat* star Lena
87. NYC Fifth Avenue retailer
88. Dim-witted one
89. Fall behind
91. He lost twice to DDE
92. Oil quota org.
94. Special ability
97. Big Atlantic sport fish
99. Like a mama who coddles
102. Sometimes sung in Canada: "_____ Save the Queen"
103. Elect an MPP
104. Complete and _____ chaos
105. **Outback instrument**
110. Sparkle, say
111. Quench
112. *La Bamba* actor Morales
113. Shania Twain hit: "_____ Still The One"
114. Nickname for tennis star Djokovic
115. Celtic tongue
116. Order to a broker
117. Bump on a log, perhaps?

DOWN

1. Commercials
2. River that bisects Calgary
3. Long-time Brit record company
4. 1984 Luba hit: "_____ Go"
5. It comes in cubes

6. European rootstock
7. Twelve sharp, say
8. Blameless, like Robbie Burns?
9. Hieroglyphs beetle
10. Foie gras spreads
11. 1977 Kansas hit line: "Once _____ above the noise and confusion"
12. Lowest female voice
13. _____ Board of Canada
14. Orally
15. Ceases
16. Long-time Edmonton Oiler Gagner, et al.
18. Cleanse with vigour
21. A pirate might have a peg one
24. Sheik's seraglio
29. Pitchers' stats
30. Sonata section
31. Gourmet, say
32. Revolt
33. Margaret Atwood's middle name
36. Purchase at Canada Post
38. Two-time Oscar winner Hackman
40. He fiddled while Rome burned
42. **Crested parrot**
44. Mad, in Mexicali
45. Slogan
46. 1987 Bryan Adams album: "_____ the Fire"
47. Former *Tonight Show* host
48. Ti-Cat competitor
49. ER order
51. "Ain't That a _____"
53. Printer/photocopier company
54. **Curry entree**
56. President Lincoln, for short
57. **Social no-no**
60. Poi tubers
61. It can be powered or granular

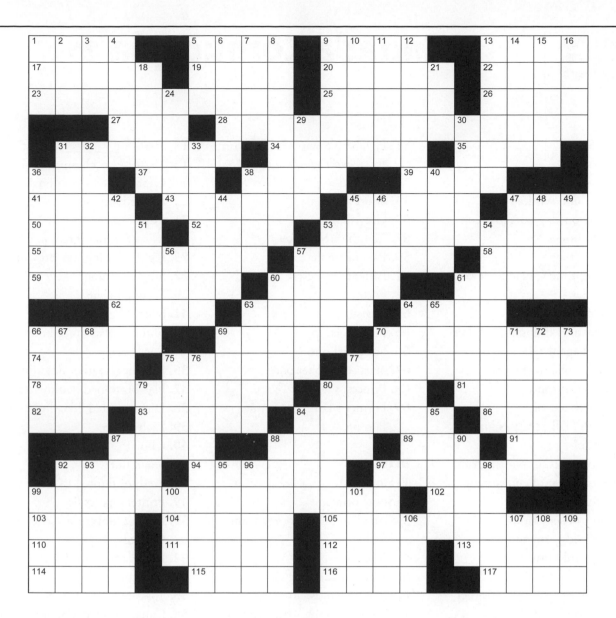

63. Little ones in the woods?
64. Sicilian wine
65. 1970s TV actress: Sue _____ Langdon
66. A bit, to Bach
67. Famous pancake place
68. "Dear" men?
69. In the thick of things
70. New Zealander's fruit?
71. Sleeve type
72. Binges
73. Black cat and sidewalk crack

75. 1989 Colin James hit: "_____ in My Arms Again"
76. Greek philosopher
77. Fairway warning
79. US civil rights assn.
80. Dangerous waves
84. _____-Tremblant
85. Homer Simpson's spouse
87. Unruffled
88. Order of the court
90. Éclat
92. Convex moulding
93. Flower feature

95. Scented oil
96. Onions' cousins
97. Canadian honour: _____ of Military Valour
98. See 88-A
99. It might be self-cleaning
100. It's next to Ukr.
101. Clamping tool
106. Canadian country singer Grand
107. Twosome
108. Mouths, anatomically
109. UK lexicon (abbr.)

Solution on page 188

ACROSS

1. Hell's half _____
5. Out of harm's way
9. Molar and wisdom
14. Hudson Bay port town
16. Arm bones
17. Led astray?
18. Long-time Canadian jewellery retailer
19. Netherlands river
20. Fearsome dinosaur, for short
21. Bind again
22. Barbecue attachment
24. Tot's transport
26. Reverberation
28. 1976 Hall & Oates hit: "_____ Smile"
30. Pub nooks, in Nottingham
32. Short term of endearment
33. Squid's liquid
35. Unit of semantics
37. Knitted garment
41. Top and bottom outfit: _____ suit
42. Wintery Canadian weather phenomenon
44. _____ Pérignon
45. Mining find
46. Hindu mystics
48. Ukrainian city
51. Elizabeth Smart CanLit classic: *By Grand Central Station I Sat Down and* _____
53. Short summary?
55. Greyish, say
57. Eighth Greek letter
59. Bass or treble
61. Patient's caregiver (abbr.)
62. Form
63. Revisit?
65. Like foolscap
66. Stretched out
67. Starts the poker pot
68. Princes, say
69. Former Manitoba premier Filmon

DOWN

1. Summits
2. Some primates
3. Canadian men's hockey team rival
4. Joule unit
5. Buttoned garment
6. Helping hands?
7. Showing off one's pecs, say
8. Antiquity, at one time
9. Toothpaste holder
10. Best of the best
11. Makes money?
12. Pay description
13. 1980 hit: "_____ So Shy"
15. 1970 Keith Hampshire Canadian #1: "The First _____ Is The Deepest"
21. Care and concern
23. Musical score threesome
25. Figure skating star Browning
27. Singular thing?
29. Feeling bugged?
31. Startle a ghost?
34. Ontario place once known as Rat Portage
36. Summer weather description
37. Flat-bottomed hauling boat
38. Disintegrated, like duds?
39. Pachyderm
40. Choler
43. Small flute
47. Fresh or farmed BC fish
49. Printer's gaffes list
50. Former Governor General Georges
52. Reservation tent (var.)
54. Hammer parts
56. Toss about ideas, say
58. Canadian media men Byfield and Rogers
60. Somerset cigarette, colloquially
62. Patty Hearst's abductors (abbr.)
63. These, in Thetford Mines
64. Choke

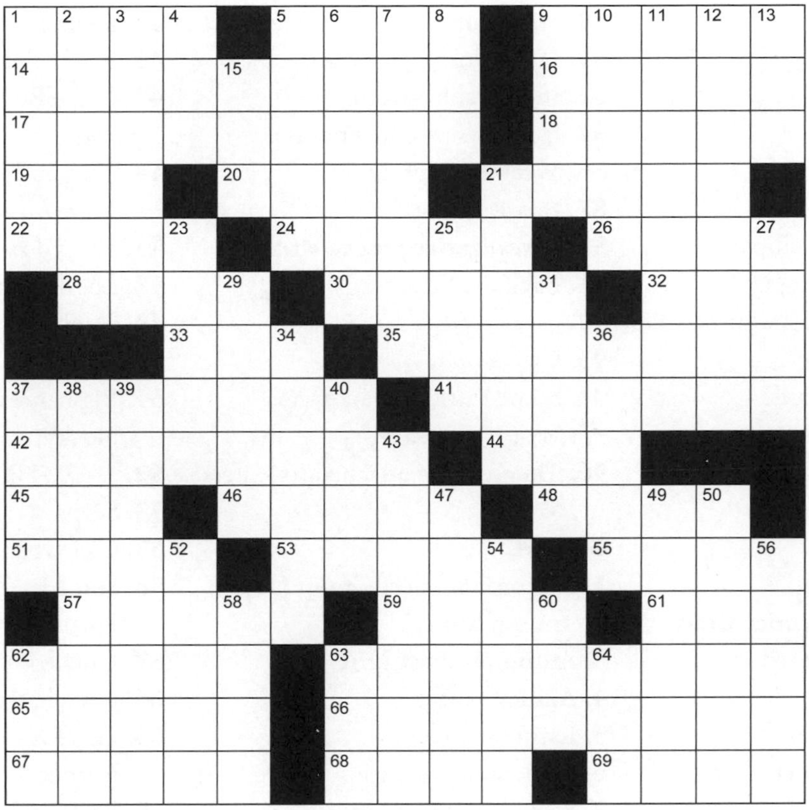

Solution on page 188

Tot-*all*-y Canadian

Do you know every name?

ACROSS

1. Most lewd
8. Toe who coached the Habs to 10 Stanley Cups
13. Carpenter's peg
18. Guangdong province port city
19. Up and about
20. Larva, previously
21. **Writer Mavis**
22. Chipped in poker chips
23. Ranee's garb
24. "Deck the Halls" refrain: Fa-_____
25. Hard-hearted attitude
27. Moist, like morning grass
29. 1940 Canadian invention: Paint _____
31. Zedong followers
32. Not quite round
34. **Saskatchewan premier Brad**
35. Chip flavour invented in Canada: _____ pickle
36. Big bloomed flower
37. Industrial strength cleaner
38. Presiding at the podium, say
43. Final moves, in chess
45. MDs
46. Fungal skin disease
47. Computing storage unit
49. Beatle John
50. Likewise
54. Ancient Hebrew
56. Martial art: _____ fu
57. Edit a clue in this puzzle?
59. Best an exotic dancer?
61. Staring intently, old style
62. Joshes
63. Admitted, for short
68. The good dishes, say
70. Copy a foreign language film?
71. Five-pin bowling score
72. Pastry ingredient
73. **Game show host Monty**
74. Flooring installer
75. Test
79. Stirred up silt
81. 1977 film: _____ *Shot*
82. Indubitably satanic?
84. It follows pro, in a phrase
86. Wear down ground
87. Synagogue leader
88. **Investigative journalist Eric**
91. Back tooth type
92. _____ *of Two Cities*
93. City in Italy
94. Some Patrick Chan jumps
95. "For _____ sake!"
96. They're often attached to loafers

DOWN

1. Regional Support Group (abbr.)
2. Triumphant cry
3. **Author/activist June**
4. Adding veneer
5. Latin list ender
6. Underwater detection device
7. Famed Egyptian king
8. Writing system for the blind
9. Door's architectural feature
10. See 19-A
11. Ship's underbelly
12. Plagues
13. Rakish
14. Muscat citizen
15. Goods for sale
16. Get rid of
17. Rich soil
25. Breaks the seventh Commandment
26. _____ Spring Island BC
27. Dumb drug user?
28. Not odd
30. Some baby birds
33. Group of two
35. With duplicitous intent
38. Lazes
39. Rideau Canal, in the winter
40. Labrador Aboriginal
41. Bright light on Broadway
42. Old CBC Radio show: *The Happy _____*
44. Niagara Falls transport: _____ *of the Mist*
45. Slims down
48. Local animal life
49. "Aloha" garlands
50. Emir's equine?
51. Big name in little building blocks
52. _____ Hills AB
53. Seep
55. Clef type
58. Some La-Z-Boy products
60. Furtive whisper
62. Unsafe building, say
64. Long letters
65. **General-turned-senator Roméo**
66. It comes before formaldehyde
67. Criminal, in slang
69. Austrian–Canadian endocrinologist Selye
70. *Toronto Star,* and others
73. Limp
75. Abnormal swelling
76. Use a photocopier
77. Yucca, for one
78. Like some jazz pieces
79. Moroccan capital
80. Comedy's opposite
83. Figure of interest?
85. European skiing mecca
88. Famed Massachusetts university (abbr.)
89. Zilch
90. Canadian natural resource

65 Actors' Aides

Sometimes stars need a little help

ACROSS

1. Leaning tower locale
5. Low male voice
9. CFB eating areas
15. Folklore giant
19. _____ even keel
20. Pin purse
21. African–American tennis great Gibson
22. _____ Ore Company of Canada
23. **Dick's military attaché?**
26. It precedes Easter Sunday
27. Absolved a bowler?
28. Salary
29. Cloth for cleaning
30. Withdraw, politically
32. _____ alcohol
33. Akin
35. Royal Ontario Museum employee
36. Rotated
38. Yolk container
39. _____ being
40. Military machine
44. Decorate anew
46. Benin people
48. *The King and I* setting
52. Gets even
54. Friend
56. Supped
57. Japanese belt
58. Greek god of the north wind
59. Whistler and Sunshine
61. Northern Ireland province
64. Like Hibernia, for example
66. BC's Pacific dogwood
67. Emulate
68. **Christopher's maintenance man?**
71. Cream-filled pastries
74. Pro _____
75. *Lou Grant* and *Phyllis*

79. Quick look
80. Lack of energy
82. Changeable
83. Murre
84. Suffers from
85. Wrath
86. Grows by heaps and bounds?
87. Profound
89. Chex or Cheerios
91. Fashionable
93. Editor's undoing?
94. Ere
96. Tropical snake
98. Amino or boric
100. Actresses Stuart and Swanson
103. Like biting humour
105. Violinist's stroke
110. _____ and Hardy
111. Greek letter
112. Assistance
113. Tricolour cat
114. Preminger or von Bismarck
115. **Ava's groundskeeper?**
119. Sharpen on a stone
120. Juno _____
121. Doozy of a singer?
122. Food gelatin
123. Tupper and Abbott, for example
124. Most sneaky
125. *National Velvet* scribe Bagnold
126. 1970s CFL star Gabriel

DOWN

1. Wild West group
2. Not suitable
3. Genie Award-winning director Polley
4. Hopping mad
5. Lake Huron locale: Grand _____
6. Lawyer (abbr.)
7. Temporarily halt a process
8. Rug fibre

9. Disfigure
10. Spanish Renaissance painter
11. Lieu
12. Southern Nova Scotia community: _____ Harbour
13. Literary contraction
14. Mandarin orange variety
15. Mechanics' containers
16. Welcome
17. Movement from Mozart
18. Step inside
24. Snakelike fish
25. Aerie newborn
31. Pitchers hope to keep this low (abbr.)
33. Sherbrooke streets
34. **Elizabeth's seamstress?**
35. Rubik's _____
37. Influence from a peer?
39. Shacks
40. Popular perfume
41. Ontario Perth Country river
42. Square one?
43. Leg bone
45. Unlocked, old style
47. Honey badger
49. Minute amount
50. Help in a holdup
51. Bog down?
53. Seasoning bulb
55. Kind of projection
59. Aries symbol
60. Fix
61. Belly buttons
62. Spleen-related, old style
63. Nightclub lights
65. Some dashes
67. Little rascal
69. Wipe the slate
70. Exploit
71. Old-time oath
72. Mr. Green game
73. Ontario or Erie

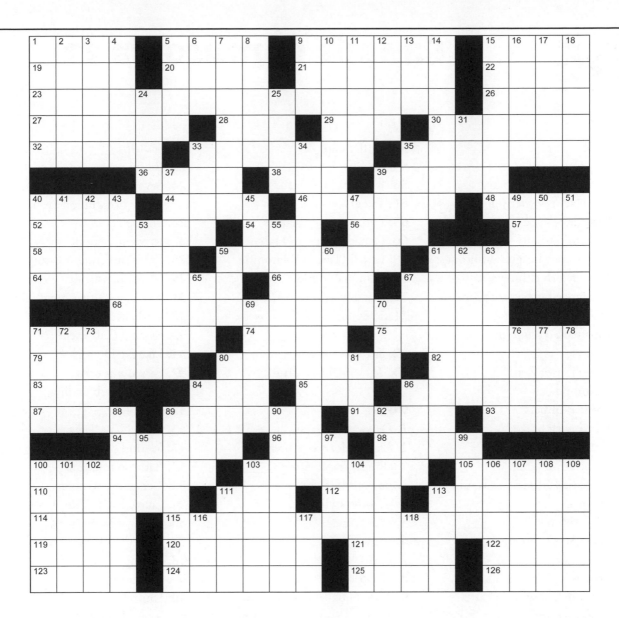

76. Clenched hand
77. Fireplace tube
78. Labour Day mo.
80. Filly's mama
81. Bit of time?
84. Not his
86. Ancient Briton
88. Bright birds?
89. Heating fuel
90. Is rife
92. Revolver

95. Old expression of disgust
97. Month before Nisan
99. Group of two
100. Radiates
101. Asian cane stick
102. _____ space
103. *The Treasure of the Sierra* _____
104. Theatre part
106. Drape fold
107. Game you win by calling?

108. *Titanic* necklace: Heart of the _____
109. Fret
111. It weighs down a waiter
113. Mucky gunk
116. Carpentry tool
117. Québec City clock setting (abbr.)
118. The greatest boxer?

Solution on page 188

ACROSS

1. Blueprint detail
5. Canadian singer Siberry
9. French sci-fi writer Jules
14. Birthday desire
15. Yemeni port city
16. Like some "League" buildings?
17. Matterhorn climbers, say
19. Rechargeable battery type, for short
20. Antifreeze compound
21. Nuance
23. Daughter of Zeus
25. Diamond stat
26. Some numbers
30. Filled with horror
35. Canadian Healthcare Association (abbr.)
36. Emulated Montréal's Émilie Heymans
38. CBC drama: *Being* _____
39. Nova Scotia provincial park: Smuggler's _____
41. Prongs
43. Sat. a.m. show?
44. Troop groups
46. Breaks in half
48. Kind of nut
49. 2014 Super Bowl performers: _____ Chili Peppers
51. Willingness
53. Coffee cup
55. Family _____
56. Keyboard key
61. Talents
65. Did up one's sneakers
66. Canada's Kain or Hart
68. Rexall Place in Edmonton
69. Balmoral hillside
70. Primary
71. 1980 hit from The Rovers: "Wasn't That a _____"
72. Some evergreens
73. They might be drunk

DOWN

1. Decorative drape
2. Alanis Morissette breakout album: *Jagged Little* _____
3. Lay orbs on
4. Too-too stylish
5. Lolita, say
6. Some plugs?
7. Earns
8. Happen next
9. 2004 book from Canadian author Alice: _____ *Munro*
10. Wickedness
11. Meal grain
12. Like a drink without ice
13. "Peter Gunn Theme" guitarist Duane
18. "With _____ in sight"
22. Bikini part
24. Seven-time national figure skating champion Stojko
26. Transpire
27. River in Geneva
28. Environmentalist Suzuki
29. Medicinal shrub
31. Menopause treatment (abbr.)
32. Garlicky mayonnaise
33. Recce a Cub Pack?
34. Like 32-D
37. Passed out cards
40. Biblical verb ending
42. Gleams, like a gem
45. 1986 Glass Tiger hit
47. Section of a script
50. Bathroom fixture
52. Gets more weapons
54. Like Chatty Cathy?
56. _____-happy
57. Old Albanian currency
58. Laptop brand
59. Red coin?
60. Unusual
62. Arrivederci synonym
63. Use needles and yarn
64. Without, in Warwick
67. Toronto's Osgoode Hall _____ School

Fortitude

You'll need it for this one . . .

ACROSS

1. Bird of prey manoeuvre
6. Openings
10. Sue Grafton mystery: _____ *for Corpse*
13. _____ Alto
17. It's beneath a volcano
18. Not at roll call
19. Thanksgiving mo. for Canadians
20. White House office name
21. Perfect
22. One who libels
24. Former Ontario Lieutenant Governor William
25. Adolescent
27. Birthplace of Mohammed
28. Greenhorn (var.)
29. 1982 film: *48 _____*
30. Stanley Park art: _____ pole
32. Ocean motion
34. Not at all tanned
35. Provide with gear
37. Serving easily, in tennis
39. **In British Columbia: Fort _____**
42. Scorched, old style
43. Calgary Stampede event horse
44. Make money
45. Crazed state
47. Polytechnic in Calgary (abbr.)
49. High school equivalency exam (abbr.)
50. Hamper the hairdresser's style?
52. Dome-shaped shrine
54. Spill the beans
56. Canada's most eastern point: Cape _____
57. **In Northwest Territories: Fort _____**
59. Where Winehouse didn't want to go
63. "Uh-uh"
65. River in France
66. Push
67. He covers all the bases?
70. Lards
72. Canadian confectioner: _____ Secord
74. One who monkeys around?
75. Derides
77. Sword handles
79. **In Ontario: Fort _____**
81. Plenty
82. Japanese–Canadian
83. Agatha Christie detective Parker
84. PC login, for example
86. Salad dressing jug
88. Chinese cuisine additive, for short
91. Rite for a Jewish newborn
92. French fighting force
94. Final demands (var.)
96. Eyebrow curve
97. Paper rustling noises
99. Rattan furniture worker
100. Raspy inhalation
101. Weeding implement
102. Leprechauns' land
103. Author Allan Poe
104. Ta-tas
105. Ontario Women's Directorate (abbr.)
106. Speak ill of (var.)
107. Tawdry

DOWN

1. **In Northwest Territories: Fort _____**
2. Water walker
3. Curved mouldings
4. Middle Eastern country
5. Near the roof of the mouth
6. Zygote predecessor
7. Having knowledge
8. Rep. or Dem.
9. Skinny
10. Vanities
11. North Pole topper
12. Old-school punishment tool
13. Covered entryway
14. Eluding
15. **In Nova Scotia: Fort _____**
16. Spread for bread
23. Species group
26. Jewish folklore figure
31. So-so spiritualists?
33. Early Mongolians
34. Male journalist?
36. **In Saskatchewan: Fort _____**
38. Religious leader?
39. Jiffies
40. Canvas covering
41. **In Ontario: Fort _____**
42. Not for
43. *The Family Circus* cartoonist Keane
46. Canadian Savings Bond, for example
48. "L'il" comic strip character
51. Suggest a deal to an athlete?
53. Like pugs and chow chows
55. Act like an angel?
58. Burden of responsibility
60. **In Ontario: Fort _____**
61. Maintain
62. City near Zurich (var.)
64. Dads, for short
67. Common Cdn. trading partner
68. **In Alberta: Fort _____**
69. Kid's frozen treat
71. Shook one's booty on the dance floor
73. Up to now
76. Expands on a plan (with "out")
78. "Haven't _____ you somewhere before?"
80. Draws in
82. Not wide

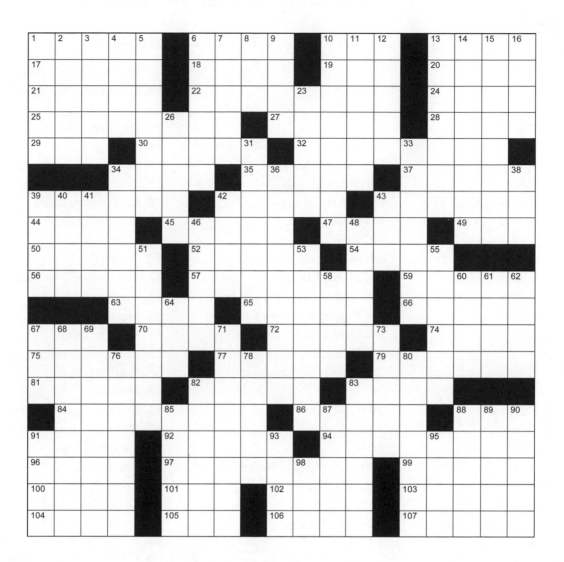

83. Throbs
85. Tortilla chip
87. Regrets, they have a few
88. Japanese animation name

89. A full head of _____
90. In Manitoba: Fort _____
91. Canadian pair skater Underhill
93. Managed with a little

95. Former CBC sitcom: _____ *in Canada*
98. 52, in old Rome

68 One + One = Yum

Good taste comes in combinations

ACROSS

1. Ballroom dance
6. Canadian Chris Hadfield tweeted from this in 2013 (abbr.)
9. Bird's perch
14. Spelunkers' spots
19. Like Mary of song?
20. 2011 NFB Web documentary: *One _____ Tower*
22. Pennsylvania religious sect
23. Famed violin craftsman
24. Cargo carrier
25. Not tight
26. Beat the pack
28. Coop nesters
29. Made slanderous statements
31. **Dairy + torte = dessert**
35. **Spread + vegetable = candy**
37. German fellow?
38. Opposite of oui
39. Church music
41. Payment to an ex
43. Flamenco instruments
44. Michael Ondaatje Giller winner: *Anil's _____*
49. Make a choice
50. Most adorable
51. Dormitory mate
52. Completely
53. Central European country (abbr.)
54. Get good directions?
57. Winery barrel
58. Unpredictable
62. Smalls display unit
63. **Spice + starch = cookie**
65. College life, say
69. With a twang
70. Alberta national park: _____ Buffalo
74. Bind, scientifically speaking
76. Dora Mavor Moore Award winner Salome

77. Virile
78. Rat
79. Mite
83. *Gone with the Wind* Oscar winner McDaniel
84. Securing with rope
85. Led the troops
87. Matadors
88. Glass containers
89. City on the Danube
90. Mottled equine
91. **Sucrose + fruit = candy**
95. **Vegetable + herb = candy**
98. Delusions of grandeur, say
99. Bathtub cleaner?
100. 1990s NBC slogan: Must _____ TV
101. Fireplace nook
102. Meet
106. Knife part
110. It's produced at Dofasco in Hamilton
111. Port worker
112. Terriers' treats
113. Rockies landmark: Kicking _____ Pass
114. Spanish appetizers
115. Bad cheque acronym
116. Canadian mysteries writer Howard

DOWN

1. Type of tub
2. Upper body limb
3. Extinct bird of New Zealand
4. **Dairy + dairy = drink**
5. "So long, señor"
6. Global monetary org.
7. A Kennedy assassin
8. Streamlined
9. Hibernia structures
10. "_____ la la!"
11. Neighbour of Que.

12. Spectacular, in the sky?
13. Elates
14. Spy who went to Canaan
15. Agave or yucca
16. Cello's orchestra neighbour
17. Ruhr Valley city
18. Backyard building
21. Engraved block
27. Pasta type
30. "See ya!"
31. African language group
32. Capital of Montana
33. Heather plants
34. Flirty
35. Takes quick notes
36. Greek Muse
40. Hasten
42. Oxford Digital Library (abbr.)
43. Repressive Russian camp
44. Orchestra percussion instrument
45. Table d'_____
46. *Lawrence of Arabia* star Sharif
47. Location
48. Peg for a pro
50. CTV show: _____ *Gas*
51. Fully prepared
53. Canadian tomato products brand name
55. Staggered
56. Venice country
58. Cough up
59. Esa Tikkanen's Oilers number
60. Biblical warrior
61. *CSI* network
64. Excessively enthusiastic
65. Greeting to a matey
66. Ghana cash
67. Prayer closing
68. Small dent
70. **Liquid + gourd = fruit**
71. Old Roman tax
72. Presidents Grant or Garfield

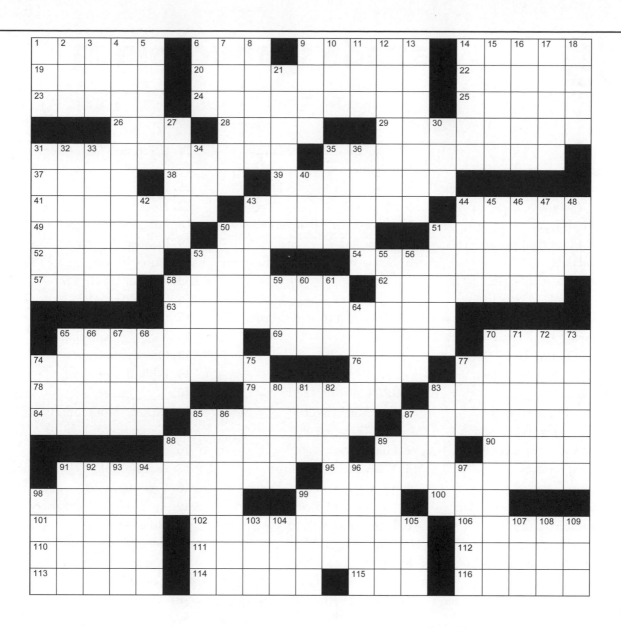

73. 1974 film: *Alice _____ Live Here Anymore*
74. Residential street abbr.
75. African language
77. Damage
80. Placid
81. Birthday marker
82. Answer an RSVP
83. Long-time HGTV Canada show: *Holmes on _____*
85. Most down in the dumps
86. Former home city of the Calgary Flames

87. Tactical Leadership Program (abbr.)
88. Family guy?
89. Pep pills
91. Caribbean capital: _____ Domingo
92. Pushy person
93. Dorothy's storms?
94. Administer a sacred oil, old style
96. Shopper's mecca: Toronto _____ Centre
97. Hasidic teacher

98. Word of contempt
99. Takes to civil court
103. Porcini
104. Spawn source
105. NHL official
107. Oscar-winning director Lee
108. *Star Wars* franchise actor Billy _____ Williams
109. New Canadian's language course (abbr.)

ACROSS

1. Image on a radar screen
5. 2013 Streep/Roberts film: *August: _____ County*
10. Hand, to Jorge
14. 1893 J.D. Edgar poem: "This Canada of _____"
15. Meat-on-a-stick entree
16. Egg-shaped
17. New Mexico locale
18. Annapolis frosh
19. Orange's outer layer
20. 1970s CTV game show: *Headline _____*
22. Sprained neck support
23. It catches Darjeeling leaves
27. What you leave behind?
31. Tugboat honks
32. Promise
33. Letter dropped by a Cockney
34. Lost soldier acronym
37. Just nothing?
41. Ottawa time setting (abbr.)
42. Loses warmth
43. Former Flame and Jet Jokinen
44. Look without blinking
45. Millhaven Institution honcho
47. Don Harron's alter ego Charlie
51. Intestinal obstruction
52. Kids' favourite store?
57. Captain Kirk, for William Shatner
58. Got to the bottom line?
61. Pop type
62. *Transformers* franchise star LaBeouf
63. Long-time Canadian furniture retailer
64. Grimm tales beast
65. Approach to an equestrian?
66. Irk
67. Peter I or II

DOWN

1. Joni Mitchell hit: "_____ Sides Now"
2. Hilo party
3. Vitamin component
4. Silent summons
5. Provincial bird of Nova Scotia
6. Latin dance style
7. Had some grub
8. Chat
9. In the blink of an _____
10. MB Red River Valley town
11. Kind of flu
12. *Twin Peaks* actor Jack
13. More senior
21. And so on (abbr.)
22. Scrubs in tubs
24. US comedic actor Ben
25. Carryalls
26. Birds of myth
27. Hobbling
28. Pre-holiday nights
29. Bearded ruminant
30. Barley bristle
33. Ancient Greek plaza
34. Combine cards?
35. It's surrounded by water
36. X _____ "xylophone"
38. Old-style seizure
39. Biblical boat builder
40. _____'easter
44. Rickety door's sound
45. Verdant
46. Some number
47. Assembly of _____ Nations
48. Greeting at 2-D
49. Archaeologist's discovery
50. Note taker
53. John A. Macdonald, by birth
54. Pigs out on pork loin?
55. Gumbo pod
56. _____ *Gynt*
58. _____ carte
59. Natural world lair
60. Hockey commentator Cherry

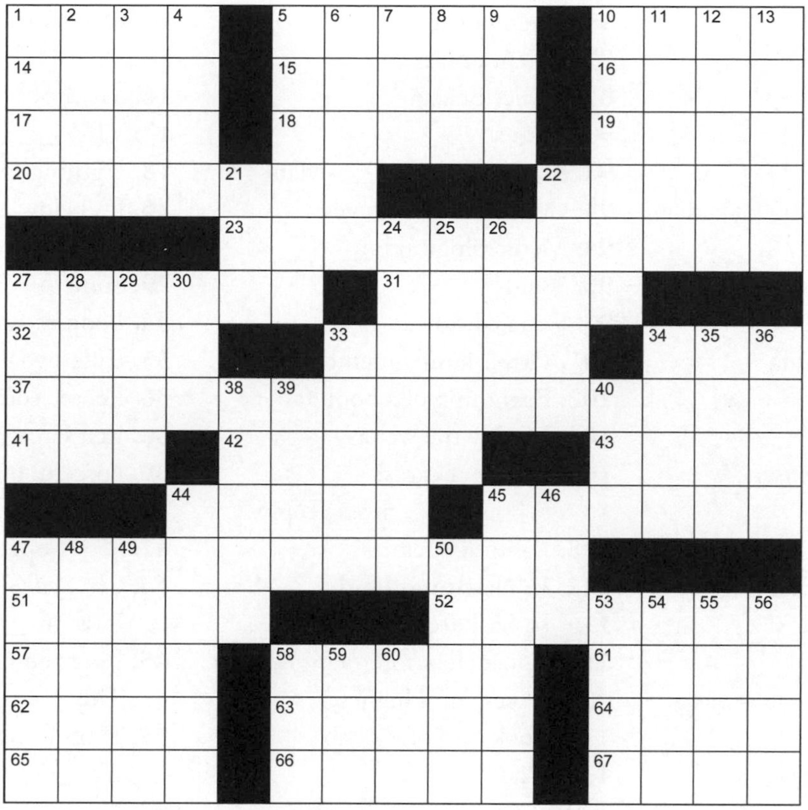

Solution on page 189

70

National Parks

Canada's beauty in all its glory

ACROSS

1. Rockies' European counterpart
5. Victoria Cross, for example
10. Toil, in Texas
15. Aloe _____
19. Jaunty rhythm
20. Escape capture
21. Mountain ridge
22. Subject of a 2005–06 Canadian government inquiry
23. Pricey sweetie?
24. Dog-_____
25. **In British Columbia**
27. **In Nunavut**
29. Awfully
30. *The _____ of the Affair*
31. Big bird
32. Lager lather
33. One–three connector
34. Coots
37. Sterilized
40. Hearing-related
44. Create interest
45. Goulash, for example
46. *CBC News* _____
48. Lily variety
49. Atlantic fish
50. MP elector
52. Seamless transitions
55. Bunk, say
56. Medicine _____ AB
57. 1980 "Whip It" band
58. Border on
60. _____ Tom
62. Drying racks
64. Flu symptom
66. Italian Middle Ages poet
67. **In Nova Scotia**
72. Soft spots?
73. "To thine own _____ be true"
74. Make
75. They work at the TSX
78. Epidemic
80. Deftness
81. _____ Wednesday
84. Royal symbol
85. Macho male?
87. Salient points
89. Spruce or sequoia
90. Injure
92. Arcade game: _____-Man
93. Céline Dion devotees
94. Meteorological line
96. Braid
98. Extra edition
101. Plover family members
102. Beginning of a book (abbr.)
104. Muddy the waters
105. Expert at cards?
107. NHL's _____ Ross Trophy
108. Political enemies?
112. **In Newfoundland**
116. **In Saskatchewan**
117. Canadian winter/summer Olympian Hughes
118. Took care of the tab
119. Places
120. Woven decorative strip
121. LP players
122. Sicilian volcano
123. Young amphibians
124. Beasts that bray
125. Little bits of Greek?
126. Appear

DOWN

1. Actors Robert or Alan
2. Time taken off work
3. Tired of baseball?
4. Hung Christmas lights
5. Get together
6. Brings good cheer
7. Wheat type
8. Acceptable
9. Conducted
10. Commuter's computer
11. Biblical peak
12. Very flattering
13. Ear-related
14. Overhaul
15. Dippy
16. Miscues
17. VIA _____
18. Fighting force
26. It's below Minnesota
28. Fateful March day
29. Some
34. Loonies and toonies
35. Killer whale
36. Echoic sound effect
38. Red Cross fluids
39. Forceful ouster
41. Fix a book
42. Secret operatives?
43. *The Red Green Show* locale: Possum _____
45. Roots and Reitmans
47. Tiny
51. 1965 Canadian #1 hit: "Shakin' All _____"
52. No _____ luck
53. Moral principle
54. Put under anaesthetic
57. Petro-Canada product
59. **In Alberta**
61. Door glass
62. Copied a gorilla?
63. Ship's rear end
65. Means of departure
67. Horses' home
68. Saudi _____
69. Hodgepodge
70. Warm up
71. TV collie
72. Walk heavily
76. Aggressive knock
77. Headliner
79. *A Summer Place* star Richard
81. Be a mediator

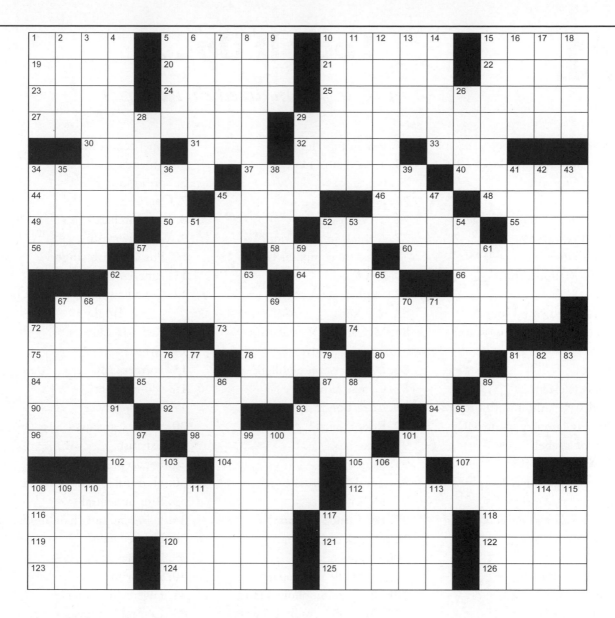

82. Pew, say
83. One of a matched set
86. Vancouver's Rogers Arena and Winnipeg's MTS Centre
88. Cameo's kin
89. Water skiers' lifelines?
91. Cell division
93. Son, in Sept-Îles

95. Ore stratum
97. Throw a salad together?
99. Curly-haired dog
100. Removes soap
101. Illinois city
103. Eyelashes
106. It follows witch or water
108. Leer at

109. UBC employee
110. NAFTA, for one
111. Catches some rays
113. Impudent attitude
114. Number under ten
115. Cheese type
117. Greek letter

Solution on page 189

71

Look It Up . . .

in these personalized dictionaries

ACROSS

1. When repeated, Shakira's 2010 World Cup song
5. Conceited
9. Unwelcome email message
13. Funds via PayPal, say
18. Foreshadowing
19. 1986 Madonna hit: "_____ Don't Preach"
20. Unstressed vowel sound
21. French fashion house since 1952
22. Lease
23. Caustic cleansers
24. Old-style announcer in town?
25. African country or currency
26. Act of a rebel
28. NWT/Yukon river
29. Turned the wheel sharply
31. _____ of Capricorn
32. **For a *Cheers* character?**
35. Environs
37. Soak
38. Ford product
39. Thicket
42. Actors' parts
44. Sty sound
46. *The Andy Griffith Show* sot
50. Assist a gambler?
51. It starts Passover
52. Jazz great Fitzgerald
53. Glenn Gould's keyboard
54. Canadian Gesner invented this oil
56. WWII leader Joseph
58. Grant permission
59. CBC News Network show: *The Passionate _____*
60. Absorb knowledge
62. Wife of 92-D
63. Scrubs
64. Elite guests
65. Frequently
67. Fungus, in Florida
68. Trees that tremble
71. Go to sea
72. Gaze fixedly
74. TTC coach
77. Armour imperfection?
78. Classical composer Gustav
80. Salve
82. Feathers one's abode?
83. *The Sun _____ Rises*
84. McCartney/Wonder hit: "_____ and Ivory"
86. *Don Giovanni* highlight
87. Genesis brother
88. Attraction to an artist?
89. Rower's boat
90. Wee
91. Salty ova
93. Greek elemental god
95. Holler
97. **For Prince William?**
102. Honk one's horn
106. Taxing crime?
107. Mentally competent
108. Early gramophone brand
110. Abnormal swelling (var.)
111. Understand
113. Trig term
114. Synonym for "dang"
115. Varnish resin
116. Court clerk
117. She lived at Green Gables
118. Canada's first international singing star Albani
119. Levels, in Liverpool
120. Paves
121. Country of 56-A (abbr.)
122. Some vintage autos

DOWN

1. _____ case scenario
2. Mideast chieftain (var.)
3. Japanese form of fencing
4. Appetizer, in Rome
5. Join ends of film
6. Spread for a BLT
7. Overturn
8. Esso purchase
9. Window mesh
10. **For a British singer?**
11. Amazement
12. Canadian sports award: Lou _____ Trophy
13. Red skin cause
14. Grilled
15. Former CBC series: *Man _____*
16. More tender
17. Acts on advice
20. Script segments
27. Exhaust
28. Potato prepping tools
30. Harmful, on the street
33. Run in neutral
34. US restaurant chain in Canada
36. Hockey halls
39. Birthday treat
40. Follow the rules
41. Fugèreville father
43. Central European river
45. National Association of Nurses (abbr.)
47. Western Samoa money
48. Get _____ a good thing
49. Plants seeds
51. Oozes
52. Military directive: At _____
53. Makeshift mattress
55. Skulks
57. Name
61. **For a famed lexicographer?**
63. Banal, to the grain grower?
64. Risky
66. Pastry type (var.)
67. For the most part
68. Teen's skin trouble
69. Tom Jones hit: "_____ a Lady"

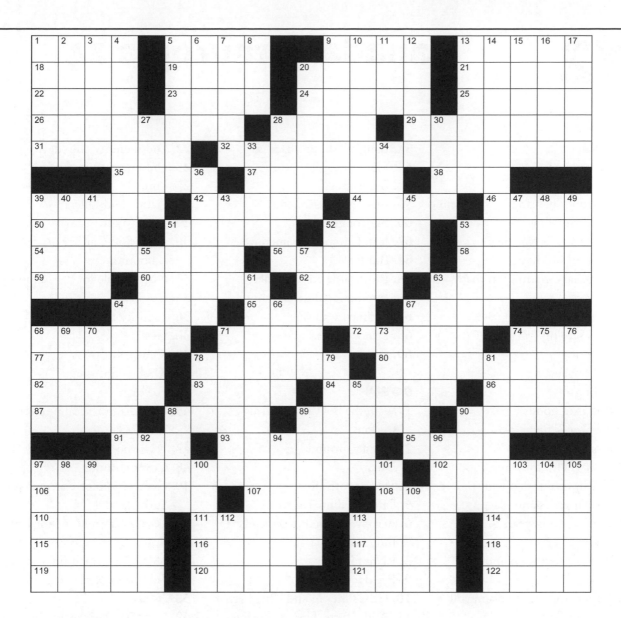

70. Italian tower town
71. Tanzanian city: Dar es _____
73. Sander or spanner
74. *Sesame Street* character
75. Apartment block component
76. Linger
78. Calendar mo.
79. Ebb
81. Like some brides who went postal?

85. Colloquial term for a town
88. Art _____
89. Samurai's religion
90. Ink _____ test
92. Egyptian underworld god
94. Teaches CP staff?
96. Artistic impressionist?
97. Inhibit
98. Soft palate part
99. Glacier mounds

100. Worrying feeling
101. 1934 Christie book: *Why Didn't They Ask _____?*
103. "The Velvet Fog" Mel
104. 1836 Texas battle landmark
105. Bye-byes, in Brighton
109. Places to rest overnight
112. Airport board info
113. 19th Greek letter

Solution on page 189

ACROSS

1. Fine pastimes?
5. First, in Florence
10. International singing star Céline
14. Caddish fellow
15. Like a Christmas tree?
16. Odd, in Orkney
17. National organization that delivers
19. Actress Miranda
20. Eggs serving (var.)
21. Type of gin
23. Hallow ending
24. Sailing
26. Brings in goods
28. Bit of mischief
31. X or 10
33. Overwhelm the opposition
34. Not in favour of a felon?
35. Vancouver Island place
38. Getting on in years
39. Get in line?
41. Part of province name
42. Shoe style
44. A touch of it can poison you
45. Lima or fava
46. Glass rock
48. Pants
49. They love to love you
51. Bangladeshi bread
53. Elevator cage
54. Big bag
56. Bhangra instruments
60. Nincompoop
62. Jean Chrétien's hometown
64. Burden
65. Ringworm, for example
66. International defence org.
67. Inclined walkway
68. Prince of Darkness
69. Got larger

DOWN

1. With the bow, in the string section
2. Wander around
3. Ditty
4. Tooth protection
5. Part of a dinner service
6. Acronym seen in a cemetery
7. Judge Lance, et al.
8. Islam follower
9. Eye doctor's field
10. CBC's Steven and Chris, say
11. Adds layers, like a seamstress
12. Group of eight
13. Middays
18. Workstation
22. Old memory chip device
25. Unknown author's abbr.
27. Lout
28. Flames and Oilers
29. Take a Yahtzee turn
30. Jubilee, in Calgary or Edmonton
32. Not suitable for consumption?
34. Compares
36. Semi-monthly tide
37. Has
39. Some soft drinks
40. Kitchen hot spot
43. For each
45. Canadian medical pioneer Frederick
47. Pelvic bones
48. Cover ground?
49. Occupation for Canada's Kiefer Sutherland
50. *Global National* anchor Friesen
52. From the Far East
55. 18th-C. German philosopher
57. Sun News Network host Jerry
58. Assess
59. Canadian winter weather woe
61. Recipe amount (abbr.)
63. Former US record co.

ACROSS

1. It can precede tourism or terrorism
4. Victoria _____
7. Toronto Maple Leaf Kessel
11. Woolly South American animals
18. Not strict
19. Blvd.
20. Alberta river
21. Rolled meat dish
22. Single try
24. Sunny courtyards (var.)
25. Lake Okanagan provincial park
26. **Dance group founded in 1939**
29. Lack of red blood cells
30. PEI-born NHLer Steve
31. Take legal action
32. Doddering
35. Sylvester Stallone character: Rocky _____
37. Proofreader's notations
39. Fit for a queen
40. Book of maps
43. Metal bar
45. Song for one
47. Title for Canada's Emma Albani
48. 2001 Kate Winslet film
49. Gave a hurrah
51. California wine valley
53. Sleuth, for short
54. Tropical drink alcohol
55. "_____-ching!"
56. Chemical weapon ingredient
58. Most stressed out
60. The US has an eastern one
63. Son of Seth
65. Skewers a chef?
66. **Nature area since 1904**
70. Mere social snub?
73. Minor biblical prophet
74. Orthodontics device
78. Meteor shower bit

80. Distinctive aspect
83. Cry of mock horror
84. Gametes
85. Paddler's blade
86. Injure one's "piggy"
88. Climber's favourable position?
90. Uniform
91. _____ of March
93. Patio locale
95. Military academy frosh
96. Lewis Carroll creature
97. WWII pistol
99. Garment size
101. Iron-related
103. Frothed
105. _____ few rounds
106. Neighbour of Ger.
107. Passes legislation
111. **Nature preserve since 1968**
115. When you might eat scones
117. Seal up cracks
118. White German wine
119. Shows up
120. First federally elected woman MacPhail
121. 1974 Munro collection: *Something _____ Been Meaning to Tell You*
122. Pipe bend
123. Gum malady
124. Teachers' favourites
125. French pronoun
126. European country (abbr.)

DOWN

1. Gorge near Guelph
2. Japanese camera company
3. Common daisy
4. Garden perennials
5. Sworn statement
6. "Abominable" Asian creature
7. Small, in Saguenay
8. Multi-string instrument

9. Most aloof
10. CFL and NHL
11. _____ code
12. Idles
13. Crowd-_____
14. Estranged, old style
15. Censures severely
16. Fuss
17. Red Chamber member (abbr.)
20. **Theatre that opened in 1914**
23. Rio Carnaval dances
27. Shania Twain hit: "_____ Needs to Know"
28. Wager
33. Most incapacitated
34. Chooses an MP
36. Language spoken in northern India
37. Optical viewing device
38. Venetian blind strip
40. Melodies
41. For real
42. Peruvian place
44. "Are you a man _____ mouse?"
46. Ran
49. Nun's virtue
50. Former *CityLine* talk show host Petty
52. Inuit jacket
55. Clobbers
57. Turndown word, in Marieville
59. He wrote *The Open Window*
61. Grocery totes
62. Genetic "fingerprint" substance
64. Sunday morning spiel (abbr.)
67. UN monetary org.
68. Scow or schooner
69. Stripper's kitchen gadget?
70. Goes bad
71. Preparatory period
72. Baker Street urchins
75. _____ Scotia
76. At any time

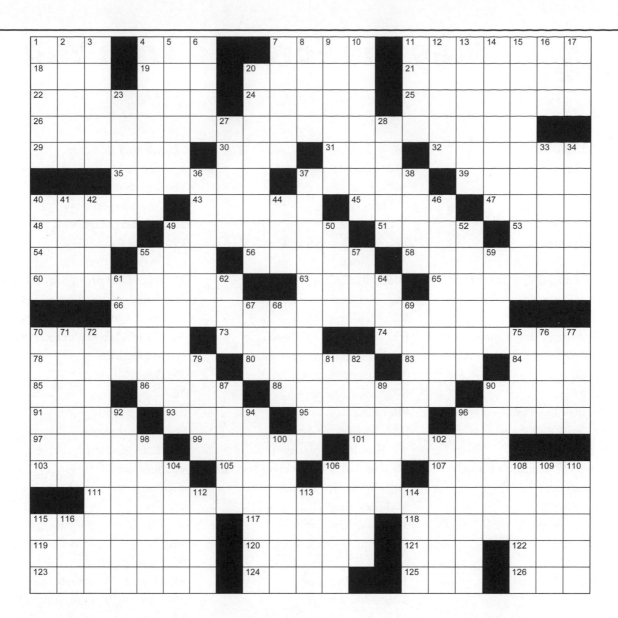

77. Captain or colonel

79. Citizenship type for some expats

81. Smoked fish delicacy

82. Top tourist destination

87. North Carolina military installation: Fort _____

89. Ancient manuscript marks

90. Display under glass

92. Hebrew-related

94. Enlarged first letter, in text

96. Nasal cavities

98. Bring back to life

100. Shelter for vehicles

102. Delete

104. Some coins

106. Heaps

108. Star, for short

109. Tutu fabric

110. Aroma

112. Loch _____ monster

113. Female family member

114. Give off light

115. Asian pagoda type

116. Monogram of Tarzan's creator

Solution on page 190

May the Force Be with You

What you seek is in the centre . . .

ACROSS

1. _____ Jaw SK
6. Leave the RV park?
12. Fatted calf locales
20. Book's alphabetical listing
21. More balanced
22. Okay
23. 1987 Rush hit: "Time Stand _____"
24. Beef sausage
25. **Bumbling French inspector**
26. Assured
28. Not all
30. Get gas?
31. Dentist's bits (var.)
32. Juno-winning singer Jordan
33. Twin or double
34. **Georges Simenon's French commissaire**
38. Fah follower
39. Niger neighbour
41. Exclamation of relief
45. Soup type
46. Toronto Zoo attraction
48. _____ brûlée
49. Métis leader Louis, et al.
50. Night light
51. Force
52. *Brave New World* drug
53. Loses feathers (var.)
54. Taught
56. German river
57. Villain
58. Sedates, old style
59. Filled with leaded glass
60. Tirades
61. Unconventional
65. Some numbers
66. Nickname of Canadian poker star Greg Mueller
69. Continuing
71. Tribunal, say
72. Pinocchio, at times
73. *Il Trovatore* and *La Traviata*
74. Maid's dressy duds?
76. Canada Post delivers letters to him
77. Allow entry
78. Alumni gatherings
79. Cultural
80. Biblical place
81. Salon service, for short
82. Retailers' pitches
83. **TV partner of Hutch**
84. Sandwich type, for short
85. Harasses a hare?
87. Satyr's cousin
88. Quell
92. *Penthouse* or *Hustler*
93. Royalty payments
98. *Hawaii 5-0* **detective sergeant**
100. Where some buddies embrace?
102. Lowest deck on a ship
103. Southern state
104. Fats Domino song: "Ain't That _____"
105. Mufti's ruling
106. Most annoying
107. Anne Murray hit: "You _____ Me"
108. Teeth cleaning twine

DOWN

1. Various (abbr.)
2. Not deceived by
3. Norse god
4. Me or I
5. Owner's bookplate
6. Sahara or Gobi
7. Roy's wife Dale
8. Early European marauder
9. *Devious Maids* star Ortiz
10. Colonial India lady
11. Abbot's underling
12. Visage
13. Annex
14. Married in secret
15. Iron Age priest
16. Speech impediment
17. Curved moulding
18. Laotian's neighbour
19. Amaze
27. Set-to for two
29. *Die Hard* **protagonist John**
32. Breaking dawn times, poetically
33. Some Queen's degs.
34. **Colin Dexter's detective chief inspector**
35. Adage
36. Things
37. Swanky soiree
38. Like chimneys
40. Knee tendons
41. Summary
42. Car rental giant
43. Roast host
44. Dandelions
46. She wants a miner's money?
47. Floral garland
48. Woos at Wimbledon?
50. Thoroughly contemporary
51. Parapet gap
53. Praying _____
55. Medieval Scottish lords
57. East Indian fig tree
59. Mulroney-era cabinet minister Beatty
61. School, in Saint-Hyacinthe
62. Like some crusaders?
63. Largest Greek island
64. **Dishevelled 1970s TV detective**
65. Tandoor-baked breads
66. Helsinki citizens
67. Dyed fabric
68. **Comic strip detective Dick**
70. A Bobbsey twin
71. Nudges

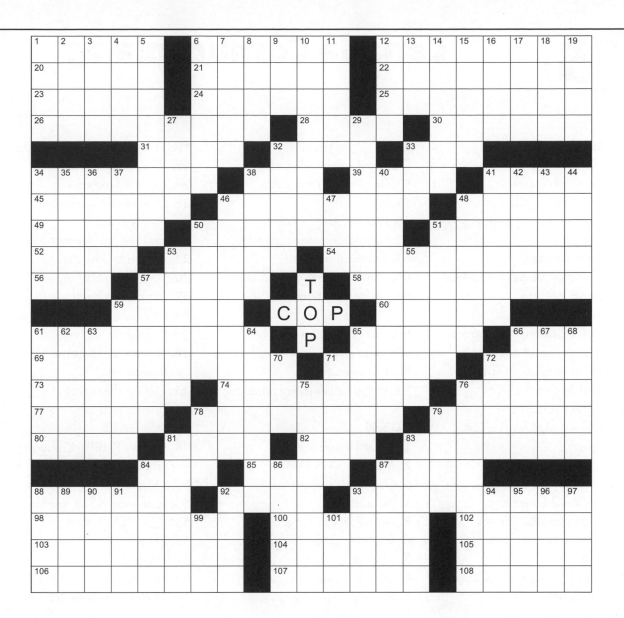

72. Former Canadian ops base in Germany
75. Determine a disease
76. Mexican impasse?
78. Soak flax in water
79. French case
81. Word repeated in a 1963 Beatles hit
83. Gave lip service?

84. Crepe's kin
86. 1990s CBC cooking show: *The _____ Peasant*
87. Lady in Laval
88. Make a trade
89. Canadian retailer since 1953: Kal _____
90. Classifications
91. Criticism

92. "Hey!" quietly
93. Boulevard
94. Russian mountain chain
95. Chorus voice
96. Cows' sounds
97. Restful vacation spots
99. Dads' mates
101. Third-person pronoun

Solution on page 190

ACROSS

1. *King Lear* has five
5. Knitting imperfection
9. Coptic bishops' titles
14. Bit of a sweet, in Sussex
15. Lay asphalt
16. Mirror damage
17. Joe Clark's Alberta birthplace
19. Shrewd
20. Nail polish, say
21. RSVP affirmative responder
23. Eye with lust in one's heart
25. Official language of India
26. Farming plot
29. They get you access?
31. They're traded on the TSX
34. Departs
35. Squirrel's hoard
37. Make noise in the night
38. Little troublemaker
39. Famed Canadian artists: _____ of Seven
41. Paddle
42. Holiday Mondays in Canada?
45. Perpetually
46. Doe's partner
47. Canadian system of measurement
49. Old name for Tokyo
50. _____ of Capri
51. Elizabethan style collars
53. *The Sopranos* star Falco
55. Awns
58. Improve engine power
62. Landlord/tenant agreement
63. Montréal university
65. Cowboy show, colloquially
66. Bruce Cockburn hit: "If a _____ Falls"
67. Sets one's sights on?
68. Salad green
69. Clairvoyant
70. Proofreader's galley notation

DOWN

1. Sign of a sore heart?
2. A beard grows here
3. Old Roman senate attire
4. Noodleheads
5. Going over the edge?
6. Washroom, for short
7. Iris area
8. Bed on a train
9. Stresses
10. Manitoba city
11. Small Australasian marsupials
12. Skin blemishes
13. Terrier breed
18. Tim Hortons order, for short
22. Poet's contraction
24. Get used to (var.)
26. Discrimination against the elderly (var.)
27. *Le _____ de Monte Cristo*
28. Return to a homeland
30. _____ Top Stuffing
32. Afrikaans village
33. QC-born ex-NHLer Lajeunesse
36. Soft fabric
40. Toronto-born Lorne Michaels, for example
43. Ties up the turkey
44. Flour separators
46. Western US range
48. Ottawa RedBlacks league (abbr.)
52. Offshoot denominations
54. First-time NYSE sale
55. _____ Québécois
56. Derrière
57. Hurtful?
59. Horizontal passage to a mine
60. 1970 Guess Who hit: "No _____"
61. Compass point
64. Aline Chrétien, _____ Chaîné

76

Who Am I? 2

ID this famous Canadian author

ACROSS

1. "Head, Shoulders, Knees and _____"
5. 1970s CTV talk-show host Alan
10. Like some cheese
14. Request
17. Indolent
18. Drupes
19. Drive
20. Greek letter
21. **She received this honour in 2013**
23. Horror film staple
24. Cambodian dictator Pot
25. Vocalist's vibrato
26. "Delicious!"
28. **University where she was writer-in-residence**
30. Broom
32. TV sitcom: *How _____ Your Mother*
34. Cloches and caps
35. Lucy _____ Montgomery
39. One who bares all in public
41. McCartney and John
42. Sirhan or Oswald
44. 1982 Canadian film: _____ *Plouffes*
45. Old European gold coins
47. Beam of sun
48. Organism structure
50. Loose loop
52. Driving necessity?
54. Actual
56. Ostia greeting
57. 2010 Michael Bublé hit: "_____ Me a River"
58. Former UN Secretary-General Hammarskjöld
61. **Film based on her "The Bear Came Over the Mountain"**
64. Ogle
65. According to, in French
66. _____ Aviv
67. Hied
68. Dem.'s opposite
70. Cause downheartedness
73. Reverse, say
75. _____ on the ground floor
79. Square dance groups
80. Lady lobster
82. Good & Plenty, for example
84. Seabird
85. Chilly sales approach?
87. Sensed
88. "Let's get going!"
89. Hades' sibling
90. Rainbow shaped
92. **Her 2004 Giller winner**
94. Cobra's kin
96. Baby's wardrobe
101. Singer Yoko
102. Stir up
104. **Her 2003 collection**
106. Torso appendage
107. Wrinkle removing appliance
108. Come together
109. Lummox
110. Ball or doll
111. Watch over
112. Some Hebrew letters
113. Two-time Oscar-winning director Kazan

DOWN

1. Bit of colour
2. Scent, in Saratoga
3. Hamburg's river
4. Look like
5. Not fortunate?
6. Crossword's cousin
7. 1002, Roman style
8. Protein in 48-A
9. In _____ of
10. Civic Holiday mo.
11. Cultivation expert
12. Bird that wades
13. Grades that don't make the grade
14. Mirror image?
15. **Her literary milieu**
16. Artists' ovens
22. Tennis shot
27. Former Ontario premier Harris
29. Quite wide
31. Nasty natured
33. Not a neat situation?
35. Some family heads, for short
36. Wood for a bat
37. Canada's southern neighbour (abbr.)
38. Goofy
40. Everywhere
41. Psyche section
43. Soapstone
45. Scuba expert
46. Canthus irritant
49. Departed
51. Scale note (var.)
53. Large pitchers
55. Desolate, old style
58. Wainscot
59. **She is . . .**
60. The art of eating well
62. *Love Story* actress MacGraw
63. Crabapple tree kin
69. Extra benefit
71. Top 1980s Woodbine jockey David
72. Old-style second-person pronoun
74. Waterproof table covering
76. Food can
77. Cause of December 2013 Ontario power outages
78. _____ Westminster BC
81. *Born Free* star
83. Chops up
85. Old name for Sri Lanka

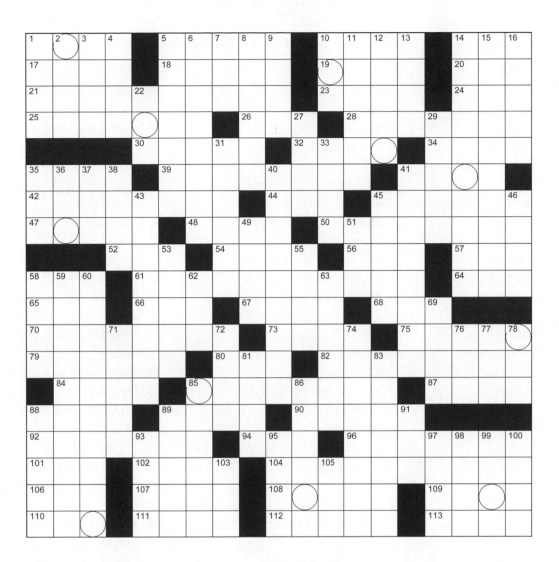

86. Gangster Al
88. Eastern European
89. African country
91. Henna one's hair
93. Habeas corpus, for example
95. Social slight
97. She, in Shawinigan

98. Home Hardware purchase
99. Order of Canada scientist Lap-Chee
100. James who sang "At Last"
103. _____ of the line
105. Soused

Use the circled letters to unscramble this author's fictional setting:

__ __ __ __ __

__ __ __ __ __ __

Solution on page 190

77

Delightful Duos

Famed comedy teams

ACROSS

1. Lofty room?
6. Woods, in Québec
10. Cotillion women
14. Painful muscle contraction
19. National agricultural group: _____ Farmers of Canada
20. Forearm bone
21. British nobility title
22. Uncle's spouse, in Saguenay
23. Environmental organization: _____ Unlimited Canada
24. File
25. Eagles vocalist Glenn
26. Trojan War epic (with "*The*")
27. Like a hard glance
29. Penned an essay
31. Divvies up
32. Hole-making tool
35. Magazine abbr.
36. Flu symptom
37. Properly arrayed
38. **Counterculture duo**
41. Faded
42. Scintilla, in Thessaloniki?
43. Like some seals
44. Captivate, in Kansas
46. Emmy-winning drama series: _____ *Men*
49. DDS and MD
50. Alexander Keith brews
51. **"*Road To . . .*" movies stars**
53. "That was close!" interjection
55. Release
57. Discovery program: *How _____ Made*
58. "Golden" king
59. Knighted lady
61. Neil Young song: "Love Is _____"
63. Festoon, old style
64. National econ. stat

67. Longing for Japan?
68. Baked ham spice bit
69. US aviation grp.
70. Article in Québec
71. _____ to go
73. Scavenging mammal
74. _____ *avis*
76. Express one's viewpoint
77. Fond-du-_____ SK
78. Varnish component
81. Some keyboard keys
84. **Magical comedy pair**
87. Layered mineral
89. BC Lions, say
91. Edmonton CFLer, for short
92. Clean-_____
93. Japanese poetry style
94. Poker term
95. Garden perennial
96. **They debuted in Atlantic City in 1946**
99. Dump of rain
101. Make petty complaints
102. Family Day mo. in some provinces
103. Bucks and boars
104. Strait of Georgia sea
105. Accepted customs
106. Property crime
108. Oust
109. Gunshot sound
110. Biological classification groups
112. Cliffside nest
116. Church donation
117. *The Razor's _____*
118. Québec singer Lapointe
119. Law enforcement forays
120. Pasture bull
121. Duct drop
122. Hazard
123. Sag

DOWN

1. Calculate a sum
2. Upsilon preceder
3. _____-tac-toe
4. Exasperates
5. Charitable organization: _____ Fibrosis Canada
6. **Radio and TV comedy spouses**
7. Oil of _____
8. Electees
9. Tree's newer layer
10. Car's condensation clearing system
11. 1999 David Suzuki book: *You are the _____*
12. *Desperate Housewives* character
13. Devious
14. **Second City spouses**
15. Wan
16. Negative particle
17. California or Colorado
18. Shoppers Drug Mart refills, for short
28. *Barbarella* star Milo
30. Go for a jog
31. Perturb
32. Amino _____
33. Crane's cry?
34. Dirty old man
36. Bosom buddy?
37. Metrical feet
39. Relieved
40. Manitoba Native group
41. Trash
45. Din
46. Runway walker
47. Without any delay
48. Students' seats
51. Cause of death determiner
52. Went undetected
54. **Their show aired on CBC**
56. *The Wizard of Oz* surname

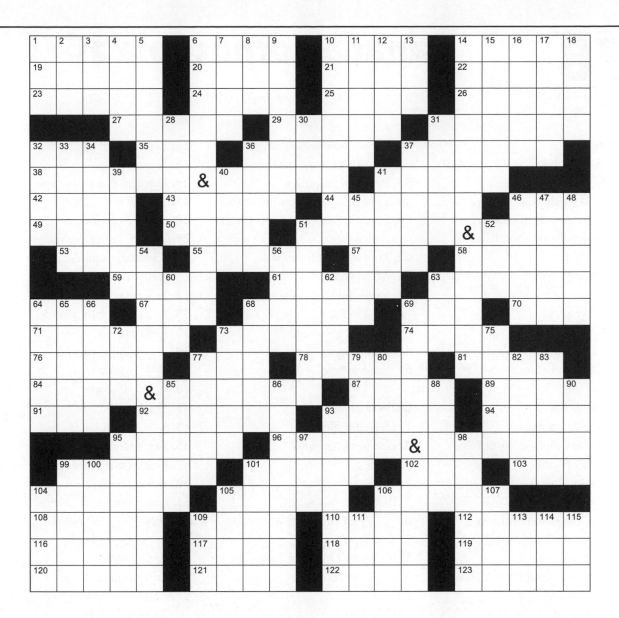

60. Actress Ryan
62. Calgary sports venue: Olympic _____
63. Ovine communication
64. Fumble blindly
65. Neck backs
66. Get gussied up
68. Go for a ride
69. **Ice Follies pair**
72. Vacationers' stopover
73. Bisect
75. Communion table
77. Depart

79. iPhone message
80. Hour segments (abbr.)
82. Last Commandment
83. French composer Erik
85. Leg part
86. Optical projector
88. *Eight Is Enough* actor Willie
90. Young _____ Christian Association
93. Game that bends you out of shape?
95. Banal saying
97. Early bible name

98. On the Rocky Mountaineer?
99. Lifeboat lowering mechanism
100. Aristocracy
101. Latin line dance
104. Hardens, like aspic
105. Earned money, say
106. Line on a graph
107. Move closer to
109. Wager
111. Onassis, informally
113. Brazilian city, for short
114. Marital agreement?
115. Psychic's alleged talent

Solution on page 190

ACROSS

1. Montréal's NHL team, for short
5. KFC side dish
9. Thumb a ride
14. American astronaut Shepard
15. Meat-and-potatoes dish
16. Mutual of _____
17. Northern New Brunswick city
19. Spread one's fingers
20. Intervene, say
21. Illegal Irish drinks
23. 1997 Céline Dion song: "_____ Talk About Love"
26. Duct
27. Plot outline
31. Some birch trees
34. Canada's highest mountain
35. Blasts of wind
37. US film director Spike
38. 1985 Camaro: _____-Z
39. "Mr. Television" Milton
40. Canadian double-gold Winter Olympian Bilodeau
41. 1960s war country, for short
42. Foot bones
43. Kitchen sifter
44. Glowers at
46. Happened
48. Fish-catching devices
49. Not temp
50. Arthur who served twice as Canada's prime minister
53. Barcelona buddies
58. Lexicographer's lesson content
59. Ontario-born cosmetics queen Arden
62. Hollywood film award
63. Metal string
64. Sarah McLachlan song: "_____ the Fire"
65. Some are Roman
66. Bad progeny?
67. Stash away

DOWN

1. Hogs the spotlight?
2. Got to the ground
3. Nude
4. Trim
5. Black eye
6. _____ La Biche AB
7. Tree type
8. It follows Dream or Miracle
9. Backpackers' lodges
10. Loom
11. Narrator
12. Canadian silver skating Olympian Patrick
13. *Airplane!* actor Robert
18. City in Italy
22. Egg-shaped
24. Big cat
25. Tropical evergreen type
27. Broken arm support
28. Sea near Australia
29. They're full of themselves
30. Canadian feminist group formed in 1971 (abbr.)
32. *Superman* star Christopher
33. Told male from female
36. Pizza piece
39. Guadeloupe capital: _____-Terre
40. _____ Canada
42. Leashes
43. _____ cum laude
45. Ska kin
47. Out of one's mind
50. Bit of physics?
51. Canadian gas station name
52. Sun _____ Network
54. Long-legged bird
55. Lady's partner
56. Bart Simpson's school bus driver
57. Long-time CBC offering: *The Tommy Hunter _____*
60. Untruth
61. British Isles country (abbr.)

79

Goin' Down the Road

Driving around Canada

ACROSS

1. _____ and found
5. Go _____ length
9. Leaning
15. Pimples
19. White-tailed flyer
20. Luxury car brand
21. Local magistrate, in Scotland
22. Stole
23. Organisms' environment
25. **Prime ministerial street**
27. Made certain
28. Ring round
30. Old-style ceramic flutes
31. Storage tubs
32. Spoke Scottish?
34. Isaac and Rebekah's boy
35. Honour _____ thieves
37. Unaided vision, say
39. 1980 Barry Manilow hit: "_____ It Through the Rain"
43. Most scanty (var.)
45. Church officer
48. "I do," for example
49. Cold word?
50. Medium-sized mandarin
53. Bit of sweat
54. Fork point
55. English Language Development (abbr.)
56. Long-time Yugoslavian president
57. _____ de Triomphe
59. Sixty-minute energy measuring unit
61. Alberta's Kananaskis Village, for example
63. Like some crop blights
65. Leases a unit
66. **Famous BC route**
70. Because
73. Medicine bottles (var.)
74. Like part of Peru
78. In-depth research report
80. _____ capita
81. Koppel, et al.
83. Brownies' org., in Orlando
84. Surf sound
85. Thaw out
87. Like activity before an earthquake
89. Trillium province chiropractic org.
90. Insect type
91. Margarine or cream cheese
93. It produces an effect
95. Contemptuous expression from GBS?
97. They might be feely?
100. Birds' abodes
101. Cookware set components
104. Ski
105. Toad's bump
106. Cover with a cerecloth
110. Honky-_____
111. Green mineral
114. **Road to Newfoundland's L'Anse aux Meadows**
116. Temporary suspensions
118. Scored on a first serve
119. Radiator protector
120. Village
121. Shopping buggy
122. CTV nightly offering
123. Chatter, colloquially
124. Relieve pressure
125. Big trees

DOWN

1. Alternative to Levi's
2. Mammal seen in West Coast waters
3. Whistler gear
4. Lab work
5. Sanctuary in the Sahara?
6. Samantha who founded War Child Canada
7. Suffix for lime or lemon
8. Mali city
9. Inane
10. Fried
11. Sue Grafton book: _____ *for Lawless*
12. Too
13. Female family member
14. Home state of the Bushes
15. Heart chamber
16. Royal Canadian Mint product
17. Former Eastern Canada carrier: Air _____
18. Gets every last drop, say
24. **Lake Ontario-to-Lake Simcoe connector**
26. Sink pipe
29. Beaver State (abbr.)
32. Male Met voice
33. Coloured with Clairol
35. Jewellery gem
36. 1930s Hollywood star Oberon
37. Profit, in Portsmouth
38. Insect type
40. Plane for Pierre
41. Treat from Tim Hortons
42. Big jugs
44. Cucumber dip, in New Delhi
46. Mike Babcock was Team Canada's in 2014
47. Decide on
51. Retailer's means of profit
52. Some sock patterns
54. "I thought _____ never leave!"
58. Hang together
60. **Highway that crosses the country**
62. Canadian jazz pianist Peterson
63. Clairvoyant's alleged ability
64. "_____ the season . . ."
67. Stun gun

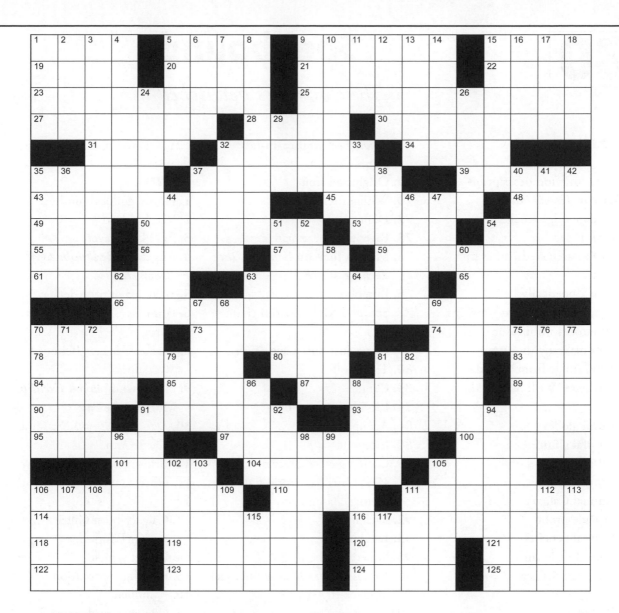

68. Brunch item (var.)
69. Dry riverbeds, in Northern Africa
70. Ladies' shoe part
71. Some golf clubs
72. Below, poetically
75. Narcissistic
76. Famed Berkshire racecourse
77. Some flatbreads
79. Fairy's relative
81. Winter Palace rulers
82. Big birds
86. New Mexico enclave

88. Emulate Elvis Stojko
91. Like testimony offered under oath
92. Easily influenced
94. CBC documentary maker McKenna
96. Sap sucking pests
98. Anger, old style
99. Attila was one
102. Early Hudson's Bay trapper's coat
103. *Kama* _____

105. Canadian fashion designer Clark
106. CBC *Power & Politics* host Solomon
107. Pleasant
108. Throw out of whack
109. Very small amount
111. Seder celebrants
112. Duration
113. Ballpark figures (abbr.)
115. Cleric's robe
117. _____ constrictor

80

Spellbound

These actresses bewitched us

ACROSS

1. "_____ never work!"
5. Acute situation description
9. **Bette in *Hocus Pocus***
15. Some Dodge trucks
19. Islamic sect
20. 1992 Barenaked Ladies hit
21. Lest
22. Black, poetically
23. American Civil War warships
25. Sultana or Thompson
26. Mount Vesuvius output
27. 1964 single from Canada's Garnett: "We'll Sing in the _____"
28. Royal globes
29. Bit of a glimpse
31. Paleontologist's find
32. Kind of market
33. Annual Calgary rodeo
35. Provide proof
38. Capital benefit?
39. Puréed fruit sauce
40. Serve the tea, say
41. _____ acid
43. Red planet
44. Electromagnetism pioneer
48. Forming a sac, anatomically
50. Loathes
52. Bit of a big machine
53. North or South state abbr.
54. High point of a tour in the Rockies?
55. Put clothes on
56. Indochinese language
57. ***The Witches of Eastwick's* Alexandra Medford**
58. Sweat drop
60. Canadian 1991 Oscar acting nominee Greene
63. Set free
65. Brown-coated ermine

67. ***Bewitched* mother-in-law Agnes**
69. Originated from
70. Without refinement
72. Digital document
73. River to the Caspian
74. **Melissa Joan on *Sabrina, the Teenage Witch***
75. Bumbling one
77. Six-time NL home run champ Mel
78. Astronauts' space-age drink
80. Ticked off
83. Central
84. Peevish, in olden days
86. Act up
88. Inception
90. Cotton seed separators
91. 1965 Canadian world figure skating champ Petra
92. Vicinity
93. Dubbing, say
95. Watering tube
96. *Save the Tiger* Oscar winner Jack
98. Watercraft
101. Burst of wind
102. They brought gifts to a manger
103. Discipline a wrongdoer
104. National historic site: Athabasca _____
105. *Candide* character
109. Valuable mineral deposits
110. Saskatchewan city: Prince _____
113. "Imagine!" in Ipswich
114. Pastry confection
115. Oddball
116. Teens' blemishes
117. Slick
118. Matching groups
119. **Nicole in *Practical Magic***
120. 1988 film from Canada's Cronenberg: _____ *Ringers*

121. Quarter or half, in music

DOWN

1. Horus' goddess mother
2. Via, for short
3. BC Place player
4. **Angela in *Bedknobs and Broomsticks***
5. Sketched out the details
6. Pointless
7. Carousel
8. Former NHLers Belfour and Westfall
9. **Helen who played *Excalibur's* Morgana Le Fay**
10. *Dancing with the Stars* judge Carrie Ann
11. British police investigative officers (abbr.)
12. _____ Vegas
13. Calgary-born Giller Prize winner Edugyan
14. Leased vehicle
15. Health deterioration
16. Humiliate
17. Changed residences
18. Small drum
24. British sweet, for short
28. Mélange
30. Releases
32. Sharp tooth
33. _____-Tracy QC
34. Marie who founded a wax museum
35. Emulated an orangutan?
36. Madam, in Madrid
37. Marsh walkways
38. Herbal remedy from a Chinese tree
39. Maine Coon
42. Actress Farrow
43. Blockbuster
45. Old-style teacher

46. Clay/silt mix
47. Coincide
49. Gaiters
50. *Charmed* star Shannon
51. Lots, colloquially
55. Tropical Atlantic fish
57. Mrs. Dithers
59. One of Canada's coasts
61. 1973 US Supreme Court decision name
62. Fellows
64. Huge
65. Average Joe?
66. CP transport
67. Muscle pain
68. Clothing

71. Take a slice?
73. Deranged
76. Distracting manoeuvre
79. Question
81. Chevrolet model
82. Long-time TV roast host Martin
84. Pierces
85. Famous conjoined twin
86. Is obligated
87. *The Wizard of Oz* baddy **Margaret**
89. Joins the army
91. Work group leader
94. Southern Ontario Native

95. **Anjelica the Grand High Witch in *The Witches***
97. Like Xmas nog
98. Dalmatians' dilemmas?
99. Halos (var.)
100. Not reactive
101. Largest lake in Italy
102. Biblical food
104. Curly do
105. Stride
106. Columbus state
107. Ice melter
108. Cause of a red eye
111. Floral necklace
112. Auction floor action
113. Short-term rage?

Solution on page 191

81

Canada Cornucopia 27

ACROSS

1. *Fruits of the Earth* character Spalding
4. Went white
8. Make modifications
14. Sleep type, for short
15. 1990s BC premier Harcourt
16. *Factory Girl* actress Miller
17. Tinker or tailor
19. Fifties waiter on wheels
20. In the thick of
21. Niagara Falls bridge
23. Geeky guys
24. Man's title
25. Artery from the heart
27. Québec's official one is the yellow birch
28. City in Ghana
30. "_____ I care!"
31. They scold you
34. Horse-and-buggy _____
35. Ballroom dance style
38. Burn slowly but surely, in Scranton
40. Blame, colloquially
41. Rock wall topper
43. List component
45. Timer in a taxi
46. Our first Sochi medal winner McMorris
50. Be worthy of a raise
52. Heating device, for short
53. Fashion magazine since 1892
54. Remedy for a seamstress?
56. Virgil poem (with "*The*")
57. Star in Aquila
58. Harassing William's sibling?
60. Idea
61. Noddy series author Blyton
62. Perceive
63. Lacking gentility
64. 2001 Hockey Hall of Fame inductee Hawerchuk
65. CFL scores, for short

DOWN

1. Lacking any moderation
2. German luxury car, colloquially
3. United _____ Loyalists
4. Out of place
5. Surrounded, in literature
6. Get the most out of
7. Alberta oil field structure
8. Spore sacs
9. Canadian singer Krall
10. Desert rodent
11. Dismounted
12. Canadian winter driving necessity
13. Knock on wood?
18. Vipers
22. Picked up a perp
24. Dunks a dory
26. Way out there
28. Crosswise, on ship
29. Knight's cladding (var.)
32. And so on, for short
33. Canadian humanitarian Stephen Lewis, to David
35. Svelte
36. Ontario university
37. *The Merry Widow*, for example
39. Children's book series pen name: _____ Snicket
42. Saved for a rainy day
44. Where trapeze artists meet
47. Prejudiced against pensioners?
48. Destroyed
49. Small anchors
51. Groups of three
53. Atlantic archipelago: Cape _____
55. Shore bird
56. Seed husk
57. Mandela's former party (abbr.)
59. California place: Santa _____

82

And the Province Is . . .

Take this tour to find out

ACROSS

1. Comic strip Andy
5. Glasses, colloquially
10. Ghana river
15. Deck
19. State an opinion
20. Fuss
21. Environments
22. Any time now, old style
23. Cancellation, colloquially
24. **Museum honouring a hometown singer**
27. Use a stylus
29. Soaks
30. Yukon region
31. Ivy League university
32. White noise
34. Former federal cabinet minister Jelinek
35. Fence supports
37. Container
38. Different
40. Furious
44. Machu Picchu people
45. Truth _____
47. April Wine hit: "Just Between _____ and Me"
48. **Early name**
49. Astrological sign
50. Fast African animal
52. Show to be true
54. Mitchell novel: *Who _____ Seen the Wind?*
55. Dearie, in Derby
56. Pasture group
57. US state rep
59. Prior to, to a poet
60. Former VP Al
61. Coins
63. Lummox
65. _____ point
66. **Annual Apple Blossom Festival locale**

70. Last Greek letter
73. Marine mammal order
74. African animals
78. Stargazer, for example
79. Bridge action
80. Wilt
81. Dirty reading
83. Dinner morsel
84. Tokyo, at one time
85. Papa
87. Atoll waters
89. One way to travel in Italy?
90. **Provincial bird**
92. University research room
94. Not old
95. _____ in the balance
96. Take the wheel
97. Outcast
99. Choose
100. Irritating
101. Where Canadian astronauts work
103. Cheaply constructed
105. Former CBC/CTV journalist Malling
106. Broadway buildings
110. Newspaper column POV
111. Some organic molecules
114. **Popular provincial park**
117. Small case
118. Old-style illness
119. Disconcerted
120. Socially unacceptable
121. Aries or Aquarius
122. Prairie writer Sinclair
123. Pips
124. Lots of murders?
125. Talk back

DOWN

1. Walking stick
2. Mary Kay rival
3. **Famous picturesque place**

4. Equitably divided
5. Remove a beard
6. Cornbread
7. Really long time
8. You might roast this on an open fire
9. Pago Pago locale
10. Long-time Grey Cup game stadium
11. Boston Garden great one
12. Dribble out
13. Canada's famed ambassador to Iran Ken
14. Fancy scarf
15. She opened a box of evils
16. Against
17. Bottle stopper
18. Leg joint
25. _____ no good
26. Lure
28. Montréal CFLers' nickname
32. Brought forth an issue?
33. Pork portion
35. Doctors' orders?
36. Outdo
37. Moosehead makes this in Saint John
39. Nunavut research base
41. Temporary committee type
42. Queen's crown
43. Painter's means of support?
45. Glossy finish
46. Islamabad spice mixtures
48. Old Rome "hello"
50. Where Canada's Norman Bethune practised
51. Coil shaped
53. Viva voce
58. Presentation bouquet
60. Spanish Romantic painter
62. Sly (var.)
63. Poker kitty
64. Eggs

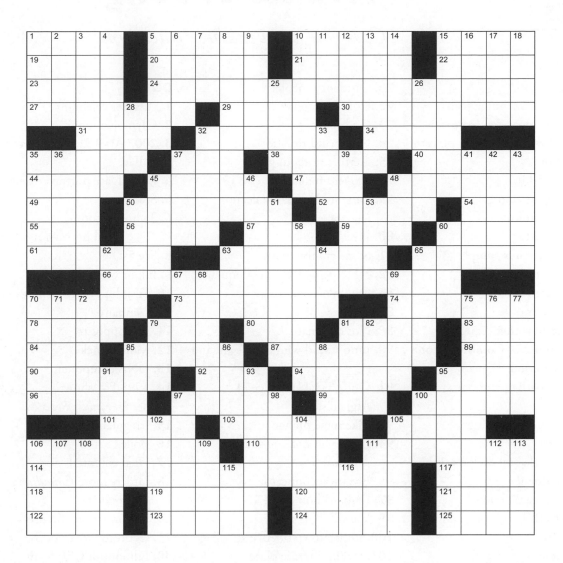

65. Craft fabrics
67. Caustic liquid
68. Sell a bike?
69. Willowdale ON MP Chungsen
70. Margarines, old style
71. Heart of things
72. Wed on the run
75. **And the province is . . .**
76. Sip
77. Orchestrated?
79. Toronto financial district street
81. *What's My Line?* panellist Sales

82. _____ Blanc
85. Reduce electrical capacity
86. Chatters like a Chihuahua?
88. Best buy?
91. Gives a new moniker
93. Witnesses, old style
95. Wealthy lady
97. Early amphibians
98. Lariat
100. Bliss Carman poem: "Low Tide on Grand _____"
102. Medieval workers

104. Monies owed
105. Group's values
106. Nicholas I, for one
107. *Les Misérables* writer Victor
108. Large birds
109. One _____ fits all
111. Big barge
112. Hauls
113. Lust and gluttony
115. Guided
116. Homer Simpson's dad

83

Five Ws of Song

Can you answer these questions?

ACROSS

1. Robed *Star Wars* humanoids
6. Wheat gets separated from this
11. Scotiabank Saddledome player
16. Map abbr.
19. Gasoline additive
20. Telephone greeting
21. Speeder's undoing
22. Lamb's mother
23. **1964 Supremes song**
26. Many centuries
27. More recent
28. Small, red monkey
29. Licorice-flavoured liqueur
31. Some House of Commons votes
33. Notable period
35. Japanese parliamentarian's regime?
37. Where Kurt Browning entertains
38. Santa's workshop exclamation?
39. Gush suddenly
41. Police car cacophonies
43. Former NHLers Hodge and Linseman
44. Leave one's car illegally
47. Painting that bares it all
48. Gordon Lightfoot hit: "Summer _____ of Life"
49. Aleppo citizen
50. Cried like a cat, in Kensington
52. BMO machine
53. Sup
54. Largest South American rodent
55. Shop around?
59. Terriers' tail motions
61. Hawaiian dish
62. Number on 70-A
63. Embarrasses
64. _____ trip
65. **1982 Men at Work smash**
69. St. Moritz peak

70. Outdoor timepiece
72. Confucian tenet
73. Go bad
74. Command to Fido
75. Getting ready to golf
76. Ancient Italian
79. Largest Hawaiian volcano: Mauna _____
80. "Gosh!"
81. Some grammarians
82. NHL penalty box, colloquially
85. Queen of spades, say
87. _____-Cola
88. Not optional
90. Juno Award winners: Tegan and _____
91. One official language of Afghanistan
93. Like some orange juice
94. *Dangerous Liaisons* star Thurman
95. Electrical connector
97. Dublin's homeland
99. View
100. Dutch town or African village
101. Odin's afterlife place
103. Hops oven
105. Carousel song: "This Was _____ Nice Clambake"
107. Hospital drips, for short
108. **1986 Van Halen single**
113. Margaret Trudeau, _____ Sinclair
114. Game ragout
115. Otherworldly
116. Cleanses oneself
117. Graduate Research Assistant (abbr.)
118. Arab world leader (var.)
119. Ancient Irish priest
120. Common Canadian precipitation

DOWN

1. Passover celebrant
2. Olympian (abbr.)
3. **2007 Avril Lavigne power ballad**
4. Dr. Kildare portrayer Lew
5. Scads
6. Twitter account?
7. "_____ sell his own mother!"
8. See 5-D
9. Ink or water
10. St. John's-based utilities holding company
11. To's opposite
12. Molten rock
13. DNA component
14. 1998 Fox show: _____ *Biggest Secrets Finally Revealed*
15. Irregularly notched
16. Boiled
17. Dual coloured
18. Orders more *Canadian Geographic*
24. Become more intense
25. Get ready to ambush
30. Edmonton CFL team
31. Auction cues
32. Cookie brand: Chips _____!
34. Semitic family language group
36. Sternum adjunct
39. Thin wood strip
40. Holiday excursion
42. Mythology anthology
45. Prejudice
46. Cosmetics giant: Mary _____
48. Farmyard fodder
51. Very evident
52. Managerial monk
54. Not warm
56. **1985 Heart hit**
57. *Sisters* star Ward
58. Glimpse, old style

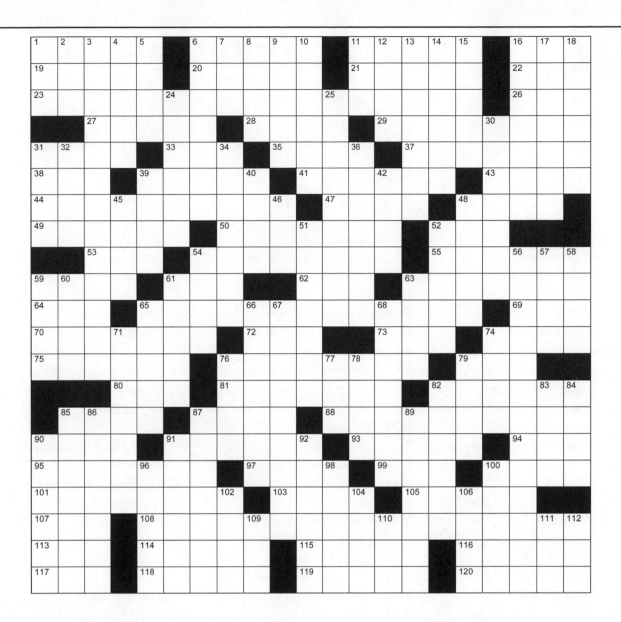

59. Alberta, Saskatchewan and
    Manitoba, collectively
60. Malarial malady
61. Parasitic virus, for short
63. Soon, archaically
65. _____ and dined
66. Diplomat's briefcase?
67. Storytelling
68. Martin Luther contemporary
71. "Sh," for example
74. Male offspring
76. Long poem
77. Part of a min.
78. Yield from a field

79. Easter flower
82. Excellent
83. _____ *La Douce*
84. 2013 Cuba-to-Florida swimmer
    Diana
85. Crime scene canine: _____ dog
86. Kazakhstan body of water
87. Randy who became the Leafs
    coach in 2012
89. Very happy
90. Accruing an RRSP
91. 2009 Travolta film: *The Taking
    of* _____ *123*
92. Spoke at a podium

96. Leather strap
98. Aromatic chemical compound
100. Pacific Northwest berry bush
102. Pinnacle
104. BC-set Discovery show:
     Highway _____ *Hell*
106. Wriggly fish
109. We breathe it
110. See 62-A
111. 22nd letter
112. Québec compass direction

ACROSS

1. Make cookies
5. Remove wallpaper
10. Young boys
14. Liquid for an etcher
15. Nursery rhyme starter word
16. Lotion emollient
17. Set against
18. Male relative
19. Colourful Québec Conservative?
20. Zone division
22. Marine wild celery a.k.a.
24. Trumpets and antlers
26. Renters
27. Strong-arm tactic
30. Hamilton's Victor Copps, to Sheila
31. Sprinted
32. Actresses Paquin and Kendrick
34. Land tracts
38. Throat-clearing noise
40. Taunting remark maker
42. Stink
43. Philosophy mavens
45. Canadian men's eight team members
47. National holiday month
48. Trifle
50. Thin vegetable farmer?
52. Famous Canadian physician Norman
56. Fall in love?
57. Like a curved nose
59. Mistreats
62. Elizabethan "guitar"
63. Contemptuous hand gesture
65. Easy pace
66. Gymnasium pads
67. Small imperial weight
68. 1970s tennis star Nastase
69. Buttonhole, say
70. Month that follows Adar
71. You wrap a scarf around this

DOWN

1. Meadow blats
2. Adolescent's facial affliction
3. Ontario city
4. Wordsmith
5. Rejecting a suitor, say
6. Number of Canadian gold medals won at Sochi
7. Queen's Plate, for example
8. Archipelago component
9. Skinned spuds
10. Newfoundland component
11. *Maclean's* columnist Fotheringham
12. Old-style second-person verb
13. *The Cat in the Hat* scribe
21. West Coast waters mammal
23. Nibble away at
25. Boom type
27. Rugged terrain cliff
28. Obama's birthplace
29. Coffee company founded in BC in 1896
33. Male and female
35. Citrusy fish dish
36. Distribute the cards
37. Inner Hebrides land mass
39. Most corny, emotionally
41. Arouse interest again
44. Aretha's essence?
46. Elitist
49. Céline Dion's first English language LP
51. 2014 golden women's hockey team member Marie-Philip
52. Healing creams
53. Exactly the same
54. All instruments at once, on a score
55. State of boredom
58. Geological time periods
60. Long narrative poem form
61. Look for
64. Ottawa Construction Association (abbr.)

Holiday cheer

ACROSS

1. Stair sections
7. Accra spending money
11. Romantic outing
15. Bachelor's blowout
19. Necessitate
20. Sharp knocks
21. "Praise the Lord!"
22. Norse myth mother of 11 sons
23. Granola kin
24. Canyon bounce
25. Telling it like it is?
27. Drowsing
28. **Song for most Canadians?**
30. Rind from a fruit
31. Photograph, for short
33. 2003 Alice Munro book: *No _____ Lost*
34. Aloof
35. Baby-to-be
37. Blame a banker?
43. **Initial song to sing?**
48. In close quarters
49. Gypsy language
50. Sympathetic syllables
51. Explorer Richard
52. It's the cat's meow?
53. Deceive: Take for _____
54. _____ Race NL
56. Depend on
57. Canadian country singer Clark
58. Golf score
59. Annual Gulf of St. Lawrence event: _____ hunt
61. Spicy tea
62. 1936 Olympics sprints great Jesse
63. **Ditty for roofers?**
67. Charlie Brown's best bud
69. Tire puncture
70. Exam
71. HBO competitor
74. Tablecloth fabric
75. Toronto-born 1928 Olympics star Myrtle
76. Calgary outdoor area: _____ Hill Park
78. Blood, in Greek mythology
80. Italian volcano
81. Gumbo or gazpacho
82. Schmaltzy stuff
83. Sore
84. Making a wild estimate?
86. **Carol for a royal trio?**
89. Financial calculations page
91. Goes sky-high
92. July-born sign
93. Minute insect
95. Macaw
96. Catholic service
100. **Song for crow's nest lookouts?**
106. Spasm
108. They sometimes attract
109. Send out a signal
110. Cry of dismay
111. 1999 Juno best single: "One _____"
112. Cheery song
113. Lawrence Welk starter: "And _____"
114. Fete
115. Tots up
116. Loch Lomond miss
117. Scott who sued Sandford in 1857
118. Appeared

DOWN

1. Draw new boundaries
2. Occupied
3. Plant tissue cylinder
4. Portrait stand
5. Irritate
6. Like sleety sidewalks
7. Buzz from a barber
8. Apiece
9. Advanced degree type (abbr.)
10. Certain atoms
11. Jive and jitterbug
12. Old-style nursemaid
13. Nunavut or Yukon
14. Endowed with spiritual wealth?
15. Old-style road stone
16. Clip a bush
17. Food Network Canada show: *Fresh with _____ Olson*
18. Shticks
26. To this point
29. Brief assessment?
32. TGIF word
35. Developed with delicacy
36. Rice Krispies sound
38. Hairdressers
39. "Little _____ has lost her . . ."
40. About-face, on the road
41. 1995 "Runaway" band
42. Russell who starred in *Felicity*
43. Golfer's sandy snare
44. "Hava Nagila" dance
45. Kuwaiti dignitary
46. Quick craze
47. Have a mortgage
51. Handsome, in Hull
54. Pop tin
55. Notwithstanding the fact that . . .
56. Fraternity letter
57. Very short time, in Tottenham
60. Dawn deity
61. Revolutionary Guevara
62. Extra periods, in sports
63. Sense of discomfort
64. Hula _____
65. Alberta national park: _____ Island

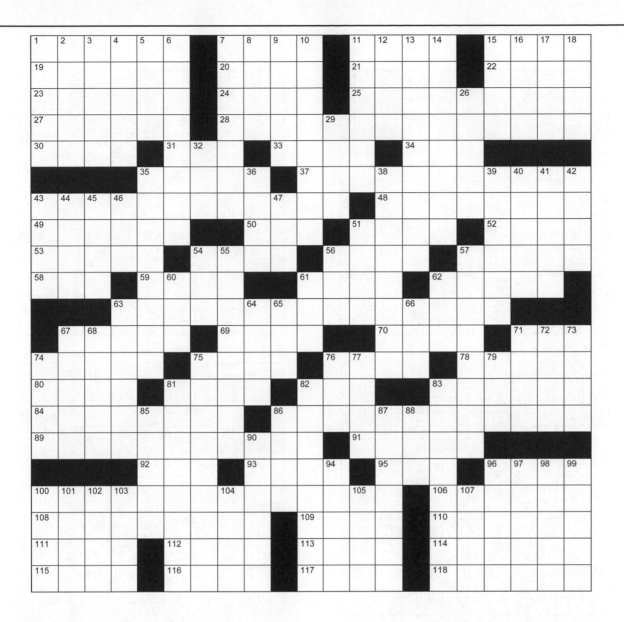

66. Reform Party senate goal (abbr.)
67. Brightened
68. Victoria landmark: _____ Harbour
71. It's below the knee
72. _____ Kong
73. Assns.
74. Furniture supports
75. Joint venture groups
76. "_____ so fast!"
77. _____ and aahs
79. See 56-D

81. Small slope
82. "Don't _____ of yourself"
83. Gardeners' machines
85. They're used to treat sailors' vapours?
86. Skin bumps
87. Cooked the capon
88. Have an _____ to the ground
90. Expels
94. Indonesian island shared by two countries
96. See 93-A

97. 1980s action series: *The _____*
98. It might weigh you down?
99. Bit of dignity?
100. Corn Belt State
101. Made haste
102. Made a copy?
103. Stir-fry pans
104. Morays
105. _____ Lake AB
107. Roller coaster rider's exclamation

Solution on page 192

1 ▪ *Name That City*

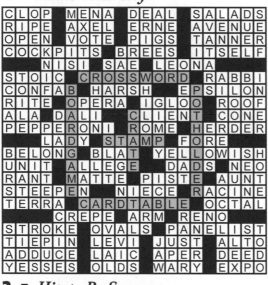

2 ▪ *Hip to Be Square*

3 ▪ *Canada Cornucopia 1*

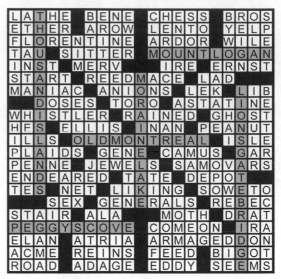

4 ▪ *Picturesque Places*

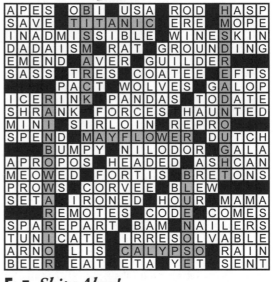

5 ▪ *Ships Ahoy!*

6 ▪ *Canada Cornucopia 2*

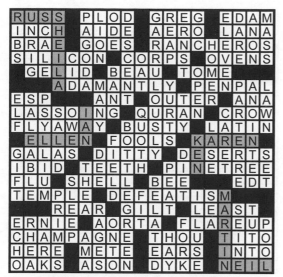

7 ▪ *They Hail from Hamilton*

8 ▪ Auto*biographical*

9 ▪ *Canada Cornucopia 3*

10 ▪ *Better to Receive?*

11 ▪ *The Fabrics of Their Lives*

12 ▪ *Canada Cornucopia 4*

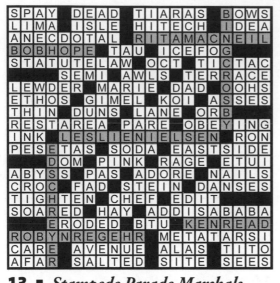

13 ▪ *Stampede Parade Marshals*

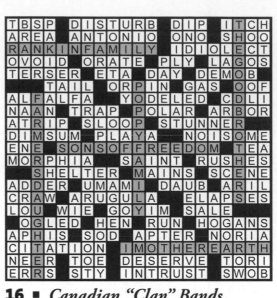

16 ▪ *Canadian "Clan" Bands*

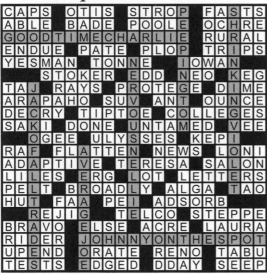

14 ▪ *'Cause You've Got Personality*

17 ▪ *Exit Strategy*

15 ▪ *Canada Cornucopia 5*

18 ▪ *Canada Cornucopia 6*

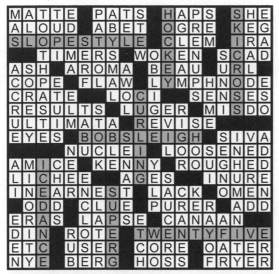

19 ■ *Shining in Sochi*

22 ■ *Who Am I? 1*

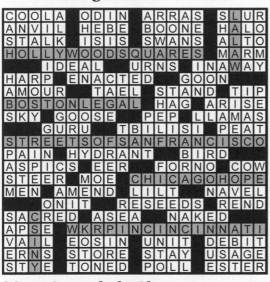

20 ■ *On with the Shows*

23 ■ *Cattle Call*

21 ■ *Canada Cornucopia 7*

24 ■ *Canada Cornucopia 8*

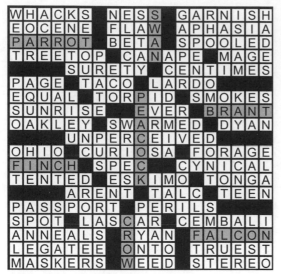

25 ■ *Meet the Flockers*

28 ■ *Leading Canadian Men*

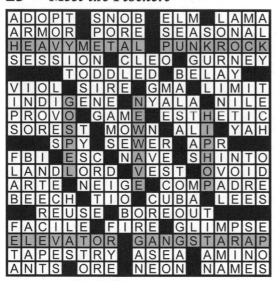

26 ■ *Get Into the Groove*

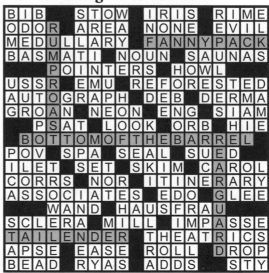

29 ■ *For Posterior's Sake*

27 ■ *Canada Cornucopia 9*

30 ■ *Canada Cornucopia 10*

31 ■ *An American in Canada*

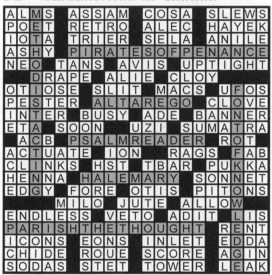

32 ■ *Mass Confusion?*

33 ■ *Canada Cornucopia 11*

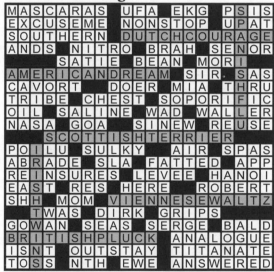

34 ■ *For a Song*

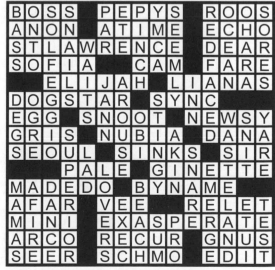

35 ■ *Around the World*

36 ■ *Canada Cornucopia 12*

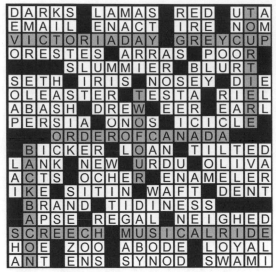

37 ■ *Only in Canada, Eh?*

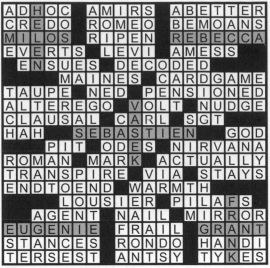

40 ■ *Tennis, Anyone? 1*

38 ■ *Say It with Food*

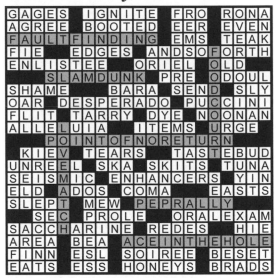

41 ■ *Tennis Anyone? 2*

39 ■ *Canada Cornucopia 13*

42 ■ *Canada Cornucopia 14*

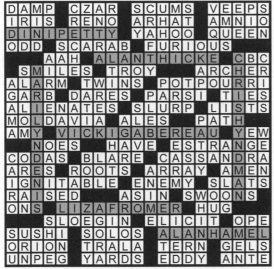

43 ■ *Let's Talk TV*

46 ■ *Best of the West*

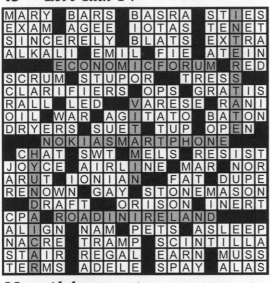

44 ■ *Alphanumeric*

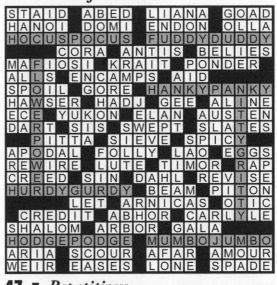

47 ■ *Repetitious*

45 ■ *Canada Cornucopia 15*

48 ■ *Canada Cornucopia 16*

49 ■ *Going to Gatineau*

50 ■ *Time Passages*

51 ■ *Canada Cornucopia 17*

52 ■ *Going with the Flow*

53 ■ *The Colour Purple*

54 ■ *Canada Cornucopia 18*

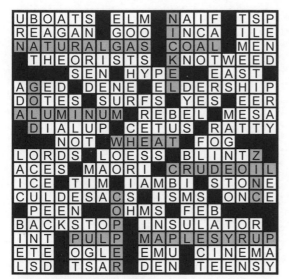

55 ▪ *It's Outta Here*

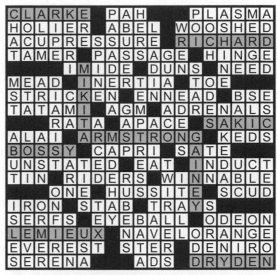

58 ▪ *Playing for Keeps*

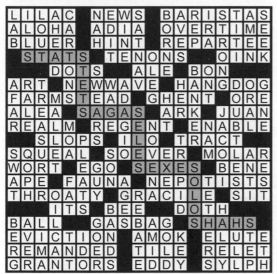

56 ▪ *A Puzzle for Anna*

59 ▪ *The Face of Human Nature*

57 ▪ *Canada Cornucopia 19*

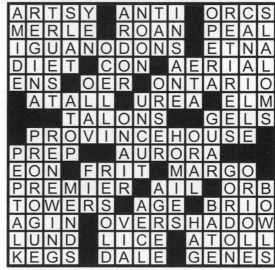

60 ▪ *Canada Cornucopia 20*

61 ■ *Ladies First*

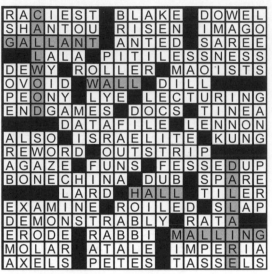

64 ■ *Tot-all-y Canadian*

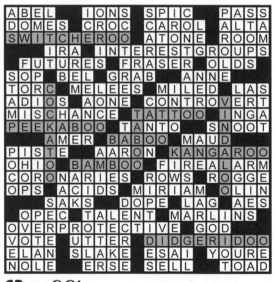

62 ■ *OO!*

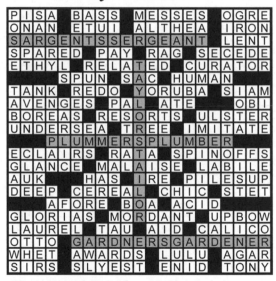

65 ■ *Actors' Aides*

63 ■ *Canada Cornucopia 21*

66 ■ *Canada Cornucopia 22*

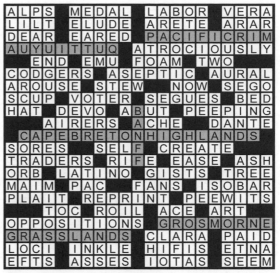

67 ■ *Fortitude*

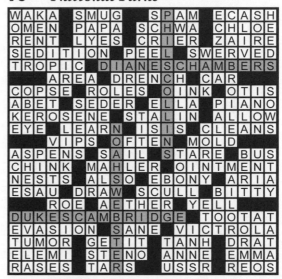

70 ■ *National Parks*

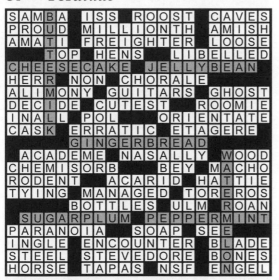

68 ■ *One + One = Yum*

71 ■ *Look It Up . . .*

69 ■ *Canada Cornucopia 23*

72 ■ *Canada Cornucopia 24*

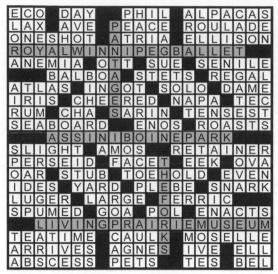

73 ▪ *Destination: Winnipeg*

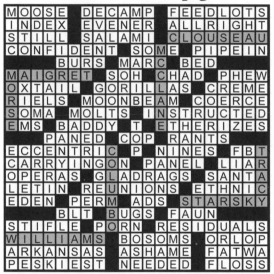

74 ▪ *May the Force Be with You*

75 ▪ *Canada Cornucopia 25*

76 ▪ *Who Am I? 2*

Unscramble: HURON COUNTY

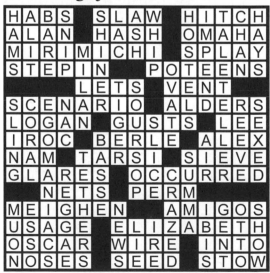

77 ▪ *Delightful Duos*

78 ▪ *Canada Cornucopia 26*